Dialogues and Games of Logic

Volume 2

Dialogues as a Dynamic Framework for Logic

Volume 1
How to Play Dialogues: An Introduction to Dialogical Logic
Juan Redmond and Matthieu Fontaine

Volume 2
Dialogues as a Dynamic Framework for Logic
Helge Rückert

Dialogues and Games of Logic Series Editors
Shahid Rahman
Nicolas Clerbout
Matthieu Fontaine

shahid.rahman@univ-lille3.fr

Dialogues as a Dynamic Framework
for Logic

Helge Rückert

© Individual author and College Publications 2011.
All rights reserved.

ISBN 978-1-84890-047-9

College Publications
Scientific Director: Dov Gabbay
Managing Director: Jane Spurr
Department of Informatics
King's College London, Strand, London WC2R 2LS, UK

www.collegepublications.co.uk

Original cover design by Laraine Welch
Printed by Lightning Source, Milton Keynes, UK

All rights reserved. No part of this publication may be reproduced, stored in a retrieval system or transmitted in any form, or by any means, electronic, mechanical, photocopying, recording or otherwise without prior permission, in writing, from the publisher.

Foreword

The content of this volume is based on the text of my PhD thesis "Dialogues as a Dynamic Framework for Logic" (2007, Leiden University, The Netherlands) which was prepared under the guidance of Prof. Göran Sundholm (*promoter*) and Prof. Erik Krabbe (*referent*).

I am very thankful to Shahid Rahman for proposing to publish this material in the book series "Dialogues and the Games of Logic" and to the editors of this series (besides Shahid Rahman himself, Nicolas Clerbout and Matthieu Fontaine) for making this possible.

Special thanks to Marion Pastoors for her help in preparing the text file for publication and to Jane Spurr from College Publications.

Helge Rückert
Mannheim (Germany), August 2011

TABLE OF CONTENTS

Introduction (English) 1

Rückert, H.
'Why Dialogical Logic?' (English) 9

Rahman, S., Rückert, H. and Fischmann, M.
'On Dialogues and Ontology. The Dialogical Approach to Free Logic'
(English) 27

Rahman, S. and Rückert, H.
'Dialogische Modallogik (für *T*, *B*, *S4* und *S5*)' (German) 43

Rahman, S. and Rückert, H.
'Dialogische Logik und Relevanz' (German) 80

Rahman, S. and Rückert, H.
'Dialogical Connexive Logic' (English) 110

Rahman, S. and Rückert, H.
'Eine neue dialogische Semantik für lineare Logik' (German) 149

Rückert, H.
'Logiques Dialogiques 'Multivalentes'' (French) 185

Bibliography 216

Introduction

What is meaning? This is a highly interesting philosophical question. A common standard answer says that the meaning of an expression is some sort of entity associated with the expression. In the field of logic this idea leads to all kinds of model-theoretic semantics. Some, unhappy with such an account of meaning because of its realistic flavour and ontological commitments, prefer an alternative account of meaning that relates meaning to use.[1] Applied to logic, this idea leads to two different kinds of approaches. According to the first the meaning of the logical particles is given via rules that determine how these particles can be used in proofs (proof-theoretical semantics). The second one characterises the meaning of the logical particles via rules that determine how these particles can be used in certain games, argumentation games (game-theoretical semantics). Within the game-theoretical approach three main traditions can be distinguished:[2]

(1) The constructivist approach of Paul Lorenzen and Kuno Lorenz, who sought to overcome the limitations of Operative Logic by providing dialogical foundations to it. The method of semantic tableaux for classical and intuitionistic logic as introduced by Evert W. Beth (1955) could thus be identified as a method for the notation of winning strategies of particular dialogue games (cf. Lorenzen/Lorenz (1978), Lorenz (1981), Felscher (1986)).

(2) The game-theoretical approach of Jaakko Hintikka who recognised at a very early stage that a two-players semantics offers a new dynamic device for studying logical systems. This approach is better known and opened many new research lines developed by Hintikka and co-authors, specially the semantic games which offer a deep and thorough insight into the notion of scope implemented by the Independence-Friendly Logic, the interrogative games which are essentially epistemic games and the formal games of theorem-proving which deal with logical truth of propositions and not with their material truth (as in the semantic games) or with one's knowledge of their truth (as in the epistemic games) Cf. Hintikka/Sandu (1996) and Hintikka (1996, 1996-1998).

---

[1] A main source of inspiration for such a view is the later Wittgenstein with his language games. His most explicit formulation of the idea of meaning as use, is the following: "For a large class of cases – though not for all – in which we employ the word "meaning" it can be defined thus: the meaning of a word is its use in language." (Wittgenstein (1953, §43))

[2] The following three paragraphs are taken from Rahman/Rückert (2001c).

Introduction

(3) The argumentation theory approach of Else Barth and Erik Krabbe (1982) (cf. also Gethmann (1979)), who sought to link dialogical logic with the informal logic or Critical Reasoning originated by the seminal work of Chaim Perelman (cf. Perelman/Olbrechts-Tyteca (1958)), Stephen Toulmin (1958), Arne Naess (1966) and Charles Hamblin (1970) and developed further by Ralph Johnson (1999), Douglas Walton (1984), John Woods (1988) and associates.

Unfortunately, for quite a long time, these three traditions followed separate paths and with some occasional exceptions did not actually pool their results in a common project.[3]

There are also interesting connections between the dialogical approach to logic and two other influential, more recent research programs:

1) *Game Theory and Logic*
One characteristic feature of the dialogical approach is that logic is studied via certain games (for example in the case of classical or intuitionistic logic via two-person zero-sum games with perfect information). So, the main interest is logical systems, and the main tool for studying them are certain games. On the other hand there is a whole mathematical discipline devoted to the systematic and formal study of games themselves: game theory. In game theory the games are the objects of investigation.

Given the above connection between logical systems and games which is characteristic for dialogical logic and other related approaches, it is a promising idea to look systematically at results from game theory and examine whether they lead, via the bridge from games to logic, to important logical results, too. This idea constitutes the basis for the research done by a whole group of logicians and other scientists under the guidance of Johan van Benthem at the ILLC (Institute for Logic, Language and Computation) in Amsterdam.[4]

2) *Adaptive Logic*
One big advantage of dialogical logic is that it easily allows for the combination of different logical systems. In general this is possible because very often different specific structural rules are decisive in order to obtain different logical systems. So, if one uses both (or more) of these specific

---

[3] Quite recently there has been a lot of interaction between the first two, however. Witness Rahman/Tulenheimo (2007), Rahman (2007) and Degremont/Rahman (2007)

[4] An enormous number of publications resulted from this big research program. Just to mention one: Van Benthem (2007)

structural rules this results in a new logical system which is in some sense a combination of these two (or more) logics.

There exists another very interesting framework for the systematic combination of different logical systems: so-called adaptive logic which was developed by Diderik Batens. This framework makes it possible to integrate two logics (one is called the upper limit logic, the other one the lower limit logic) into one proof system with a well defined consequence relation.[5]

I think, it might be very rewarding to compare dialogical logic and adaptive logic with respect to the similarities and the differences in the ways how logical systems are combined in these two general logical frameworks. A first step in this direction has already been done by Rahman/Van Bendegem (2002).

This is a collection of seven papers on dialogical logic, most of them co-authored by Shahid Rahman. It starts with the overview paper 'Why Dialogical Logic?' which could serve as an introduction to the other six papers. Those other papers, ordered according to the time when they had been written (which is different from the order of their first publication) are related by one central theme. As each of them presents dialogical formulations of a different non-classical logic, they show that dialogical logic provides a powerful and flexible general framework for the development and study of various logical formalisms and combinations thereof. So, especially for logical pluralists who do not believe in "the one and only correct logic", but who take an instrumentalist attitude towards logic and see different logical systems as formal tools for different purposes, dialogical logic is an interesting and fruitful alternative to model-theoretic and other logical methodologies.

Most of the papers were first published in an internal memo series at the University of Saarbrücken before they were submitted to an international journal. For this volume all the papers have been corrected, clarified and amended at various places. Furthermore the three German papers have been adapted to new German orthography and stylistically revised. The layout and composition of the papers has been unified and a single bibliography for the whole volume can now be found at the end. As each paper is supposed to be self-contained and can be read independently from the others, it was impossible to avoid some redundancies, especially when presenting the basic features of standard dialogical logic in each paper. Here are some remarks on each of the papers assembled in this collection:

---

[5] Again there are lots of publications by Diderik Batens and his collaborators. So, let me just give the URL of the Adaptive Logics Home Page: http://logica.ugent.be/adlog/al.html.

Introduction

Rückert, H.: 'Why Dialogical Logic?', in: Wansing, H. (ed.): Essays on Non-Classical Logic (Advances in Logic - Vol. 1), New Jersey, London, Singapore, Hong Kong 2001, p. 165-185

This paper grew out of a German talk called "Wodurch sich der dialogische Ansatz in der Logik auszeichnet" I had given on occasion of the XVIII. German Congress for Philosophy, Constance, October 1999. An extended abstract of this talk was published in the congress proceedings (see Rückert (1999a)).

    The paper is a general presentation and defence of the dialogical approach from the standpoint of logical pluralism. It counters some prejudices against dialogical logic, stresses the advantages of the framework (specifically the distinctions between the game level and the strategic level, between structural rules and particle rules and between logical validity as general validity and logical validity as formal validity), and gives an overview of most of the Rahman/Rückert-papers contained in this collection.[6]

Rahman, S., Rückert, H. and Fischmann, M.: 'On Dialogues and Ontology. The Dialogical Approach to Free Logic', Logique et Analyse 160 (1997), p. 357-374

This paper was written together with one of the students who took part in our graduate course "Erweiterungen der Dialogischen Logik", Matthias Fischmann. It was first published in the memo series (memo no. 24, October 1998) and then accepted for publication in the international journal Logique et Analyse. In the paper it is shown that reflections on ontological assumptions that lead to so-called free logics can be captured in the dialogical framework by special structural rules that apply to the attack and defence of quantified statements.

    Rahman (2001) is an interesting paper that combines ideas about free logics from this paper with dialogical formulations of paraconsistent and intuitionistic logic.

Rahman, S. and Rückert, H.: 'Dialogische Modallogik (für T, B, S4 und S5)', Logique et Analyse 167-168 (1999), p. 243-282

This paper provides dialogical formulations of the most basic systems of modal logic. The most important new concept introduced in it is the one of a dialogue context, which corresponds, roughly speaking, to the concept of a possible world used in other approaches. The paper was first published in the memo series (memo

---

[6] For another, more recent, general presentation and defence of dialogical logic see Rahman/Keiff (2004).

no. 25, November 1998) and was later accepted for publication in Logique et Analyse.

There is some related work which started from this paper: Thus Patrick Blackburn (2001) has generalised the dialogical approach to modal logic to formulate dialogical versions of so-called hybrid logics (modal logic with nominals to name specific possible worlds) and Ulrich Nortmann (2001), by manipulating the rule which prohibits unnecessary moves (the no-delaying-tactics rule), extends the approach to provability logic.. Shahid Rahman (2006) has shown how to deal with so-called non-normal modal logics within the dialogical framework.

Rahman, S. and Rückert, H.: 'Dialogische Logik und Relevanz', Universität des Saarlandes, memo no. 27, December 1998

In this paper ideas about relevance are captured by imposing a certain relevance criterion which must be met by the winning strategies for a formula to be relevantly valid. We used here the strictest criterion possible and thus received a logical system with very high standards of relevance. In contrast to that, the best known systems of relevance logic generally use weaker standards of relevance which leads to stronger logics with more valid formulas. For this reason, after publishing the paper in the memo series, we didn't submit it in this form to an international journal, but had the plan to expand the paper some day in order to add dialogical versions of the standard systems of relevance logic with weaker criteria of relevance, too. This plan has so far not been realised and is a desideratum for future research.

An interesting idea that is not already present in this paper, is the following: Instead of adding criteria of relevance at the strategic level one could build them in already at the game level itself. This can be done with the help of certain subdialogues which make it possible that a player in the dialogue challenges the other one and asks him to show in this subdialogue that what he stated in the main dialogue meets the criterion of relevance at stake.

Rahman, S. and Rückert, H.: 'Dialogical Connexive Logic', in: Rahman, S. / Rückert, H. (ed.): New Perspectives in Dialogical Logic, Synthese 127 (1/2) (2001), p. 105-139

We first published a German paper on dialogical connexive logic in the memo series (cf. Rahman/Rückert (1998b)) and then revised it thoroughly for the English version which was published in Synthese. The English version of the paper was presented by Shahid Rahman and me at the New Perspectives in Dialogical Logic conference (Saarbrücken, June 1999) and by myself at the Logic and Games workshop (Amsterdam, November 1999)[7] and at the Connexive Logic and Beyond workshop (Siena, June 2000).

The system of connexive logic developed in this paper by the introduction of a new connective, the connexive conditional, seems to be very close to a connexive logic which was formulated approximately at the same time and completely independently from ours by Graham Priest (1999) who used a model-theoretic semantics. It might be promising to examine more closely whether these two systems of connexive logic, formulated within completely different semantic frameworks, are indeed equivalent to each other.[8]

Rahman, S. and Rückert, H.: 'Eine neue dialogische Semantik für lineare Logik', previously unpublished paper (written in 2000/01)

This previously unpublished paper was written in 2000/01 and presents a dialogical semantics for linear logic. We didn't submit it for publication because the dialogical semantics only captures one variety of linear logic and the equivalence proofs were still missing. So, we planned to expand this important material to a more comprehensive dialogical treatment of linear logic (the result arguably would be of book size) and publish it then. But owing to the geographic academic separation with Shahid Rahman and myself working at different locations collaboration became more difficult and this project is still awaiting realisation.

From a methodological viewpoint the paper is quite stimulating as it sheds some new light on the nature of non-classical logics. According to one viewpoint one receives new non-classical logical systems by changing the set of structural rules against a fixed set of particle rules. This feature is shared by dialogical logic and so-called substructural logics (see for example Restall (2000)). In the context of substructural logics this methodological idea is sometimes called 'Došen's Principle'.

On the other hand linear logic is well known for its many different logical particles. So, one could formulate an alternative methodological principle according to which new non-classical logics can be received by introducing new logical constants. In Rahman/Rückert (2001b) we referred to this idea by naming it after the inventor of linear logic 'Girard's Principle'.[9]

---

[7] An extended abstract for this talk was published in the workshop reader. Cf. Rückert (1999b).

[8] Another very interesting paper on connexive logic is Pizzi/Williamson (1997). For an overview on connexive logic see Heinrich Wansing's online entry in the *Stanford Encyclopedia of Philosophy*: http://plato.stanford.edu/entries/logic-connexive/#Bib.

[9] This name was suggested by Heinrich Wansing (1994).

Introduction

Our paper on linear logic shows that Girard's logical particles can be reconstructed dialogically by the help of certain structural rules that only apply locally, i.e. with respect to certain particles, and not in general. So what is needed are not new particle rules, but only a specific kind of new structural rules.

This result seems to suggest a certain compromise between the two principles mentioned above: Contrary to how it may first appear, Došen's Principle and Girard's Principle don't contradict each other. One can not only generate new logical systems by either changing the structural rules or by introducing new logical particles, but it is possible to proceed according to both devices at the same time, by introducing new particles with the help of a special kind of structural rules. Further future research about these methodological ideas might lead to more clarity and relevant technical results.

Rückert, H.: 'Logiques Dialogiques 'Multivalentes'', Philosophia Scientiae 8 (2), 2004, p. 59-87

This paper was written for a special issue of the journal Philosophia Scientiae dedicated to logic and game theory, edited by Manuel Rebuschi and Tero Tulenheimo.

As there is no place for truth-values in dialogical logic, it was necessary to add a new concept corresponding to the concept of a truth-value in other approaches in order to be able to give a dialogical reconstruction of many-valued logics. This new concept was the one of a mode of assertion. So, with the help of different modes of assertion it became possible to give a dialogical semantics for the standard systems of many-valued logics without using values. A bit paradoxical perhaps, but it worked![10]

---

[10] For other work using games in connection with many-valued logics see for example Giles (1974) and Ciabattoni/Fermüller/Metcalfe (2004).

Introduction

There are many people to whom I am grateful because of their kindness to me, but let me just mention two of them:

1) Shahid Rahman, the "Pope of Dialogical Logic", who first introduced me to the fascinating world of logic, who later worked with me to produce the papers in this collection, and, most importantly, who is a good friend on whose support I can always count.

2) My mother Monika Rückert, a strong woman who was and still is always there for me. This volume is dedicated to her.[11]

Helge Rückert
Mannheim (Germany), April 2007

---

[11] I would like to thank Andrew Morton for orthographic, grammatical, and stylistic improvements, and Alexis Georgi for necessary help with various text processing programs.

Why Dialogical Logic?

Helge Rückert

Abstract:
The aim of this paper is to present the dialogical approach to logic as an interesting alternative to the model-theoretic approach. In the introduction I plead for pluralism concerning logical systems and logical methodology before giving a short outline of Dialogical Logic. Then, I discuss and reject several prejudices against Dialogical Logic. I present three conceptual distinctions that are characteristic of the dialogical approach to logic (namely, formal vs. general truth, level of games vs. level of strategies and particle rules vs. structural rules) and their fruitfulness for logical research is demonstrated at the hand of some examples.

1 Introduction

This paper was originally published in a volume called *Essays on Non-Classical Logic*. Any logical system that differs from classical two-valued propositional and first order logic can be called non-classical, for example intuitionistic logic, modal logics, relevance logics and such-like. Non-classical logics in this sense are not the main issue of this paper, even though they play an important part in the argumentation.

Instead I consider different approaches to logic or logical methodology. The goal is to defend the dialogical approach, that – at present – seems to be of secondary interest in logical research.[1] I will try to show in what aspects the dialogical approach differs from other logical methods and what its advantages are.

A first dichotomy subdivides logical methodology into syntactic and semantic approaches. Whereas the first deals with axiomatic systems, model-theoretic and proof-theoretic (systems of natural deduction, for example) approaches predominate the second category. Dialogical Logic, together with related approaches like Hintikka's better known GTS (Game Theoretical

---

Rückert, H.: 'Why Dialogical Logic?', in Wansing, H. (ed.): *Essays on Non-Classical Logic* (Advances in Logic – Vol. 1), New Jersey, London, Singapore, Hong Kong 2001, p. 165-185

[1] There are some signs that the situation is changing and that there is a new start of research in Dialogical Logic (see Rahman/Rückert (2001a)).

Semantics)² constitutes a third alternative on the semantic side of the dichotomy: game-theoretical logical methodology.

The goal of this paper is not to press the superiority of the dialogical approach to all other semantic methodologies, not even to claim that it alone should be used in future logical research. I will not only plead for pluralism concerning the different logical systems, but also for pluralism concerning the different logical methodologies. This means that it is appropriate to use different logical methods to pursue different aims. In my opinion, for many aims Dialogical Logic is a fruitful alternative to the more common model-theoretic or proof-theoretic approaches and it deserves more attention than it gets at present.

In the sequel I defend logical pluralism, and I give a short introduction to the dialogical approach. Furthermore some prejudices that are – among other things – responsible for the fact that Dialogical Logic often is completely unknown or considered exotic are corrected. Finally, some peculiarities and some resulting advantages of Dialogical Logic are discussed. I would be happy if this paper could contribute a little bit to change the uncaring attitude towards Dialogical Logic.

1.1 Pluralism concerning Logics and Logical Methodology

I plead for logical pluralism, i.e. I think that among the different logical systems developed so far (and still to be developed), including classical logic, as well as the so-called non-classical logics, there is no system that represents the only correct logic. Thus I do not plead for a certain logic as intuitionistic logic, or a version of relevance logic, but for working with a multitude of formal instruments. Which logical system is the most adequate always depends on the context of application and on the purposes for which one wants to use the formal tools. Thus, different logical systems are formal instruments for different purposes.

The task of the logician should be – among other things – to develop many different interesting logical systems, in which the motivations and underlying ideas are formally worked out. Especially for these purposes I consider the dialogical approach to logic as very suitable, because it often provides the possibility to formally treat interesting ideas in a very simple way. Another advantage is that such formally treated ideas can often be easily combined.

But I do not want to voice the opinion that the dialogical approach provides the best of all available logical methodologies. Even on the methodological level the choice of tools depends on the purposes. Thus – in many contexts – it could be the best choice to use the model-theoretic approach, a Gentzen calculus or another

---

[2] Hintikka's (1998) treatment of branching quantifiers in his IF-Logic (Independence Friendly Logic) receives considerable attention from logicians. It would be interesting to examine whether Hintikka's ideas can be reconstructed in dialogical terms.

logical method. However, I do think that Dialogical Logic is a fruitful alternative for logical research, especially for developing and combining new logics, and I think that it could be used fruitfully more often than is presently the case.

1.2 Dialogical Logic: a short Outline

Dialogical Logic was suggested at the end of the 1950s by Paul Lorenzen and then worked out by Kuno Lorenz.[3] In a dialogue two parties argue about a thesis respecting certain fixed rules. The defender of the thesis is called Proponent (**P**), his rival, who attacks the thesis is called Opponent (**O**). Each dialogue ends after a finite number of moves with one player winning, while the other loses. The rules are divided into structural rules and particle rules. The structural rules determine the general course of a dialogue game, whereas the particle rules show which moves are allowed to attack the moves of the other player or to defend one's own moves.

Structural Rules

(SR 0) (starting rule):
The initial formula is uttered by **P**. It provides the topic of the argumentation. Moves are alternately uttered by **P** and **O**. Each move that follows the initial formula is either an attack or a defence.

(SR 1) (no delaying tactics rule):
Both **P** and **O** may only make moves that change the situation.[4]

(SR 2) (formal rule):
P may not introduce atomic formulas, any atomic formula must be stated by **O** first.

(SR 3) (winning rule):
X wins iff it is Y's turn but he cannot move (either attack or defend).

---

[3] Some of the most important early texts about Dialogical Logic are collected in Lorenzen/Lorenz (1978).

[4] This rule replaces Lorenz' *Angriffsschranken*. It still needs to be made clear on a formal basis.

(SR 4i) (intuitionistic rule):
In any move, each player may attack a (complex) formula asserted by his partner or he may defend himself against the last attack that has not yet been answered.

or

(SR 4c) (classical rule):
In any move, each player may attack a (complex) formula asserted by his partner or he may defend himself against any attack (including those that have already been defended).[5]

---

[5] Both in SR 4i and SR 4c we have stated the so-called symmetric versions of these rules. It is possible to diminish the rights of **O** without any changes on the level of strategies in the following way: For **P** the rules remain unchanged, but **O** is only allowed either to defend himself against the last move of **P** or to attack this move. These versions of the rules SR 4i and SR 4c are called asymmetric, because now **P** has more rights than **O**.

Why Dialogical Logic?

Particle Rules

$\vee, \wedge, \rightarrow, \neg, \forall, \exists$	Attack	Defence
$\neg A$	A	$\otimes$ (No defence, only counterattack possible)
$A \wedge B$	?L(eft) --------- ?R(ight) (The attacker chooses)	A --------- B
$A \vee B$	?	A --------- B (The defender chooses)
$A \rightarrow B$	A	B
$\forall_x A$	$?_n$ (The attacker chooses)	$A[n/x]$
$\exists_x A$	?	$A[n/x]$ (The defender chooses)

The given structural and particle rules define the intuitionistic (with SR 4i) and the classical (with SR 4c) dialogue games. Validity is defined as follows:

> *Validity (definition):*
> A formula is valid in a certain dialogical system iff **P** has a formal winning strategy for this formula. (To have a formal winning strategy means, that for any choice of moves by your opponent you have at least one possible move at your disposition, so that you finally win.)

It can be shown that with these rules and this definition of logical validity the same valid formulas are obtained as in the common approaches to logic. (To get intuitionistic logic use the intuitionistic rule, and to get classical logic use the classical rule.)[6]

---

[6] Such proofs can be found for example in Barth/Krabbe (1982), in Krabbe (1985), and in Rahman (1993).

Example 1 (with either SR 4i or SR 4c):

	O			P	
				$((a{\to}b){\wedge}a){\to}b$	(0)
(1)	$(a{\to}b){\wedge}a$	0		b	(8)
(3)	$a{\to}b$	1		?L	(2)
(5)	a	1		?R	(4)
(7)	b	3		a	(6)

P wins

Example 2 (with SR 4c):

	O			P	
				$\forall_x(P_x{\vee}\neg P_x)$	(0)
(1)	$?_n$	0		$P_n{\vee}\neg P_n$	(2)
(3)	?	2		$\neg P_n$	(4)
(5)	P_n	4		$\otimes$	
(3')	?	2		P_n	(6)

P wins

Remarks concerning the examples:
Here, as in the following, very simple examples are chosen, so that with the help of just one dialogue it is easy to see whether **P** has a winning strategy for the formula in question or not. For example 1 it makes no difference whether you use SR 4i or SR 4c, but the formula in example 2 is only valid in classical logic.

Explication of the notation: The moves of **O** are written down in the **O**-column, the ones of **P** in the **P**-column. The numbers in brackets on the left and right margin represent the order in which the moves were made. Move number (0) is the thesis that is argued about in the dialogue. Attacks are characterised by numbers without brackets that indicate which move of the partner is attacked. Defences are always written down in the same line as the corresponding attacks. Such pairs of attacks and corresponding defences are called rounds.

(As you can see in example 2, when playing according to the classical rule, it is possible for **P** to defend himself again against an attack that has already been answered before. To note down this renewed defence, we repeat the corresponding attack, but please keep in mind, that this is not a move in the dialogue, but only a notational convention, which is indicated by an apostrophe as in (3') of example 2.)

2 Prejudices against Dialogical Logic

Dialogical Logic is generally regarded as exotic and sometimes even completely unknown. Here, three prejudices that – among other things – have led to the fact that the dialogical approach is in this unfortunate situation will be formulated and then rejected.[7]

2.1 'Dialogical Logic is a Constructivistic Logic'

It is indeed correct that Dialogical Logic was developed in the context of the constructivist program of the so-called school of Erlangen, and that it was used in these surroundings to defend intuitionistic logic. But it is totally wrong to identify Dialogical Logic with intuitionistic or constructivistic logic. Instead, Dialogical Logic represents a general framework[8] within logical methodology, comparable to, say, Gentzen's sequent-calculus formulations, with the help of which classical, intuitionistic, and many other logics can be examined, just by using different dialogue rules. It seems that among the successors to the constructivistic school of Erlangen there is now a tendency to see Dialogical Logic as an inappropriate tool for the foundation (*Begründung*) of logic (see Hartmann (1998)).

---

[7] There might be other prejudices against Dialogical Logic. For instance, it should not be concealed that dialogical logicians made some mistakes when working out and presenting their approach. Naturally these mistakes have had a negative influence on the reception of Dialogical Logic (see Felscher (1986)), but mistakes can often be corrected and in a lot of cases this has already been done.

[8] 'Framework' is here used in a non-technical sense, of course; I don't wish to propose Dialogical Logic as rival to, say, LF or ALF.

2.2 'Dialogical Logic is Limited to Classical and Intuitionistic Logic'

It is right that with some exceptions[9] the dialogical approach to logic was for a long time only worked out for classical and intuitionistic logic.[10] But in the last few years, together with Shahid Rahman, I have made several proposals to extend it to other logics, too. We have developed dialogical free, paraconsistent, modal, relevance and connexive logics.[11] We have shown that results that were reached within a model-theoretic framework, can also be obtained dialogically. But it is even more interesting that, using dialogical methods, it has been possible to treat of certain notions for which there was no perspicuous semantics, examples being certain systems of paraconsistent, relevance and connexive logics.

It is evident that these few papers about non-classical logics formulated within the dialogical framework cannot compete with the immense literature about non-classical logics treated with the help of model theory. But this does not imply that it would also be impossible to reach a comparable amount of interesting results with the dialogical approach,[12] if one invested as much time, work and money in such a kind of logical research.

2.3 'Dialogical Logic Complicates Things Unnecessarily'

It is correct that there are several distinctions in Dialogical Logic that cannot be found in other approaches to logic. But these distinctions do not complicate simple logical procedures essentially (for example the test whether a formula is valid in a certain logic still is a trivial matter in most cases), but they offer conceptual possibilities for certain purposes.

---

[9] Fuhrmann (1985) for example presents a dialogical reconstruction of Anderson/Belnap's (1975) First Degree Entailment Logic and in Lorenzen (1987) some steps towards dialogical modal logics can be found.

[10] Fuhrmann (1985, p. 51) writes: "Die Diskussion um die Dialogische Logik ist bisher ausschließlich aus dem Blickwinkel klassischer bzw. konstruktiver Positionen geführt worden. Relevanzlogiken und parakonsistente Logiken sind nicht angemessen in Betracht gezogen worden."

[11] See Rahman/Rückert/Fischmann (1997), Rahman/Carnielli (2000) and Rahman/Rückert (1998a, 1999 and 2001b).

[12] One early interesting technical result obtained by using dialogical methods is Lorenz' (1978) proof of functional completeness of the intuitionistic connectives, that differs considerably from the model-theoretic proof of McCullough (1971). A comparison of Lorenz' result with the proof-theoretic completeness theorems of Prawitz (1978) and Zucker/Tragesser (1978) might be of interest.

The impression that Dialogical Logic is unnecessarily complicated probably arises when one is not used to the dialogical approach. But with some training it is easy to see that playing dialogues and checking formulas for winning strategies is as easy as writing down truth-tables or Beth-tableaux. For some time students at Saarbrücken learned the dialogical approach simultaneously with the common model-theoretical approach to logic, and it is remarkable that at least when treating quantifiers most of them had less trouble with the dialogical approach.

3 Advantages of Dialogical Logic

In Dialogical Logic there are several distinctions that are not available in other frameworks, for example in the model-theoretic approach. These distinctions offer interesting possibilities for logical research. In the sequel I present some examples.

3.1 The Distinction between General and Formal Truth

The standard defintion of logical truth or validity reads as follows: "A proposition A is logically true iff it is true under *all* interpretations." Thus, validity is usually seen as a generalisation of truth. It is also called 'formal truth', because it depends only on the logical form of the proposition in question and not on the interpretation of its constituents:

> "The logical truths, then, are those true sentences which involve only logical words *essentially*. What this means is that any other words [...] can be varied at will without engendering falsity." (Quine (1976, p. 110))

Now, if we turn to Dialogical Logic the concept of logical truth or validity can be split into two conceptually different notions, namely 'general truth', corresponding to the common conception, and 'formal truth', where 'formal' is understood in a strict sense.

Validity as General Truth

In Dialogical Logic we should think of truth as the existence of a winning strategy for **P**. To formulate validity as 'general truth' within the dialogical framework, we have to introduce so-called material dialogues by adding the following structural rule that replaces the formal structural rule:

SR 5 (rule for material dialogues):
Atomic formulas standing for true propositions may be uttered, atomic formulas standing for false propositions must not be uttered.

With the help of the following definition we have reached a dialogical reformulation of the common view of validity:

Validity as general truth (definition):
A formula is valid iff there is a winning strategy for **P** in every material dialogue about this formula. This means that **P** must have a winning strategy for this formula for each possibility of assigning truth-values to the atomic formulas.

Here, it makes no difference whether using the intuitionistic or the classical structural rule. In any case the resulting logic will be the classical one.[13] Please notice that when playing material dialogues it is always presupposed that all elementary propositions have a definite truth-value, namely 'true' or 'false'.

Validity as Formal Truth

This is different when we turn to the usual definition of validity in Dialogical Logic, namely validity as formal truth:

Validity as formal truth (definition):
A formula is valid iff there is a *formal* winning strategy for **P** in a dialogue about this formula. This means that **P** must have a winning strategy when the formal structural rule is in use.

This way of seeing validity differs conceptually from the common way, because here validity is not just general truth, validity does not just require the existence of winning strategies for **P** for a certain totality of dialogues, but the existence of a winning strategy for **P** in a certain kind of dialogue game, namely in a formal dialogue for the formula in question.
  Also, it is not presupposed that all elementary propositions have a truth-value, are either true or false. Thus, the dialogical concept of formality is stricter than the usual one: The form is not only independent of the truth or falsity of the

---

[13] Besides using the classical structural rule or working with material dialogues, there is a third possibility to reconstruct classical logic in the dialogical approach: A formula is valid in classical logic iff **P** has a formal winning strategy for it in intuitionistic dialogues with additional *tertium non datur* hypotheses.

elementary propositions, but it is even independent of whether the elementary propositions have truth-values.[14]

The fruitfulness of the distinction between formal and general truth still needs to be worked out in detail, but it should be obvious that it offers an interesting conceptual instrument for logical research.

3.2 The Distinction between the Level of Games and the Level of Strategies

The distinction between the level of dialogue games where questions of meaning and sense are located and the level of strategies where questions about truth and validity are located is not available in other semantic logical approaches.[15] Usually the meaning of the connectives is defined by using concepts of correctness such as 'true' and 'false', for example. In dialogues it is possible that the players make moves that are bad moves from a strategic point of view, and a player may even lose who could have won if he had played in a different way. This acceptance of strategically bad moves on the level of games seems to be unnecessary, but this is not the case. The level of games is important, too, and stands in its own right.

As an example I will try to show that the distinction between the level of games and the level of strategies allows an almost trivial proof of the disjunctive property for dialogical intuitionistic logic. Usually this proof is rather complicated for Gentzen sequent-calculi that allow more than one formula on the right-hand side of a sequent, but when using dialogical methods it is not.

The disjunctive property of intuitionistic logic says that $A \vee B$ is valid iff A is valid or B is valid:

$$\models A \vee B \Leftrightarrow \models A \text{ or } \models B$$

The proof from the right to the left is unproblematic. If **P** has a formal winning strategy for A or for B, it is evident that he has a winning strategy for $A \vee B$: **P** starts the dialogue by stating the thesis $A \vee B$, and **O** attacks it with '?'. In order to win **P** then just has to choose the disjunct he has a winning strategy for. If he has a winning strategy for A (or B) he has to choose A (or B respectively) to answer **O**'s attack.

---

[14] Thus with respect to the elementary propositions it is not required that there is either a winning strategy for **P** or for **O**. What is required is that there is a way of arguing about the elementary propositions. This means, they must have sense or meaning, but not necessarily a truth-value. (For the possibility in Dialogical Logic of separating the senses or meanings of propositions from their having truth-values see the next section.)

[15] There might be a few other approaches – as, for example, Martin-Löf's (1984) Intuitionistic Type Theory – which have built in analogous distinctions.

The proof from the left to the right seems much more difficult, but it also becomes almost trivial in Dialogical Logic, because of the distinction between the level of games and the level of strategies. On the level of games intuitionistic logic is characterised by the so-called intuitionistic structural rule:

(SR 4i) (intuitionistic rule):
In any move, each player may attack a (complex) formula asserted by his partner or he may defend himself against the last attack that has not yet been answered.

The crucial point of this rule with regard to the present argumentation is that **P** is not allowed to defend himself against an attack of **O** he has already answered, unless **O** renews his attack. In our example this means that **P** is not allowed to defend himself again with B (or A) against the attack '?' on $A \vee B$ if he has already defended himself with A (or B respectively).

Now we go to the level of strategies and recall the definition of validity in the dialogical approach: A formula is valid iff **P** has a formal winning strategy for it. Thus, from the left to the right the metatheorem of the disjunctive property says, that if **P** has a winning strategy for $A \vee B$ he also has a winning strategy for at least one of the two disjuncts. And to have a winning strategy means for **P** that he is able to win the dialogue no matter how **O** plays.

If we look at the beginning of a dialogue with the thesis $A \vee B$, it is clear that the first move of **O** has to be the attack '?' and that **P** has to reply A (or B) in the second move. Now, the dialogue continues with an argumentation about A (or B respectively) alone, if **O** does not renew his attack on $A \vee B$. Consequently, if **P** has a winning strategy for $A \vee B$, he must also have a winning strategy for at least one of the two disjuncts alone, *quod erat demonstrandum.*

So we see that with the help of Dialogical Logic the proof of the disjunctive property of intuitionistic logic becomes almost trivial. It results directly from combining the intuitionistic structural rule on the level of games with the definition of validity that is formulated on the level of strategies. Here it is irrelevant whether we use the symmetric or the asymmetric structural rule. As strategy tableau-systems (i.e. decision methods for checking whether **P** has a formal winning strategy or not) for symmetric dialogues correspond to intuitionistic semantic tableau-systems for Gentzen sequent-calculi in which more than one formula on the right-hand side of a sequent is allowed, we have obtained – by using dialogical methods – a very easy proof of the disjunctive property, and, modulo the equivalence-proof concerning tableaux and dialogue-formulations, also for the Gentzen systems mentioned above.[16]

---

[16] This argumentation is worked out in detail in Rahman/Rückert (1998/99). This paper also includes a discussion of the philosophical background and consequences.

3.3 The Distinction between the Particle Rules and the Structural Rules

In Dialogical Logic the rules are divided into particle rules and structural rules. The particle rules determine for each logical particle how the corresponding formulas can be attacked and defended. The structural rules determine the general course of a dialogue.[17]

Now it is very interesting to see that you can get to different logical systems by only changing the set of structural rules while retaining the same set of particle rules. For example, dialogical classical and intuitionistic logic differ only in one structural rule, and you can get to a paraconsistent or a free logic by adding certain structural rules. Thus, the differentiation between particle rules and structural rules makes it very simple to generate new logics by combining certain structural rules.

The division into particle and structural rules is an essential feature also of Display Logic.[18] In Display Logic the idea that alternate systems are to be obtained by modifying structural rules against the background of a fixed set of connective rules is sometimes referred to as *Došen's Principle*:

> "[T]he rules for the logical operations are never changed: all changes are made in the structural rules." (Došen (1988, p. 353))

Thus, the proof-theoretic approach of Display Logic working with modifications of Gentzen style sequent-calculi and Dialogical Logic apply the same methodology for presenting non-classical logics and combinations of them. In this respect both could be seen as parts of a common enterprise. In any case, a detailed comparison of Dialogical Logic and Display Logic remains an interesting task.

Here, I will first present the main ideas of dialogical free, paraconsistent, modal and relevance logics, and then I will discuss the possibilities of combining them.[19]

---

[17] Thus every rule governing a dialogue game that is no particle rule is called a structural rule. Perhaps it is appropriate to refine the category of structural rules, for example the class of formal rules (for atomic formulas, for attacking negations or for introducing new constants) seems to be of particular interest.

[18] Display Logic was inaugurated by Belnap (1982). Further work has been done for example by Wansing (1998).

[19] Dialogical connexive logic is not appropriate for my present purpose, because there not only the structural rules but also the particle rules, at least for the subjunction, have to be extended (see Rahman/Rückert (2001b)).

Dialogical Free Logic

The main idea of dialogical free logic is to make the quantifiers stronger so that they carry existential import: if a player in a dialogue uses a certain constant to defend an existential quantifier or to attack a general quantifier he simultaneously admits that this constant denotes an existing object. As in formal dialogues **P** is only allowed to use information that **O** has admitted first, we can add the following structural rule to our usual set of rules to define free (and inclusive) formal dialogue games:

> *SR 6 (formal rule for constants):*
> Only **O** may introduce constants. (A constant is introduced iff it is used for the first time to defend an existential quantifier or to attack a general quantifier.)

With the help of this rule we get a basic dialogical system of free logic.[20] A simple example shows that in the so defined dialogical free logic fewer formulas are valid than in non-free logics:

Example 3 (free logic):

	O			P	
				$P_n \to \exists_x P_x$	(0)
(1)	P_n		0	$\exists_x P_x$	(2)
(3)	?		2		
O wins					

P loses because he is not allowed to defend himself against the attack in move (3): No constant has been introduced so far. (Note that n has not been introduced even if it appears in the dialogue.)

Dialogical Paraconsistent Logic

The main point concerning paraconsistent logics is that not every contradiction should make the whole system trivial. This means *ex falso sequitur quodlibet* should not be valid in general. In Rahman/Carnielli (2000) several proposals for extending Dialogical Logic are made that lead to this effect. An interesting idea is

---

[20] This basic system is similar to some versions of so-called outer domain systems of free logic (see Bencivenga (1986)), but it is inclusive, i.e. it allows the universe of discourse to be empty. It is also possible to invent more sophisticated dialogical free logics, for example with an indefinite number of pairs of quantifiers (see Rahman/Rückert/Fischmann (1997)).

that only contradictions on the atomic level should be excluded from implying anything.[21] For this purpose we have to add the following structural rule:

SR 7 (formal rule for negative literals):
P is allowed to attack the negation of an atomic formula iff **O** has attacked the same formula before.

Example 4 (paraconsistent logic):

	O			**P**	
				$(a \land \neg a) \to b$	(0)
(1)	$a \land \neg a$	0			
(3)	a		1	?L	(2)
(5)	$\neg a$		1	?R	(4)

O wins

P loses because he is neither allowed to defend himself with b (because of SR 2) nor to attack $\neg a$ with a because **O** has not done the same before.

Dialogical Modal Logic

To get to dialogical modal logics it is not sufficient to change the set of structural rules, but here we have to introduce new particle rules for the modal operators 'necessary' and 'possible'. The new concept of a dialogue context also has to be introduced.[22] In dialogical modal logics a dialogue game is played by stating formulas in different dialogue contexts. If a player states 'necessarily p' in a dialogue context n he commits himself to state p in all dialogue contexts that are admissible from n. Correspondingly, if a player states 'possibly p' he commits himself to defend p in at least one admissible dialogue context.

---

[21] One way to defend this approach is to distinguish between two sorts of negations, a negation *de re* and a negation *de dicto* (see Sinowjew (1970)). If there is a contradiction with a negation *de dicto* (possible only on the atomic level), the system does not become trivial, because in dialogical paraconsistent logics such a contradiction gets isolated in a certain sense, so that it cannot be used to infer anything (see Rahman (2001)). Wittgenstein is a precursor of such an idea: "You might get $p.\sim p$ by means of Frege's system. If you can draw any conclusion you like from it, then that, as far as I can see, is all the trouble you can get into. And I would say, "Well then, just don't draw any conclusions from a contradiction."" (Diamond (1976, p. 220))

[22] Dialogue contexts are the dialogical counterparts to possible worlds in model-theoretic modal semantics.

Why Dialogical Logic?

Particle Rules for the Modal Operators

□, ◊	Attack	Defence
□A (in dialogue context α)	? (in an admissible dialogue context β, chosen by the attacker)	A (in β)
◊A (in dialogue context α)	? (in α)	A (in an admissible dialogue context β, chosen by the defender)

For each modal logic system we must determine by supplementary structural rules which dialogue contexts are admissible. In Rahman/Rückert (1999) the dialogical approach to modal logics has been worked out for classical and intuitionistic versions of *T*, *B*, *S4* and *S5*. It should not be very difficult to reconstruct other modal logic systems by mere modifications of the structural rules.[23]

Dialogical Relevance Logic

In Rahman/Rückert (1998a) we have made a proposal for a very strict dialogical relevance logic (even uniform substitution is no longer valid).[24] In this case we get to this non-classical logic not by changing the set of rules on the level of dialogue games, but by formulating a criterion that the winning strategy of **P** has to fulfil: The winning strategy should contain no redundant parts.

---

[23] Nortmann (2001) presents a dialogical version of the modal logic system *G*.

[24] The name 'dialogical relevance logic' is perhaps misleading, because our system differs considerably from the usual systems called relevance logic. Our system is rather a formal logical version of the well-known Gricean maxims for conversation (cf. Grice (1989)). It still needs to be examined whether commonly known systems of relevance logic can be formulated in dialogical terms by changing the set of structural rules. One step in this direction was taken by Fuhrmann (1985).

Relevant validity (definition):
A formula is relevantly valid iff there is a formal winning strategy for **P** that contains no redundant parts (this means that **P** would have no winning strategy left if he didn't have all of his possible move choices at his disposition).

Example 5 (relevance logic):

O				P	
				$(a \wedge b) \rightarrow b$	(0)
(1)	$a \wedge b$	0		b	(4)
(3)	b		1	?R	(2)

P wins (but not relevantly)

Even if **P** has a formal winning strategy for this formula, it is not relevantly valid, because he does not need to use the attack '?L' against move (1) of **O** to win.

Combinations of Logics

In dialogical free and paraconsistent logic only the set of structural rules was changed, in dialogical modal logic new particle rules and new structural rules had to be added and in relevance logic a new definition of relevant validity was introduced. But it is decisive for the possibility of combining different non-classical dialogical logics, that the changes are all at different locations in the dialogical framework, so that it is no problem at all to combine them. The ideas presented here already offer two to the power of five possibilities for different dialogical systems (please keep in mind that you can always choose between the intuitionistic and classical structural rule), for example intuitionistic non-free modal relevance logic or classical free non-modal relevance logic.

It is clear that not all of these different possibilities are equally interesting. Perhaps some of them do not have a field of application at all. But at least some of them seem to be very interesting: in Rahman (1999a) a combination of free and paraconsistent logics is proposed to treat fictional entities. This idea is worked out in more detail in Rahman (2001), where a further combination with intuitionistic and classical features is developed: The players can argue classically with regard to existing objects but have to use the intuitionistic structural rule concerning fictions.

4 Concluding Remarks

With this paper I intended to defend the dialogical approach to logic in a general way rather than work out one dialogical logic system extensively. Thus a more detailed examination of every example and step in the argumentation was not possible. If the reader has the impression that many themes have not been treated in detail, he should have a look at the corresponding articles referred to in the text. In this paper it was my goal to correct some prejudices concerning Dialogical Logic and to stimulate more interest in it by presenting some possibilities for logical research that the dialogical approach offers.[25]

---

[25] I wish to thank Shahid Rahman (Lille), Goeran Sundholm (Leiden) and an anonymous referee for helpful suggestions, and Karl Hudson for correcting my English.

On Dialogues and Ontology
The Dialogical Approach to Free Logic

Shahid Rahman*, Helge Rückert and Matthias Fischmann

Abstract:
Being a pragmatic and not a referential approach to semantics, dialogical logic does not understand semantics as mapping names, propositions and relationships into the real world to obtain an abstract counterpart of it, but as dealing *(handeln)* with them in a particular way. This allows a very simple formulation of free logic the core of which can be expressed in a nutshell, namely: in an argumentation, it sometimes makes sense to restrict the introduction of singular terms in the context of quantification to a formal use of them. That is, the proponent is allowed to use a constant iff this constant has been explicitly conceded by the opponent.

More technically, we show a new, dialogical way to build free logic systems for first-order logic with classical and intuitionistic features and present their corresponding tableaux.

1 Introduction

1.1 Free Logics

The proposition "God does not exist" contains a paradox sometimes referred to as Plato's beard: if God does not exist and the proposition should be true, standard referential semantics for quantified logic fails to give meaning to the name "God". But, given compositionality, since the meaning of a sentence is combined from the meanings of its parts, "God does not exist" does not evaluate.

It is easy to see that related difficulties appear in every formula that contains singular terms. In standard logic, it is impossible to state that God is either good or evil without presupposing his existence, or that the round square is round, or even that the flying horse can fly. We always get caught by the lack of (referential) meaning of some of the parts of the sentences.

Several modifications to standard logic have been proposed to deal with formulae containing *referential gaps* while still defending reference (for instance,

---

* My work on this article has been supported by the Fritz-Thyssen-Stiftung which I wish to thank expressly.

Russell's (1905) theory of descriptions renders them false by translating "The P is Q" to $\vee(x)\ (P(x) \wedge \wedge(y)\ (P(y) \rightarrow x=y) \wedge Q(x))$. But they all suffer the same shortcoming: Logic and ontology are conceptually distinct topics, but reference as a tool for giving meaning to formulae necessarily mixes them up. Only such names can be used to build meaningful formulae that denote some entity.[1]

An interesting class of more or less non-standard approaches to give meaning to singular terms is called *free logics*. The name is due to Lambert (1962 and 1963) who first used it in 1960 for a system free of any existence assumptions about entities.[2] Bencivenga (1986) gave one of the most fruitful definitions in his introduction to free logics:

> "A free logic is a formal system of quantification theory [...] which allows for some singular terms in some circumstances to be thought of as denoting no existing object, and in which quantifiers are invariably thought of as having existential import."

Interestingly Quine's (1980) ontological criterion that "to be is to be the value of a bound variable" still holds; it even becomes the fundamental principle of most free logics. Existence is still part of our logic, expressed by the quantifiers: "everything" means "everything *that exists*", "anything" is "any *existing* thing". The crucial difference is that existence does not influence the truth or falsity of sentences containing singular terms that escape the scope of quantification in the same way as in Quine's point of view.

Many different free semantics have been presented, but basically they can be split into two main categories:

1. In *outer domain* systems, reference still holds, but "God" may either denote an object from a domain of existents D_E or from a newly created domain of non-existents D_N. In some flavours of outer domain free logics, D_N is more complex and can itself contain more than one domain.

2. Systems based on modality are somewhat more sophisticated. Every singular term either denotes an existing entity or it does not denote at all; *there simply are no such things like non-existents*. To make a non-

---

[1] Cf. Hintikka (1958). Castaneda (1974) wrote about Plato-Meinongian objects. Though he was mainly interested in ontology and not in logics, the formal nature of his style would be useful to develop non-free logical systems to argue about fictive or contradictory entities.

[2] Although free semantics had not yet been given birth to then and Lambert's concerns were purely syntactic this obviously was what he had in mind when designing his proof system. Cf. also Leonard (1956).

denoting singular term meaningful, models related to Kripke's possible worlds are used in one or the other way (e.g. by mapping formulae containing referential gaps to truth values using a convention like van Fraassen (1966a) did, or by directly evaluating the referential gaps in possible worlds like in Bencivenga (1981)).

We will not go into the details of free logics based on reference nor will we discuss advantages and drawbacks (cf. Read (1995, chapter 5)). Instead, we will present a different approach that proposes a pragmatic view on the relations between ontology and logic. We base this approach on *dialogues*.

1.2 Dialogues

Dialogical logic, suggested by Paul Lorenzen in 1958 and developed by Kuno Lorenz in several papers from 1961 onwards (cf. Lorenzen/Lorenz (1978)[3]), was introduced as a pragmatic semantics for both classical and intuitionistic logic.

The dialogical approach studies logic as an inherently pragmatic notion with help of an overtly externalised argumentation formulated as a *dialogue* between two parties taking up the roles of an *opponent* (**O** in the following) and a *proponent* (**P**) of the issue at stake, called the principal *thesis* of the dialogue.

P has to try to defend the thesis against all possible allowed criticism *(attacks)* of **O**, thereby being allowed to use statements that **O** may have made at the outset of the dialogue. The thesis *A* is logically valid if and only if **P** can succeed in defending *A* against all possible allowed criticism of the opponent. In the jargon of game theory: **P** has a *winning strategy* for *A*.
An interesting fact is that dialogues don't understand semantics as mapping names and relationships into the real world to obtain an abstract counterpart of it, but as acting upon them in a particular way.

1.3 Contents of this Paper

In this paper, we show how the ideas behind free logics can be captured with the dialogical approach to logic. In Section 2, we introduce an intuitionistic and a classical version of a very basic system called **DFL** that fits the definition of Bencivenga cited above. In Section 3, the notion of quantifiers of **DFL** is extended into several directions, some of them motivated by non-dialogical free semantics, others simply by the fact that dialogues open new perspectives on the topic.

---

[3] Further work has been done by Rahman (1993) in his PhD thesis.

2 The Core System

This section introduces **DFL**, a simple system of dialogues that *is free* and *inclusive*. A logic is inclusive if it does not require any entity to exist at all (expressed in standard referential semantics, the domain of correspondence is allowed to be empty). But first, we need some formal definitions.

2.1 Formulae

A formula is a term generated according to the well-known standard conventions using constants (τ, σ,...), variables (x, y, z,...), predicates (*P, Q, R*,...), logical connectives ($\wedge$, $\vee$, $\rightarrow$, $\neg$) and quantifiers ($\bigwedge$ and $\bigvee$).

A formula is said to be atomic if it has the form $P(\tau_1,...)$ for some predicate *P* and constants τ_i. Formulae that are not atomic are called complex. Atomic formulae are represented by small letters (*a, b*,...), formulae that might be complex by capitals (*A, B*,...).

2.2 Dialogues again

A dialogue is a sequence of labelled *formulae* that are stated by either **P** or **O**.[4] The label of a formula describes its role in the dialogue, whether it is an aggressive or a defensive act. An *attack* is labelled with $?_{n/...}$, while $!_{n/...}$ tags a defence. (*n* is the number of the formula the attack or defence reacts on, the dots are sometimes completed with more information. The use of indices of labels will be made clear in the following.)

In dialogical logic the meaning in use of the logical particles is given by two types of rules which determine their *local (particle rules)* and their *global (structural rules)* meaning. The particle rules specify for each particle a pair of moves consisting of an attack and (if possible) the corresponding defence. Each such pair is called a *round*. An attack *opens* a round, which in turn is *closed* by a defence if possible.

Before presenting a dialogical system **DFL** for free logics, we need the following definition:

- A constant τ is said to be *introduced by* X if (*i*) X states a formula *A* $[\tau/x]$ to defend $\bigvee(x)A$ or (*ii*) X attacks a formula $\bigwedge(x)A$ with $?_{n/\tau}$, and

---

[4] Sometimes, we use X and Y to denote **P** and **O** with X ≠ Y.

2.3 The System DFL

DFL is closely related to Lorenz' standard dialogues for both intuitionistic and classical logic. The particle rules are identical, and the sets of structural rules differ in only one point, namely when fixing the way constants are dealt with.

Before we present the formal definition of **DFL**, we have a look at a simple propositional dialogue as an example for notational conventions:

	O		P	
		$(a \wedge b) \to a$		(0)
(1)	$?_0 a \wedge b$	$!_1 a$		(4)
(3)	$!_2 a$	$?_{1/\text{left}}$		(2)
P wins				

Formulae are labelled in (temporal) order of appearance. They are not listed in the order of utterance, but in a way that every defence appears on the same level as the corresponding attack.

Informally, the argument goes like this:

P: "If a and b, then a."

O: "Given a and b, show me that a holds."

P: "If you concede a and b, you should also concede each of them alone. Thus, please concede the left part."

O: "Ok, agreed: a."

P: "If you can say that a, so can I."

O runs out of arguments; **P** wins.

The particle rules are given in Figure 1. The first row contains the form of the formula in question, the second one possible attacks to this formula, and the last one possible defences to those attacks. (The symbol '⊗' indicates that no defence is possible.)

The Dialogical Approach to Free Logic

formula	attack	defence
$A \wedge B$	$?_{n/\text{left}}$	$!_m A$
	$?_{n/\text{right}}$	$!_m B$
$A \vee B$	$?_n$	$!_m A$
		$!_m B$
$\neg A$	$?_n A$	$\otimes$
$A \rightarrow B$	$?_n A$	$!_m B$
$\bigwedge(x)A$	$?_{n/\tau}$	$!_m A\,[\tau/x]$
$\bigvee(x)A$	$?_n$	$!_{m/\tau} A\,[\tau/x]$

Figure 1: Particle Rules
(orig. *Partikelregeln*) for **DFL**

Note that the symbol $?_{n/\ldots}$ is a move – more precisely it is an attack – but not a formula. Thus if one partner in the dialogue states a conjunction, the other may initiate the attack by asking either for the left side of the conjunction ("show me that the left side of the conjunction holds", or $?_{n/\text{left}}$ for short) or the right one ("show me that the right side of the conjunction holds", or $?_{n/\text{right}}$). If one partner in the dialogue states a disjunction, the other may initiate the attack by requiring to be shown any side of the disjunction ($?_n$). As already mentioned, the number in the index denotes the formula the attack refers to. The notation of defences is used in analogy to that of attacks. Rules for quantifiers work similarly.

Next, we fix the way formulae are sequenced to form dialogues with a set of structural rules (orig. *Rahmenregeln*):

(DFL0)
Formulae are alternatingly uttered by **P** and **O**. The initial formula is uttered by **P**. It does not have a label, but provides the topic of argument. Every formula below the initial formula is either an attack or a defence to an earlier formula of the other player.

(DFL1)
Both **P** and **O** may only make moves that change situation.[5]

(DFL2) (*formal rule for atomic formulae*)
P may not introduce atomic formulae: every atomic formula must be stated by **O** first.

(DFL3) (*formal rule for constants*)
Only **O** may introduce constants.

(DFL4) (*winning rule*)
X wins iff it is Y's turn but he cannot move (either attack or defend).

(DFL$_I$5) (*intuitionistic rule*)
In any move, each player may attack a (complex) formula asserted by his partner or he may defend himself against the last not already defended attack.

DFL is an intuitionistic as well as a classical semantics. To obtain the classical version simply replace (DFL$_I$5) by the following rule:

(DFL$_C$5) (*classical rule*)
In any move, each player may attack a (complex) formula asserted by his partner or he may defend himself against any attack (including already defended) of his partner.[6]

If we need to make explicit which system is meant, we write **DFL$_I$** or **DFL$_C$** instead of **DFL**.

A **DFL** dialogue is finite, since the particle rules satisfy the subformula property and (DFL1) ensures that no player may enter a loop iterating a finite sequence of arguments infinitely often.

The crucial rule that makes **DFL** behave like a free logic is (DFL3). To see the difference between standard and free dialogues (those with and those without (DFL3)), consider another example. Without (DFL3), we would obtain the following dialogue proving that if nothing is a vampire, Nosferatu is no vampire:

---

[5] Fuhrmann (1985) has used the same formulation. Intuitively, it replaces Lorenz' *Angriffsschranken*, but this point still remains to be made clear on a formal basis. The idea is that the situation changes if and only if **O** introduces a new atomic formula. See the appendix to Rahman/Rückert (1999).

[6] This rule is actually redundant, but we keep it to make the point explicit.

	O	P	
		$\bigwedge(x) \neg P(x) \to \neg P(\tau)$	(0)
(1)	$?_0 \bigwedge(x) \neg P(x)$	$!_1 \neg P(\tau)$	(2)
(3)	$?_2 P(\tau)$	$\otimes$	
(5)	$!_4 \neg P(\tau)$	$?_{1/\tau}$	(4)
	$\otimes$	$?_5 P(\tau)$	(6)

P wins

If we play the same dialogue again in **DFL**, things look different:

	O	P	
		$\bigwedge(x) \neg P(x) \to \neg P(\tau)$	(0)
(1)	$?_0 \bigwedge(x) \neg P(x)$	$!_1 \neg P(\tau)$	(2)
(3)	$?_2 P(\tau)$	$\otimes$	

O wins

We observe that **P** runs out of arguments. He cannot attack (1) any more, because no single constant has been introduced so far, and he may not introduce one on its own. He also cannot defend himself against the atomic formula in (3) due to the particle rule for negation.

It is easy to see that **DFL** fits Bencivenga's definition. It is a formal system containing quantifiers, and existence can be defined according to Quine's dictum: "God exists" is formalized as $\bigvee(x)$ (x is God). Obviously, if we enter the denotational point of view at all, constants may be thought of as sometimes not denoting an existing entity.

To conclude this section, we would like to point out an interesting consequence of the inclusiveness of **DFL**. The rules do not allow closed formulae to be valid if they occur in an existential quantification (in the empty universe they would not be true for a single object):

	O	P	
		$\bigvee(x) (P(\tau) \to P(\tau))$	(0)
(1)	$?_0$		

O wins

According to the rules, **P** has to use a constant to defend (0). Since no such constant has been introduced so far, he cannot move.

The Dialogical Approach to Free Logic

2.4 Winning Strategies and Dialogical Tableaux for DFL

As already mentioned validity is defined in dialogical logic via winning strategies for **P**, i.e. the thesis *A* is logically valid iff **P** can succeed in defending *A* against all possible allowed criticism of **O**. In this case, **P** has a *winning strategy* for *A*.

A systematic description of the winning strategies available can be obtained from the following considerations:

- If **P** shall win against any choice of **O**, we will have to consider two main different situations, namely the dialogical situations in which **O** has stated a complex formula and those in which **P** has stated a complex formula. We call these main situations the **O**-cases and the **P**-cases, respectively.

In both of these situations another distinction has to be examined:

1. **P** wins by *choosing* an attack in the **O**-cases or a defence in the **P**-cases, iff he can win *at least one* of the dialogues he has chosen.

2. When **O** can *choose* a defence in the **O**-cases or an attack in the **P**-cases, **P** can win iff he can win *all of the* dialogues **O** can choose.

The closing rules for dialogical tableaux are the usual ones: A branch is closed iff it contains two copies of the same formula, one stated by **O** and the other one by **P**. A tree is closed iff each branch is closed. A closed tree for some formula *A* presents a winning strategy for *A*.

For the intuitionistic tableaux, the structural rule about the restriction on defences has to be considered. The idea is quite simple: The tableaux system allows all the possible defences (even the atomic ones) to be written down, but as soon as determinate formulae (negations, conditionals, universal quantifiers) of **P** are attacked, all others will be deleted. Those formulae which compel the rest of **P**'s formulae to be deleted will be indicated with the expression '$[O]_{[O]}$' (or '$[P]_{[O]}$') which reads *save* **O**'s *formulae and delete all of* **P**'s *formulae stated before*.

To obtain free tableaux from those described above, add the following restriction to the closing rules and recall the rule (DFL3) for constants in 2.3:

DFL-*restriction*
Check that for every step in which **P** chooses a constant (i.e. for every **P**-attack on a universally quantified **O**-formula and for every **P**-defence of an existentially quantified **P**-formula) this constant has been already introduced by **O** (by means of an **O**-attack on a universally quantified **P**-formula or a defence of an existentially

quantified **O**-formula).

This restriction can be technically implemented by a device which provides a label (namely a star) for each constant introduced by **O**. Thus, the **DFL**-restriction can be simplified in the following way:

DFL-*restriction with labels*
Check that for every step in which **P** chooses a constant this constant has already been there labelled with a star.

All these considerations can be expressed by means of the tableaux systems for classical and intuitionistic **DFL** (see Figure 2 for **DFL$_C$-T** and Fig. 3 for **DFL$_I$-T**).[7]

[O]-cases	[P]-cases
[O] $A \lor B$	[P] $A \lor B$
---------	---------
<[P]?> [O] A | <[P]?> [O] B	<[O]?> [P] A, <[O]?> [P] B
[O] $A \land B$	[P] $A \land B$
---------	---------
<[P]?$_{left}$> [O] A, <[P]?$_{right}$> [O] B	<[O]?$_{left}$> [P] A, <[O]?$_{right}$> [P] B
[O] $A \rightarrow B$	[P] $A \rightarrow B$
---------	---------
[P] A... | <[P] A> [O] B	[O] A, [P] B
[O] $\neg A$	[P] $\neg A$
---------	---------
[P] A, $\otimes$	[O] A, $\otimes$
[O] $\bigwedge(x)A$	[P] $\bigwedge(x)A$
---------	---------
<[P]?$_\tau$> [O] A [τ/x] (τ has been labelled with a star before)	<[O]?$_{\tau*}$> [P] A [τ/x] (τ is a new constant)
[O] $\bigvee(x)A$	[P] $\bigvee(x)A$
---------	---------
<[P]?> [O] A [$\tau*/x$] (τ is a new constant)	<[O]?> [P] A [τ/x] (τ has been labelled with a star before)

Figure 2: Rules for classical **DFL**-tableaux.

---

[7] See details on how to build the tableaux systems from the above considerations in Rahman (1993) and Rahman/Rückert (1998/99). The use of these tableaux systems follows the very well known analytic trees of Smullyan (1968). Cf. also Felscher (1986).

Observe that the formulae below the line represent pairs of attack-defence moves, i.e. they represent rounds. Also note that the expressions between the symbols '<' and '>', such as <[P]?> or <[O]?_left> are moves – more precisely they are attacks – but not statements.

[O]-cases	[P]-cases
[O] $A \vee B$	[P] $A \vee B$
------------	------------
<[P]?> [O] A | <[P]?> [O] B	<[O]?> [P] A, <[O]?> [P] B
[O] $A \wedge B$	[P] $A \wedge B$
------------	------------
<[P]?_left> [O] A, <[P]?_right> [O] B	<[O]?_left> [P] A, <[O]?_right> [P] B
[O] $A \rightarrow B$	[P] $A \rightarrow B$
------------	------------
[P] A... | <[P] A> [O] B	[O]_{[O]} A, [P] B
[O] $\neg A$	[P] $\neg A$
------------	------------
[P] A, $\otimes$	[O]_{[O]} A, $\otimes$
[O] $\wedge(x)A$	[P] $\wedge(x)A$
------------	------------
<[P]?_\tau> [O] A [τ/x] (τ has been labelled with a star before)	<[O]?_{\tau*}> [P]_{[O]} A [τ/x] (τ is a new constant)
[O] $\vee(x)A$	[P] $\vee(x)A$
------------	------------
<[P]?> [O] A [$\tau*/x$] (τ is a new constant)	<[O]?> [P] A [τ/x] (τ has been labelled with a star before)

Figure 3: Rules for intuitionistic **DFL**-tableaux

Let us look at two examples, namely one for **DFL_C-T** and one for **DFL_I-T**, where we will use again the notation introduced in section 2.3 for keeping track of the moves in a dialogue. First, we run the classical tableau for $\wedge(x) \neg P(x) \rightarrow \neg P(\tau)$.

[P] $\wedge(x) \neg P(x) \rightarrow \neg P(\tau)$ (1)
[O] $\wedge(x) \neg P(x)$ (2)
[P] $\neg P(\tau)$ (3)
[O] $P(\tau)$ (4)

The tree remains open

The tableau remains open for **P** cannot choose τ to attack the universal quantifier of **O**. The following **DFL_I-T** strategy is slightly more complex.

[P]	~~∧(x)P(x) → ¬∨(x)¬P(x)~~	(1)
[O][O]	∧(x)P(x)	(2)
[P]	~~¬∨(x)¬P(x)~~	(3)
[O][O]	∨(x)¬P(x)	(4)
[O]	¬P(τ*)	(5)
[O]	P(τ)	(6)
[P]	P(τ)	(7)

The tree closes

3 Extensions

In this section, we will analyse several extensions to **DFL** that target the modification of the set of quantifiers.

3.1 DFL with Four Quantifiers (DFL-4Q)

Church (1965) proposed a semantics to prove free logics useless that, ironically, turned out to be one of the very first free semantics instead. It is based on the assumption that existence is nothing more than an ordinary predicate, say **E!**. The use of **E!** in combination with the standard (non-free) quantifiers yields a logic that looks very much like **DFL**.

Formally, take ∀ and ∃ as the quantifiers well-known from standard classical logic, and define two more quantifiers ∧ and ∨ as follows.

$$\wedge(x)A \equiv_{def} \forall(x)(\mathbf{E!}x \to A) \quad (1)$$

$$\vee(x)A \equiv_{def} \exists(x)(\mathbf{E!}x \wedge A) \quad (2)$$

As Leblanc/Thomason (1968) (and others at the same time) have pointed out this leads directly to a semantics with two domains, one matching the scope of the existential predicate **E!** (the *inner domain*) and one containing all entities, existing or not (the *outer domain*).

Of course we cannot use definitions like (1) and (2) to describe a system of dialogues.[8] A new system **DFL-4Q** with two pairs of quantifiers, one with

---

[8] Instead, in dialogical logics, semantics is always designed by a set of appropriate particle and structural rules.

The Dialogical Approach to Free Logic

existential import ($\wedge$ and $\vee$)[9] and one without ($\forall$ and $\exists$), is obtained from **DFL** by adding the following two particle rules:

formula	attack	defence
$\forall(x)A$	$?_{n/\tau}$	$!_m A\,[\tau/x]$
$\exists(x)A$	$?_n$	$!_{m/\tau} A\,[\tau/x]$

3.2 Many Quantifiers (DFL^n and DFL$^{<n>}$)

Consider the situation expressed by the following proposition:

> The novel contains a passage in which Sherlock Holmes dreams that he shot Dr. Watson.

There is an underlying reality that the novel is part of, the outer reality of the story told in the novel, and an even outer reality of the dream of the protagonist. To formalize this situation in **DFL-4Q** we run out of quantification classes. To distinguish between the reality of Conan Doyle writing stories, Holmes's reality and the reality of Holmes's dream, we need at least three pairs of quantifiers expressing the three levels of reality.[10]

The solution is simple. Think of the pair of quantifiers of **DFL** as having upper index 0 and add new pairs of quantifiers with higher indices, as many as we need to express every level of reality (or fiction) that possibly could appear.

We call the so derived dialogical logic **DFL^n** The new particle rules to be added to **DFL** are:

---

[9] Note that $\wedge$ and $\vee$ are used in **DFL-4Q** in exactly the same way as in **DFL**.

[10] Hugh MacColl (1837-1909), the father of formal non-classical logic, developed a system of logic which contains the seeds of a many sorted free logic that is somewhat related to the idea of outer domains, though expressed in different terms (cf. MacColl (1906, p. 42-45)). He distinguishes objects that have a meaning independent of discourse, the *real existents,* and the *non-existents* that are of symbolic nature and escape the ontological implications real entities carry with them. See Rahman (1997, 1999a and 2001) for a detailed discussion about the subject.

The Dialogical Approach to Free Logic

formula	attack	defence
$\bigwedge^i(x)A$	$?_{n/\tau}$	$!_m A\,[\tau/x]$
$\bigvee^i(x)A$	$?_n$	$!_{m/\tau} A\,[\tau/x]$

The extended set of quantifiers requires a new notion of introduction:

- A constant τ is said to be *introduced at level i* iff it is used to attack a universal quantifier of level i or to defend an existential quantifier of level i and has not been used in the same way before.

We adapt (DFL3) to **DFL^n**:

(DFL^{n}3) (*first extended formal rule for constants*)
At each level of quantification, other than the $\forall\exists$-level, constants may only be introduced by **O**.

These formulations yield a logic containing a pair of standard quantifiers and arbitrary many more disjunct pairs of quantifiers dealing with different sorts of reality and fiction. In some contexts, it might be useful to have a logic where these different realities are ordered in a hierarchy. We call the system that establishes this ordering **DFL$^{<n>}$**; it results from modifying (DFL3) again:

(DFL$^{<n>}$3) (*second extended formal rule for constants*)
P may introduce a constant τ on a level m iff **O** has introduced τ on some level n with $n < m$ before.

Consider two further examples. The first states that in **DFL^n**, whenever P has an instance in the scope of one or another $\bigvee$-quantifier, it has an instance in the scope of $\exists$; the second makes use of the ordering in **DFL$^{<n>}$**.

	O			P	
			$(\bigvee^1(x)P(x) \vee \bigvee^2(x)P(x))) \to \exists(x)P(x)$		(0)
(1)	$?_0\ \bigvee^1(x)P(x) \vee \bigvee^2(x)P(x))$		$!_1\ \exists(x)P(x)$		(6)
(3)	$!_2\ \bigvee^1(x)P(x)\,[!_2\ \bigvee^2(x)P(x)]$		$?_1$		(2)
(6)	$!_4\ P(\tau)$		$?_3$		(4)
(7)	$?_6$		$!_7\ P(\tau)$		(8)
P wins					

40

O	P
	$(\vee^1(x)P(x)\wedge\wedge^2(x)(P(x)\rightarrow Q(x)))\rightarrow\vee^1(x)Q(x)$ (0)
(1) $?_0 \vee^1(x)P(x)\wedge\wedge^2(x)(P(x)\rightarrow Q(x))$	$!_1 \vee^1(x)Q(x)$ (2)
(3) $?_2$	$!_3 Q(\tau)$ (14)
(5) $!_4 \wedge^2(x)(P(x)\rightarrow Q(x))$	$?_{1/\text{right}}$ (4)
(7) $!_6 \vee^1(x)P(x)$	$?_{1/\text{left}}$ (6)
(9) $!_8 P(\tau)$	$?_7$ (8)
(11) $!_{10} P(\tau)\rightarrow Q(\tau)$	$!_{5/\tau}$ (10)
(13) $!_{12} Q(\tau)$	$?_{11} P(\tau)$ (12)

P wins

Obviously, there are formulae valid in **DFL**$^{<n>}$ that are not valid in **DFL**^{n}. This example makes use of the fact that if some formula holds on a lower level of quantification, it may be used on a higher level as well.

4 Related Work

Bencivenga (1986) wrote a very illuminating introduction to referential free logics based on reference, including some involving modality or more exotic ideas. Many of his older articles contain the theories summarized there (cf. Bencivenga (1978 and 1980)).

This article is one of a series based on the seminar "Erweiterungen der Dialogischen Logik" ("Extensions to Dialogical Logic") held in Saarbrücken in summer 1998 by Shahid Rahman and Helge Rückert. The same seminar has motivated the publication of Rahman (1999a and 2001), Rahman/Carnielli (2000), Rahman/Rückert (1998a, 1999 and 2001b), and Rückert (2001).

5 Conclusion and Open Problems

In this paper several dialogical systems for free logics have been developed. These systems open a new approach to the problem of ontological presuppositions in logical argumentations.

A purely referential approach with the same goal has been proposed by van Fraassen (1966a and 1966b)). His idea is to ignore the fact that certain terms in first order quantified logics do not denote, and takes atomic formulae that lack a truth value to be either true or false, based on some arbitrary propositional convention. An important difference between this so called *supervaluational semantics* and **DFL** is that **DFL** is inclusive while supervaluations are exclusive. It would be interesting to analyse how **P** could be allowed to introduce constants in a controlled manner (making **DFL** exclusive) and prove an equivalence theorem that connects free *dialogical* logics with van Fraassen's ideas.

Definite descriptions have always been a major motivation for free logics.

Whether the dialogical approach to free logics offers a new understanding of the problems involved remains to be examined.[11]

---

[11] We would like to thank Erik Krabbe (Groningen) for careful proof-reading of an earlier draft of this article and fruitful comments and suggestions.

Dialogische Modallogik (für *T*, *B*, *S4* und *S5*)[*]

Shahid Rahman und Helge Rückert[**]

Zusammenfassung:
In diesem Aufsatz wird der dialogische Ansatz in der Logik, der von Paul Lorenzen angeregt, und von Kuno Lorenz für die klassische und die effektive (bzw. intuitionistische) Junktoren- und Quantorenlogik ausgearbeitet wurde, so erweitert, dass in ihm auch Modallogik betrieben werden kann.

    Nach einer Einleitung wird im ersten Abschnitt das bisherige Regelwerk um die Partikelregeln für die Modaloperatoren sowie die modalen Rahmenregeln erweitert, so dass klassische und effektive modale Dialoge für die Systeme *T, B, S4* und *S5* gespielt werden können. Zu diesem Zweck muss der neue Begriff des Dialogkontextes eingeführt werden. Im zweiten Abschnitt werden die entsprechenden Strategientableaux dargeboten, zusammen mit Angaben, wie diese in ein bekanntes Entscheidungsverfahren übersetzt werden können. Der Aufsatz endet mit einigen Schlussbemerkungen.

Rahman, S. und Rückert, H.: 'Dialogische Modallogik (für *T, B, S4* und *S5*)', *Logique et Analyse* 167-168 (1999), S. 243-282

[*] Kuno Lorenz zum 66. Geburtstag.

[**] Die in diesem Aufsatz entwickelte Dialogische Modallogik haben wir im Ansatz zum ersten Mal in einem im Sommersemester 1998 unter dem Titel „Erweiterungen der Dialogischen Logik" an der Universität des Saarlandes von uns gehaltenen Seminar vorgestellt. Wir möchten uns bei allen Teilnehmern dieses Seminars recht herzlich bedanken, insbesondere bei Jung-Bae Son, der bei der Vorbereitung einer früheren Fassung mitgearbeitet hat.
    Ebenso möchten wir uns bei allen bedanken, die diese frühere Fassung gelesen, und uns mit ihren Anmerkungen weitergeholfen haben. So danken wir Marcel Guillaume (Grenoble) und Erik Krabbe (Groningen) für ihre nützlichen Hinweise und Anregungen, Jacques Dubucs (Paris), der uns auf einige mögliche Missverständnisse in Bezug auf die Formulierung der modalen Rahmenregeln aufmerksam gemacht hat, Ulrich Nortmann (Saarbrücken) für seine Anmerkungen zur Nicht-Verzögerungsregel, sowie einem anonymen Referee für sein ausführliches Gutachten.

Dialogische Modallogik (für T, B, S4 und S5)

Einleitung

Der dialogische Ansatz war lange Zeit bis auf einige Ausnahmen nur für die klassische und effektive Junktoren- und Quantorenlogik ausgearbeitet worden, was schon durch Paul Lorenzen und Kuno Lorenz bei der Entwicklung der Dialogischen Logik geleistet worden ist (Lorenzen/Lorenz (1978)). Zu den wenigen Versuchen, diesen Ansatz auch für andere Teilbereiche der Logik fruchtbar zu machen, gehören u.a. die Arbeiten von A. Fuhrmann zur Relevanzlogik (siehe z.B. Fuhrmann (1985)), sowie einige Ausführungen zur Modallogik in Haas (1984), Kamlah/Lorenzen (1967), Krabbe (1986) und Lorenzen (1987)

Diese Ansätze zu einer dialogischen Modallogik stellen so etwas wie Vorgänger zu unserem Aufsatz dar, sie erscheinen uns allerdings als unbefriedigend. Einige prinzipielle Schwächen werden in diesem Aufsatz korrigiert, indem u.a. die folgenden Forderungen beachtet werden:

(1) In der dialogischen Fassung der Modallogik sollen zumindest die gängigsten Systeme (*T, S4, S5*) rekonstruiert werden können.

(2) Die Modaloperatoren ($\Box$ und $\Diamond$) sollen wie die übrigen logischen Partikeln (Junktoren, Quantoren) durch Partikelregeln eingeführt werden.

(3) Der Unterschied zwischen klassischer und effektiver Modallogik soll sich alleine durch die alternative Verwendung der klassischen bzw. der effektiven Rahmenregel ergeben.

(4) Das schon bestehende dialogische Gerüst für die Junktoren- und Quantorenlogik soll erhalten bleiben, die Modallogik soll also eine echte Erweiterung des schon bestehenden Ansatzes darstellen, in der der nicht-modale Teil unverändert als Spezialfall wiederzufinden ist.

Zunächst sei als Ausgangspunkt die Junktoren- und Quantorenlogik im dialogischen Ansatz dargestellt:[1]

---

[1] Eine mathematisiertere Formulierung der dialogischen Junktoren- und Quantorenlogik findet sich z.B. in Felscher (1986).

Dialogische Modallogik (für T, B, S4 und S5)

Rahmenregeln

RR 1 (Ablauf):
Ein Dialog besteht aus einer endlichen Folge von Dialogschritten oder Zügen, in denen zwei Gesprächspartner, der Proponent **P** und der Opponent **O**, abwechselnd Argumente (von **O** bzw. **P** gesetzte Aussagen) gemäß den Partikelregeln und den übrigen Rahmenregeln vorbringen. Der erste Dialogschritt ist das Setzen der These des Dialogs durch **P**. Jeder weitere Dialogschritt oder Zug besteht im Vorbringen eines Arguments durch einen der beiden Dialogpartner. Jedes Argument ist entweder ein Angriff auf eine vorangehende Behauptung des Gegners oder eine Verteidigung auf einen vorhergehenden gegnerischen Angriff gemäß den Partikelregeln, jedoch nicht beides zugleich.

RR 2 (Dialogende):
Ein Dialog ist beendet, wenn dem Spieler am Zug kein nach den Regeln erlaubtes Argument mehr zur Verfügung steht. Einen beendeten Dialog hat derjenige gewonnen, der den letzten Zug gemacht hat, sein Gegner hat den Dialog verloren.

RR 3 (e) (effektive Rahmenregel):
X darf nach eigener Wahl ein beliebiges von Y (X und Y stehen für **O** bzw. **P**, wobei X ≠ Y) gesetztes Argument angreifen, soweit dies die Partikelregeln und die übrigen Rahmenregeln zulassen, oder sich auf den letzten noch unbeantworteten Angriff von Y verteidigen.

oder

RR 3 (k) (klassische Rahmenregel):
X darf nach eigener Wahl ein beliebiges von Y gesetztes Argument angreifen oder sich auf einen beliebigen Angriff von Y verteidigen, soweit dies die Partikelregeln und die übrigen Rahmenregeln zulassen.

RR 4 (keine Verzögerungen):
X darf ein Argument von Y nur dann ein weiteres Mal angreifen bzw. sich auf einen Angriff ein weiteres Mal verteidigen (letzteres ist nur bei klassischer Rahmenregelung erlaubt), wenn sich dadurch neue Zugmöglichkeiten ergeben.[2]

---

[2] Diese Regel, die mit ähnlichem Wortlaut auch schon in Fuhrmann (1985) verwendet wurde, birgt einige Probleme. Im Anhang findet sich eine ausführlichere Formulierung.

Dialogische Modallogik (für T, B, S4 und S5)

RR 5 (formale Rahmenregel):
P darf nur solche Primaussagen als Argumente setzen, die **O** bereits zuvor gesetzt hat. **O** darf Primaussagen jederzeit setzen (soweit dies die Partikelregeln und die übrigen Rahmenregeln zulassen). Primaussagen sind (im formalen Dialog) nicht angreifbar.

Dialogische Modallogik (für T, B, S4 und S5)

Partikelregeln

∨, ∧, →, ¬, ⋀, ⋁	*Angriff*	*Verteidigung*
$A \vee B$	?	A -------- B (Der Verteidiger hat die Wahl)
$A \wedge B$	?L(inks) -------- ?R(echts) (Der Angreifer hat die Wahl)	A -------- B
$A \rightarrow B$	A	B
$\neg A$	A	⊗ (Keine Verteidigung möglich. Nur Gegenangriff spielbar)
$\bigwedge_x A$	$?_n$ (Der Angreifer hat die Wahl)	$A\,[n/x]$
$\bigvee_x A$	?	$A\,[n/x]$ (Der Verteidiger hat die Wahl)

Dialogische Modallogik (für T, B, S4 und S5)

Die angegebenen Rahmen- und Partikelregeln definieren die effektiven (bei RR 3(e)) bzw. klassischen (bei RR 3(k)) formalen Dialogspiele.[3] Logische Gültigkeit wird folgendermaßen definiert:

Def. Gültigkeit:
Eine Formel heiße in einer bestimmten Dialogischen Logik gültig, wenn **P** unter den entsprechenden Regeln eine (formale) Gewinnstrategie hat. (Eine Gewinnstrategie zu haben, bedeutet, zu allen Zugwahlen des Gegners immer mindestens selbst eine Zugmöglichkeit zur Verfügung zu haben, sodass man schließlich den Gewinn erzwingen kann.)[4]

Es kann gezeigt werden, dass bei effektiver bzw. klassischer Rahmenregelung sich genau die Formeln als gültig erweisen, die auch in anderen Ansätzen als effektiv bzw. klassisch gültig gelten.[5]

(Anmerkung: Bei den Regeln RR 3 (e) und RR 3 (k) haben wir die symmetrische Variante angegeben. Symmetrisch deshalb, da **O** und **P** jeweils gleiche Rechte und Pflichten haben. Es kann gezeigt werden, dass sich die Rechte von **O** einschränken lassen, die Klasse der Formeln, für die **P** eine Gewinnstrategie hat, aber unverändert bleibt. Der Einfachheit halber verwenden wir im Folgenden in den Beispielen die sogenannten asymmetrischen Rahmenregeln, bei denen sich gegenüber den symmetrischen Varianten nur folgendes ändert: **O** darf nur jeweils entweder den letzten Zug von **P** angreifen oder sich auf diesen verteidigen.)

---

[3] Formal deshalb, weil eine formale Rahmenregel verwendet wird, im Gegensatz zu materialen Dialogspielen, die in diesem Aufsatz nicht betrachtet werden.

[4] Der Begriff der Gewinnstrategie kann mit Hilfe einer rekursiven Definition folgendermaßen präzisiert werden: Es gibt eine Gewinnstrategie für **P**, wenn die Ausgangsstellung (nach Setzen der These) eine Gewinnstellung für **P** ist. Eine Stellung ist eine Gewinnstellung für **P**, wenn **P** zu jeder möglichen Zugwahl von **O** mindestens einen Zug zur Verfügung hat, der den Dialog gewinnt oder wieder zu einer Gewinnstellung für **P** führt.

[5] Diesbezügliche Beweise finden sich u.a. in Barth/Krabbe (1982), Krabbe (1985) und Rahman (1993).

Dialogische Modallogik (für T, B, S4 und S5)

Beispiel 1 (bei RR 3 (e) oder RR 3 (k)):

	O			P	
				$((a{\to}b)\land a){\to}b$	(0)
(1)	$(a{\to}b)\land a$	0		b	(8)
(3)	$a{\to}b$		1	?L	(2)
(5)	a		1	?R	(4)
(7)	b		3	a	(6)

P gewinnt

Beispiel 2 (bei RR 3 (k)):

	O			P	
				$\bigwedge_x(P_x\lor\neg P_x)$	(0)
(1)	$?_n$	0		$P_n\lor\neg P_n$	(2)
(3)	?	2		$\neg P_n$	(4)
(5)	P_n	4		$\otimes$	
(3')	?	2		P_n	(6)

P gewinnt

Anmerkungen zu den Beispielen:
Hier wie in der Folge sind die Beispiele so einfach gewählt, dass man anhand eines Dialoges auch direkt sehen kann, ob **P** eine Gewinnstrategie hat oder nicht. Während für Beispiel 1 kein Unterschied zwischen effektiver und klassischer Rahmenregelung besteht, ist die Formel aus Beispiel 2 nur bei letzterer gewinnbar.

Zur Notation: In der **O**-Spalte sind die Züge von **O** notiert, in der **P**-Spalte diejenigen von **P**. Die Zahlen am linken und rechten Rand geben an, in welcher Reihenfolge die Züge vorgebracht wurden. Der 0. Zug stellt das uneigentliche Anfangsargument dar, um das in der Folge argumentiert wird. Angriffe sind durch eine Zahl am inneren Rand gekennzeichnet, die angibt, gegen welchen Zug sich der Angriff richtet. Die Verteidigung auf einen Angriff steht immer in derselben Zeile wie dieser. Einen Angriff mit zugehöriger Verteidigung, also eine komplette Zeile, bezeichnet man als Runde.[6]

(Wie in Beispiel 2 ersichtlich kann es bei klassischer Rahmenregelung

---

[6] In der Literatur zur Dialogischen Logik sind auch andere Konventionen zur Notation von Dialogen gebräuchlich. Insbesondere werden die einzelnen Züge meist in der Reihenfolge notiert, in der sie auch im Dialog ausgeführt werden. Diese Notation kann unter Umständen bei der Beweisführung von Metatheoremen von Vorteil sein. Wir haben uns dagegen dafür entschieden, jeweils Angriff und zugehörige Verteidigung in einer Zeile zu notieren, da dies zum einen für das eigenständige Spielen von Dialogen hilfreich ist (man sieht stets, welche Angriffe noch nicht verteidigt sind), und da zum anderen der Begriff der Runde für die Formulierung von Strategientableaus wichtig ist (siehe Abschnitt 2).

möglich sein, dass sich **P** auf einen Angriff, auf den er sich zuvor schon verteidigt hat, noch einmal (anders) verteidigt. Um für diese zweite Verteidigung in der Notation Platz zu schaffen, wird der entsprechende Angriff noch einmal notiert. Man beachte aber, dass es sich dabei nicht um einen Zug im Dialog handelt, was durch einen Strich wie bei (3') in Beispiel 2 angedeutet wird.)

1 Modale Dialoge

1.1 Dialogkontexte

Um die Regeln für den Umgang mit Formeln, die Modaloperatoren enthalten, formulieren zu können, ist es zunächst nötig, den neuen Begriff *Dialogkontext* einzuführen.[7] Die Dialogische Logik soll so erweitert werden, dass ein Dialog in mehreren Dialogkontexten ablaufen kann, d.h. dass die Züge unter unterschiedlichen Bedingungen gesetzt werden können. Die nicht-modalen Dialoge ergeben sich so als Spezialfall, bei dem der Dialog durchgehend im Ausgangsdialogkontext verbleibt.

Ein Dialogkontext ist dadurch charakterisiert

(1) aus welchem anderen Dialogkontext er innerhalb des Dialoges eröffnet wurde,

(2) welche Züge in diesem Dialogkontext von **O** und **P** gesetzt worden sind, und

(3) welche Primaussagen in diesem Dialogkontext gesetzt werden dürfen.

Dialogkontexte unterscheiden sich insbesondere also dadurch, welche Primaussagen gesetzt werden dürfen. In der Folge wollen wir uns nur noch mit formalen Dialogen beschäftigen, in denen **P** nicht weiß, welche Primaussagen sich in einem gegebenen Dialogkontext erfolgreich verteidigen lassen. Er darf deshalb selbst in jedem Dialogkontext nur diejenigen Primaussagen verwenden, die **O** in diesem Dialogkontext schon zugestanden hat. Bei modalen Dialogen muss deshalb die formale Rahmenregel (RR 5) auf Dialogkontexte relativiert werden:

---

[7] Bei den Dialogkontexten handelt es sich um die dialogischen Gegenstücke zu den möglichen Welten in der Standard-Kripke-Semantik für Modallogik (für eine Einführung in die nicht-dialogische Modallogik siehe z.B. Hughes/Cresswell (1978)). Der Begriff der *Dialogebene* in Inhetveen (1982) ist mit unserem Begriff des Dialogkontextes verwandt.

Dialogische Modallogik (für T, B, S4 und S5)

RR 5 (m) (formale Rahmenregel für modale Dialoge):
P darf in einem Dialogkontext nur solche Primaussagen als Argumente setzen, die **O** bereits zuvor in dem selben Dialogkontext gesetzt hat. **O** darf Primaussagen jederzeit setzen (soweit dies die Partikelregeln und die übrigen Rahmenregeln zulassen). Primaussagen sind (im formalen modalen Dialog) nicht angreifbar.

Die übrigen Rahmenregeln bleiben in ihrer bisherigen Form bestehen.

Zur Notation:
Für spätere Zwecke ist es günstig, ein Nummerierungssystem, sowie einige Definitionen einzuführen:

a) Der Ausgangs-Dialogkontext, in dem die These des Dialoges gesetzt wird, erhält die Nummer 1.

b) Der erste Dialogkontext, der aus dem Dialogkontext mit der Nummer n eröffnet wird, erhält die Nummer *n*.1, der zweite die Nummer *n*.2, und entsprechend der *m*-te die Nummer *n.m*.[8]

c) Ein Dialogkontext *n* heiße einem Dialogkontext *n.m* übergeordnet, entsprechend heiße *n.m* *n* untergeordnet.

d) Ein Dialogkontext *n* stellt für *n.m.l* einen übergeordneten Dialogkontext 2. Stufe dar, *n.m.l* dagegen bzgl. *n* einen untergeordneten Dialogkontext 2. Stufe. Entsprechend seien Über- und Unterordnung für beliebige Stufen definiert.

e) Bei der Notation eines modalen Dialoges wird bei Wechsel des Dialogkontextes jeweils ein Querstrich gezogen, und links oben in der **O**-Spalte die Nummer die Dialogkontextes notiert, in dem die Argumentation fortgeführt wird.

---

[8] Dieses Nummerierungssystem entspricht genau demjenigen für die möglichen Welten in Fitting (1993).

Dialogische Modallogik (für T, B, S4 und S5)

1.2 Partikelregeln für □ und ◊

Die Partikelregeln für den Notwendigkeits- und den Möglichkeitsoperator[9] werden folgendermaßen eingeführt:

□,◊	*Angriff*	*Verteidigung*
□A (in Dialogkontext α)	? (in einem zulässigen Dialogkontext β, den der Angreifer wählt)	A (in β)
◊A (in Dialogkontext α)	? (in α)	A (in einem zulässigen Dialogkontext β, den der Angreifer wählt)

Anmerkungen:
Durch □A verpflichtet man sich, A in einem Dialogkontext, den der Angreifer nach den gleich anzugebenden modalen Rahmenregeln wählen kann, zu verteidigen. Durch ◊A ist man darauf festgelegt, A in mindestens einem Dialogkontext, den man gemäß den modalen Rahmenregeln selbst wählen kann, verteidigen zu können.

Der Angriff auf ein □A bzw. die Verteidigung eines ◊A sind die einzigen Gelegenheiten in einem Dialog, den Dialogkontext zu wechseln. Das heißt u.a. auch, dass die in der Einleitung angegebenen Partikelregeln für Junktoren und Quantoren für die modalen Dialoge erhalten bleiben, mit der zusätzlichen Bestimmung, dass der angegriffene Zug, der Angriff und die Verteidigung immer im gleichen Dialogkontext zu stehen haben.

Um das Regelwerk für die modalen Dialoge zu komplettieren, kommen wir nun zu den modalen Rahmenregeln, die angeben, welche Dialogkontexte bei einer Dialogkontext-Wahl zulässig sind.

---

[9] Wir folgen in diesem Aufsatz der allgemein üblichen Notation mit '□' für den Notwendigkeits- und '◊' für den Möglichkeitsoperator. Vielleicht ist es eine Überlegung wert, statt dieser Zeichen wie in Lorenz (1995) 'Δ' und '∇' zu verwenden, da die Modaloperatoren offensichtliche Parallelen zu den Quantoren aufweisen.

Dialogische Modallogik (für T, B, S4 und S5)

1.3 Modale Rahmenregeln

Wie schon zuvor erwähnt, ist ein Dialogkontextwechsel nur im Falle eines Angriffes auf ein $\Box A$ oder der Verteidigung eines $\Diamond A$ möglich. Diese beiden Fälle zusammen genommen bezeichnen wir als Dialogkontext-Wahlen.

Die unterschiedlichen Modallogik-Systeme *T, B, S4* und *S5* unterscheiden sich in ihrer dialogischen Fassung nur in den modalen Rahmenregeln, die diese Dialogkontext-Wahlen reglementieren. Diese bestehen aus drei Teilen, die Unterschiede ergeben sich nur aus dem dritten.

RR6.1:
Bei einer Dialogkontext-Wahl kann **O** jeden beliebigen schon vorhandenen Dialogkontext wählen oder einen neuen eröffnen.[10]

Während **O** bei Dialogkontext-Wahlen also keinerlei Beschränkungen unterliegt, darf **P** nur bestimmte schon vorhandene Dialogkontexte wählen (neue Dialogkontexte eröffnen darf er prinzipiell nicht).

Für alle vier Systeme gilt, dass **P** bei einer Dialogkontext-Wahl den Dialogkontext nicht unbedingt wechseln muss, sondern ihn auch beibehalten kann (wie es bei Junktoren und Quantoren ja die Pflicht ist):

RR 6.2:
Bei einer Dialogkontext-Wahl ist es **P** erlaubt, den Dialogkontext beizubehalten.[11]

---

[10] Aus strategischen Überlegungen ergibt sich sehr leicht, dass es für **O** nie ein Fehler sein kann, einen neuen Dialogkontext zu eröffnen. Dies liegt daran, dass **P** bei formaler Rahmenregelung nur gewinnen kann, wenn er eine Primformel, die **O** in einem Dialogkontext gesetzt hat, übernimmt, um erfolgreich anzugreifen, oder sich zu verteidigen. Deshalb wird **P** bestrebt sein, die Argumentation möglichst immer in solchen Dialogkontexten stattfinden zu lassen, in denen **O** möglichst viele (bzw. die richtigen) Formeln schon selbst gesetzt hat. Analog wird **O**, um den Gewinn von **P** möglichst zu verhindern, immer versuchen, die Argumentation, in neue Dialogkontexte überzuleiten, in denen er noch nichts zugegeben hat.

In der Folge nehmen wir deshalb immer an, dass **O** bei Dialogkontext-Wahlen immer einen neuen Dialogkontext eröffnet (wenn die Nicht-Verzögerungsregel dies erlaubt). Für den Fall, dass er das nicht tun würde, und einen schon vorhandenen Kontext wählte, so würde dieser damit automatisch zu einem untergeordneten Dialogkontext gegenüber dem Dialogkontext, in dem die Wahl stattgefunden hat. (So kann es dann auch vorkommen, dass ein Dialogkontext gegenüber einem anderen sowohl unter- als auch übergeordnet ist.) Entsprechend sind die Definitionen der Unter- oder Überordnung beliebiger Stufe zu erweitern.

[11] Diese Regel entspricht der Reflexivität der Relation *R,* die in der Standard-Semantik zwischen den möglichen Welten besteht. Lässt man diese Regel weg, erhält man die

Dialogische Modallogik (für T, B, S4 und S5)

Bezüglich der dritten Teilregel unterscheiden sich *T, B, S4* und *S5*.[12]

RR 6.3 (T):
Bei einer Dialogkontext-Wahl kann **P** einen schon vorhandenen untergeordneten Dialogkontext 1. Stufe wählen.

RR 6.3 (B):
Bei einer Dialogkontext-Wahl kann **P** einen schon vorhandenen unter- oder übergeordneten Dialogkontext 1. Stufe wählen.[13]

RR 6.3 (S4):
Bei einer Dialogkontext-Wahl kann **P** einen schon vorhandenen untergeordneten Dialogkontext beliebiger Stufe wählen.[14]

RR 6.3 (S5):
Bei einer Dialogkontext-Wahl kann **P** einen beliebigen schon vorhandenen Dialogkontext wählen.[15]

---

dialogischen Gegenstücke zu den Systemen ohne Reflexivität, in denen Beispiel 3 (siehe später) für **P** nicht mehr gewinnbar ist.

[12] Die modalen Rahmenregeln sind so formuliert, dass **P** in den Systemen *B, S4* und *S5* gegenüber *T* zusätzliche Zugmöglichkeiten erhält, aber keine einbüßt. Deshalb ist jede in DML-T-k (bzw. DML-T-e) gültige Formel auch in allen anderen klassischen (bzw. effektiven) Systemen gültig. Entsprechende Verhältnisse bestehen auch zwischen *B*- und *S5*-Gültigkeit, sowie zwischen *S4*- und *S5*-Gültigkeit.

[13] Dass auch ein übergeordneter Dialogkontext gewählt werden kann, entspricht der Symmetrie von R in der Standard-Semantik.

[14] Die Änderung von *T* zu *S4*, die darin besteht, dass in *S4* untergeordnete Dialogkontexte beliebiger Stufe ausgewählt werden können, entspricht der Hinzunahme der Transitivität von R in der Standard-Semantik.

[15] In der Standard-Semantik ist R reflexiv, symmetrisch und transitiv.

Dialogische Modallogik (für T, B, S4 und S5)

1.4 Übersicht

Die angegebenen Regeln liefern eine dialogische Fassung der vier modallogischen Systeme *T, B, S4* und *S5,* jeweils in einer effektiven und einer klassischen Variante. Der Übersichtlichkeit halber sei kurz angegebenen, durch welche Rahmenregeln diese acht dialogischen Modallogik-Systeme charakterisiert sind (die Partikelregeln stimmen bei allen überein):

(1) *DML-T-k (Dialogische Modallogik, System T, klassisch):*
RR 1 + RR 2 + RR 3 (k) + RR 4 + RR 5 (m) + RR 6.1 + RR 6.2 + RR 6.3 (T)

(2) *DML-T-e (Dialogische Modallogik, System T, effektiv):*
RR 1 + RR 2 + RR 3 (e) + RR 4 + RR 5 (m) + RR 6.1 + RR 6.2 + RR 6.3 (T)

(3) *DML-B-k (Dialogische Modallogik, System B, klassisch):*
RR 1 + RR 2 + RR 3 (k) + RR 4 + RR 5 (m) + RR 6.1 + RR 6.2 + RR 6.3 (B)

(4) *DML-B-e (Dialogische Modallogik, System B, effektiv):*
RR 1 + RR 2 + RR 3 (e) + RR 4 + RR 5 (m) + RR 6.1 + RR 6.2 + RR 6.3 (B)

(5) *DML-S4-k (Dialogische Modallogik, System S4, klassisch):*
RR 1 + RR 2 + RR 3 (k) + RR 4 + RR 5 (m) + RR 6.1 + RR 6.2 + RR 6.3 (S4)

(6) *DML-S4-e (Dialogische Modallogik, System S4, effektiv):*
RR 1 + RR 2 + RR 3 (e) + RR 4 + RR 5 (m) + RR 6.1 + RR 6.2 + RR 6.3 (S4)

(7) DML-S5-k (Dialogische Modallogik, System S5, klassisch):
RR 1 + RR 2 + RR 3 (k) + RR 4 + RR 5 (m) + RR 6.1 + RR 6.2 + RR 6.3 (S5)

(8) DML-S5-e (Dialogische Modallogik, System S5, effektiv):RR 1 + RR 2 + RR 3 (e) + RR 4 + RR 5 (m) + RR 6.1 + RR 6.2 + RR 6.3 (S5)

Dialogische Modallogik (für T, B, S4 und S5)

1.5 Beispiele

Es seien einige charakteristische Beispiele durchgeführt, die die Unterschiede zwischen den Systemen deutlich machen:

Beispiel 3 (DML-T-e):

1	O			P	
				$\Box a \to a$	(0)
(1)	$\Box a$	0		a	(4)
(3)	a		1	?	(2)

P gewinnt

P kann aufgrund der formalen Rahmenregel (RR 5 (m)) sich nicht schon im zweiten Zug mit a verteidigen. Deshalb ist es nötig, zuerst Zug (1) von **O** anzugreifen. Der Verbleib im Ausgangsdialogkontext wird dabei durch RR 6.2 ermöglicht. Diese Formel ist auch in allen sieben anderen Systemen gewinnbar.

Beispiel 4 (DML-B-e):

1	O		P	
			$a \to \Box\Diamond a$	(0)
(1)	a	0	$\Box\Diamond a$	(2)
1.1				
(3)	?	2	$\Diamond a$	(4)
(5)	?	4	(siehe 1)	
1				
	(aus 1.1)		a	(6)

P gewinnt

Zum Gewinn dieser Formel ist es nötig, in Zug (6) bei der Verteidigung von $\Diamond a$ in den übergeordneten Dialogkontext 1 zurückzukehren. Diese Formel ist deshalb in den *B*- und *S5*-Systemen, aber nicht in den *T*- und *S4*-Systemen gewinnbar.

(*Anmerkung:* Da mit Zug (6) die Verteidigung auf den Angriff in Zug (5) in einem anderen Dialogkontext steht als dieser, ist es hier nicht möglich, unserer Notationskonvention zu folgen, dass Angriff und zugehörige Verteidigung immer in derselben Zeile stehen sollen. Dies wird hier wie in der Folge durch Verweise wie '(siehe 1)' und '(aus 1.1)' angedeutet.)

Dialogische Modallogik (für T, B, S4 und S5)

Beispiel 5 (DML-T -e):

1	O			P	
(1)	$\Box(a\to b)$	0		$\Box(a\to b)\to(\Box a\to\Box b)$	(0)
(3)	$\Box a$	2		$\Box a\to\Box b$	(2)
				$\Box b$	(4)
1.1					
(5)	?	4		b	(12)
(7)	$a\to b$	1		?	(6)
(9)	a	3		?	(8)
(11)	b	7		a	(10)
P gewinnt					

In allen Systemen gewinnbar.

Beispiel 6 (DML-S4-e):

1	O			P	
(1)	$\Box a$	0		$\Box a\to\Box\Box a$	(0)
				$\Box\Box a$	(2)
1.1					
(3)	?	2		$\Box a$	(4)
1.1.1					
(5)	?	4		a	(8)
(7)	a	1		?	(6)
P gewinnt					

Zum Gewinn dieser Formel ist es erforderlich, dass **P** die Möglichkeit hat, zum Angriff auf Zug (1) den untergeordneten Dialogkontext 2.Stufe 1.1.1 aufzusuchen, was nur in den *S4*- und *S5*-Systemen erlaubt ist.

Dialogische Modallogik (für T, B, S4 und S5)

Beispiel 7 (DML-S5-e):

1	O		P	
(1)	$\Diamond a$	0	$\Diamond a \to \Box \Diamond a$	(0)
			$\Box \Diamond a$	(2)
1.1				
(3)	?	2	$\Diamond a$	(4)
(5)	?	4	(siehe 1.2)	
1				
	(siehe 1.2)	1	?	(6)
1.2				
(7)	a		(aus 1)	
	(aus 1.1)		a	(8)

P gewinnt

In Zug (8) wird bei der Verteidigung von $\Diamond a$ aus Zug (4) weder der Dialogkontext beibehalten, noch ein neuer Dialogkontext eröffnet, oder ein schon vorhandener unter- oder übergeordneter Dialogkontext ausgewählt, sondern ein sozusagen 'nebengeordneter' (1.2 gegenüber 1.1), was nur in den *S5*-Systemen erlaubt ist.

Beispiel 8 (DML-T-k):

1	O		P	
(1)	$\neg \Box \neg a$	0	$\neg \Box \neg a \to \Diamond a$	(0)
(3)	?	2	$\Diamond a$	(2)
	$\otimes$		(siehe 1.1)	
		1	$\Box \neg a$	(4)
1.1				
(5)	?	4	$\neg a$	(6)
(7)	a	6	$\otimes$	
	(aus 1)		a	(8)

P gewinnt

Zug (8) ist nur bei klassischer Rahmenregelung erlaubt. Dieses Beispiel zeigt daher, dass im effektiven Fall beide Modaloperatoren nötig sind, und nicht aufgrund der Gültigkeit von $\neg \Box \neg A \leftrightarrow \Diamond A$ beziehungsweise $\neg \Diamond \neg A \leftrightarrow \Box A$ wie im klassischen Fall auf einen reduziert werden können.

Dialogische Modallogik (für T, B, S4 und S5)

1.6 Die Barcan-Formeln

Bei den bisher angegebenen Regeln sind die sogenannten Barcan-Formeln[16] $\wedge_x \square P_x \to \square \wedge_x P_x$ und $\lozenge \vee_x P_x \to \vee_x \lozenge P_x$ in allen Systemen gültig:

Beispiel 9 (DML-T-e):

1	O			P	
(1)	$\wedge_x \square P_x$	0		$\wedge_x \square P_x \to \square \wedge_x P_x$	(0)
				$\square \wedge_x P_x$	(2)
1.1					
(3)	?		2	$\wedge_x P_x$	(4)
(5)	$?_n$		4	P_n	(10)
1					
(7)	$\square P_n$		1	$?_n$	(6)
1.1					
(9)	P_n		7	?	(8)

P gewinnt

In allen Systemen gültig. Der Dialog um die andere Barcan-Formel verläuft entsprechend.

Nun ist die Gültigkeit der Barcan-Formeln aber nicht unumstritten. So hat zum Beispiel Kripke (1963b) gegen ihre Gültigkeit argumentiert, wenn (in modelltheoretischer Terminologie ausgedrückt) die Individuenbereiche (*universes of discourse*) der einzelnen möglichen Welten sich unterscheiden könnten. D.h. dass es in manchen möglichen Welten Individuen geben könnte, die in anderen nicht existieren.

Im dialogischen Ansatz können solche ontologischen Überlegungen durch eine Reglementierung des Gebrauchs von Konstanten im Zusammenhang mit Quantoren umgesetzt werden.[17] Im Fall der Barcan-Formeln kann Kripkes Idee durch die folgende Einschränkung eingefangen werden:

- Zum Angriff auf eine Allaussage $\wedge_x A$ mit $?_n$ oder zur Verteidigung einer Einsaussage $\vee_x A$ mit $A[n/x]$ darf **P** die Konstante n in einem bestimmten Dialogkontext α nur dann benutzen, wenn diese entweder in α schon vorkommt, oder wenn sie im gesamten Dialog noch nicht vorkommt, also gänzlich neu ist.

---

[16] Vgl. Barcan (1962).

[17] Für eine ausführliche Diskussion dieses Punktes vergleiche Rahman/Rückert/Fischmann (1997).

Dialogische Modallogik (für T, B, S4 und S5)

Jetzt ist im obigen Dialog Zug (6) von **P** nicht mehr erlaubt, sodass **O** gewinnt. Auch die andere Barcan-Formel ist nun nicht mehr gültig. In der Folge beschäftigen wir uns wieder ausschließlich mit der dialogischen Modallogik ohne diese Einschränkung.

2 Modale Strategientableaux

In der Dialogischen Logik wird Gültigkeit mit Hilfe der Strategien definiert. Eine Aussage ist demnach in der dialogischen Deutung der Logik genau dann gültig, wenn der Proponent über eine Gewinnstrategie für diese Aussage verfügt. Oder anders ausgedrückt: Die Aussage A ist dialogisch genau dann gültig, wenn A gegen alle Zugwahlen des Opponenten formal verteidigt werden kann.

Um eine systematische Darstellung der Strategien zu formulieren, die **P** haben muss, um die Gültigkeit einer Aussage nachweisen zu können, führen wir zunächst eine einfache Notation ein. Um die Gewinnstellungen aufzählen zu können, unterscheiden wir zunächst die Spielstellungen, in denen **P** eine Formel gesetzt hat (**P**-Fälle), von den Fällen, in denen **O** eine Formel gesetzt hat (**O**-Fälle) – dabei wird jeweils ein Angriffs- und der entsprechende Verteidigungszug zu einer Runde zusammengestellt. Wenn sowohl in den **O**-Fällen als auch in den **P**-Fällen **P** die Wahl über den weiteren Dialogverlauf hat, genügt es, wenn er bei nur einem Dialogverlauf gewinnen kann. Wenn dagegen **O** die Wahl hat, muss **P** alle möglichen Dialogverläufe gewinnen können. Man kann demnach Regeln für den Dialogverlauf aufstellen, die immer nur von Gewinnstellungen zu Gewinnstellungen führen. So verzweigt sich z.B. die strategische Gewinnregel für die Adjunktion beim **P**-Fall, nicht aber beim **O**-Fall:

O-Regel		P-Regel	
Opponent	*Proponent*	*Opponent*	*Proponent*
...	...	...	...
$A \vee B$			$A \vee B$
$A \mid B$	<?>	<?>	A
		...	...
			$A \vee B$
		<?>	B
Da hier **O** die Wahl hat, gilt: Kennt **P** Gewinnvarianten für beide Verteidigungen, so kann er damit immer gewinnen.		Hier hat **P** die Wahl: Kennt er eine Gewinnvariante für mindestens einen Dialogverlauf, dann kann er immer gewinnen.	

Dialogische Modallogik (für T, B, S4 und S5)

Erläuterung: Angriffe, die selbst keine angreifbaren Formeln darstellen (Anfragen), klammern wir mit Hilfe der Zeichnen '<' und '>' ein. Nun zur Subjunktion:

O-Regel		P-Regel	
Opponent	Proponent	Opponent	Proponent
...	...	...	...
$A \rightarrow B$			$A \rightarrow B$
...| B	A |...	A	$[B]$
Wenn **O** die Subjunktion $A \rightarrow B$ als Argument vorgebracht hat, greift **P** mit A an. **O** kann A angreifen oder sich mit B verteidigen. **P** muss also eine Gewinnvariante für beide Wahlen von **O** kennen.		Hier ist B in eckige Klammern gesetzt, da **P** nicht unmittelbar mit B antworten muss. Er kann zunächst die bisherigen Argumente (einschließlich A) von **O** angreifen – er bleibt dabei aber zur Verteidigung von B verpflichtet, es sei denn, der Dialog kommt vorher zu einem Ende.	

Die Strategieregeln können im Falle der anderen Junktoren auf ähnliche Weise angegeben werden:

O-Regel		P-Regel	
Opponent	Proponent	Opponent	Proponent
...	...	...	...
$\neg A$			$\neg A$
	A	A	
Opponent	Proponent	Opponent	Proponent
...	...	...	...
$A \wedge B$			$A \wedge B$
A	<?L>	<?L> | <?R>	$A \mid B$
...	...		
$A \wedge B$			
B	<?R>		

Für die Quantoren müssen noch die folgenden strategischen Überlegungen betrachtet werden: Wenn **O** eine Konstante auswählen kann, dann wird er, um die Spielweise von **P** zu erschweren, der, um eine gewonnene Endstellung mit Primaussagen erreichen zu können, eventuell auf die Züge von **O** angewiesen ist, immer eine neue Konstante auswählen, also eine, die noch nicht im Dialog vorkam. **P** dagegen, wird aus analogen Gründen versuchen, keine neuen Konstanten einzuführen (vgl. Fußnote 10).

O wählt die Konstante, wenn **P** eine Allaussage als Argument vorgebracht hat, und wenn er selbst eine Einsaussage behauptet hat, die er gegen einen Angriff von P verteidigt:

Dialogische Modallogik (für T, B, S4 und S5)

O-*Regel*		P-*Regel*	
Opponent	*Proponent*	*Opponent*	*Proponent*
...	...	...	...
$\vee_x A$			$\wedge_x A$
A [n/x]	<?>	<?$_n$>	A [n/x]
(*n* ist neu)		(*n* ist neu)	

P dagegen wählt die Konstante, wenn **O** eine Allaussage als Argument vorgebracht hat, und wenn er selbst eine Einsaussage behauptet hat, die er gegen einen Angriff von **O** verteidigt:

O-*Regel*		P-*Regel*	
Opponent	*Proponent*	*Opponent*	*Proponent*
...	...	...	...
<?>	$\vee_x A$	$\wedge_x A$	<?$_n$>
	A [n/x]	A [n/x]	
	(*n* muss nicht neu sein)		(*n* muss nicht neu sein)

Nun bleibt schließlich der Fall der Primaussagen zu betrachten, der die für **P** gewonnenen Endstellungen definiert. **P** hat eine formale Gewinnstrategie um eine von **O** gesetzte Primaussage (**O**-Regel), wenn er selbst diese Primaussage als Argument verwenden kann. **P** hat eine formale Gewinnstrategie um eine von ihm gesetzte Primaussage (**P**-Regel), wenn **O** sie zuvor selbst als Argument vorgebracht hat. Mit anderen Worten, die Gewinnstrategie um eine Primaussage fällt bei der **O**-Regel mit der Strategie bei der **P**-Regel zusammen:

Opponent	**Proponent**
...	...
a	
	a

2.1 Tableaux für Junktoren und Quantoren

Von diesen Überlegungen ausgehend lassen sich zwei Tableaux-Systeme – eines für die klassische und eines für die effektive Junktoren- und Quantorenlogik – aufbauen, die den Zusammenhang zwischen Dialogischer Logik und semantischen Tableaux herstellen. (Hier ist aber zu beachten, dass beim dialogischen Ansatz die Tableaux durch die Partienebene begründet werden. Genauer: Die Partikel- und Rahmenregeln der Partienebene legen die pragmatische Semantik fest, die auf der Strategieebene der Tableaux, auf der der Begriff der Gültigkeit angesiedelt ist, vorausgesetzt wird.)

Dialogische Modallogik (für T, B, S4 und S5)

1) Klassische Tableaux

(O)-*Fall*	**(P)**-*Fall*
(**O**)$A \vor B$	(**P**)$A \vee B$
<(**P**)?> (**O**)A | <(**P**)?> (**O**)B	<(**O**)?> (**P**)A, <(**O**)?> (**P**)B
(**O**)$A \wedge B$	(**P**)$A \wedge B$
<(**P**)?L> (**O**)A, <(**P**)?R> (**O**)B	<(**O**)?L> (**P**)A | <(**O**)?R> (**P**)B
(**O**)$A \to B$	(**P**)$A \to B$
(**P**)A, ... | <(**P**)A> (**O**)B	(**O**)A, (**P**)B
(**O**)$\neg A$	(**P**)$\neg A$
(**P**)A, $\otimes$	(**O**)A, $\otimes$
(**O**)$\wedge_x A$	(**P**)$\wedge_x A$
<(**P**)?$_n$> (**O**)$A[n/x]$ (n muss nicht neu sein)	<(**O**)?$_n$> (**P**)$A[n/x]$ (n ist neu)
(**O**)$\vee_x A$	(**P**)$\vee_x A$
<(**P**)?> (**O**)$A[n/x]$ (n ist neu)	<(**O**)?> (**P**)$A[n/x]$ (n muss nicht neu sein)

Erläuterungen:
Die Schließungsregeln sind die üblichen: Ein Baum ist geschlossen, wenn alle Zweige geschlossen sind. Ein Zweig ist genau dann geschlossen, wenn er ein Paar der Form (**O**)a, (**P**)a enthält. In der Sprache der Dialoge: **P** hat genau dann eine Gewinnstrategie für einen möglichen Dialogverlauf (entspricht in etwa einem Zweig des Tableaus), wenn dieser Dialog mit einer Primaussage von **P** endet, die vorher von **O** gesetzt wurde.

Dialogische Modallogik (für T, B, S4 und S5)

2) *Effektive Tableaux*

Die Regeln für die effektiven Tableaux enthalten an bestimmten Stellen Formeln mit dem tiefgestellten Suffix '(**O**)' (z.B. (**P**)$_{(O)}A$). Die Anwendung solcher Regeln bewirkt, dass sämtliche vorher gesetzten **P**-bezeichneten Formeln, die auf dem selben Zweig vorkommen, gelöscht werden (durch Ausstreichen dargestellt).[18] Dadurch wird die effektive Rahmenregel von der Partieebene auf die Strategieebene übertragen. Um diese Übertragung zu leisten, genügt es, wenn man das Suffix '(**O**)' bei der **P**-Verteidigung allquantifizierter Aussagen, sowie bei den Junktoren einsetzt, bei denen **P** das Recht hat, die dazugehörige Angriffsbehauptung von **O** selbst anzugreifen – das heißt bei der Subjunktion und der Negation.

(**O**)-*Fall*	(**P**)-*Fall*
(**O**)$A \vor B$	(**P**)$A \vor B$
---	---
<(**P**)?> (**O**)A | <(**P**)?> (**O**)B	<(**O**)?> (**P**)A, <(**O**)?> (**P**)B
(**O**)$A \wedge B$	(**P**)$A \wedge B$
---	---
<(**P**)?L> (**O**)A, <(**P**)?R>(**O**)B	<(**O**)?L> (**P**)A | <(**O**)?R> (**P**)B
(**O**)$A \to B$	(**P**)$A \to B$
---	---
(**P**)A,... | <(**P**)A> (**O**)B	(**O**)$_{(O)}A$, (**P**)B
(**O**)$\neg A$	(**P**)$\neg A$
---	---
(**P**)A, $\otimes$	(**O**)$_{(O)}A$, $\otimes$
(**O**)$\wedge_x A$	(**P**)$\wedge_x A$
---	---
<(**P**)?$_n$> (**O**)$A[n/x]$	<(**O**)?$_n$> (**P**)$_{(O)}A[n/x]$
(*n* muss nicht neu sein)	(*n* ist neu)
(**O**)$\vee_x A$	(**P**)$\vee_x A$
---	---
<(**P**)?>(**O**)$A[n/x]$	<(**O**)?> (**P**)$A[n/x]$
(*n* ist neu)	(*n* muss nicht neu sein)

---

[18] Die Verwendung des Buchstabens '**O**' im Suffix soll also andeuten, dass nur noch die **O**-bezeichneten Formeln dieses Zweiges erhalten bleiben. Bei **P**-bezeichneten Formeln, die oberhalb einer Verzweigung stehen, und damit also zu beiden folgenden Zweigen gehören, muss beachtet werden, dass sie eventuell nur für einen Zweig ausgestrichen werden.

Dialogische Modallogik (für T, B, S4 und S5)

Wir haben damit Strategien für symmetrische Rahmenregeln aufgestellt, haben aber bei den Beispielen die asymmetrischen Rahmenregeln angewendet. Nun kann aber gezeigt werden, dass eine Aussage, die bei symmetrischer Rahmenregelung gewinnbar ist, auch bei asymmetrischer Rahmenregelung gewinnbar ist, und umgekehrt – der symmetrische Fall erlaubt nur zusätzliche Züge, die strategisch betrachtet redundant sind.[19] Um asymmetrische effektive Strategientableaux zu bilden, genügt es, wenn man das Suffix '(**O**)' bei jeder **P**-Regel einsetzt. Dies ergibt folgendes System:

(**O**)-*Fall*	(**P**)-*Fall*
(**O**)$A \vee B$	(**P**)$A \vee B$
<(**P**)?> (**O**)A | <(**P**)?> (**O**)B	<(**O**)?> (**P**)$_{(O)}A$, <(**O**)?> (**P**)$_{(O)}B$
(**O**)$A \wedge B$	(**P**)$A \wedge B$
<(**P**)?L> (**O**)A, <(**P**)?R>(**O**)B	<(**O**)?L> (**P**)$_{(O)}A$ | <(**O**)?R> (**P**)$_{(O)}B$
(**O**)$A \rightarrow B$	(**P**)$A \rightarrow B$
(**P**)A,... | <(**P**)A> (**O**)B	(**O**)$_{(O)}A$, (**P**)B
(**O**)$\neg A$	(**P**)$\neg A$
(**P**)A, $\otimes$	(**O**)$_{(O)}A$, $\otimes$
(**O**)$\wedge_x A$	(**P**)$\wedge_x A$
<(**P**)?$_n$> (**O**)$A[n/x]$ (*n* muss nicht neu sein)	<(**O**)?$_n$> (**P**)$_{(O)}A[n/x]$ (*n* ist neu)
(**O**)$\vee_x A$	(**P**)$\vee_x A$
<(**P**)?>(**O**)$A[n/x]$ (*n* ist neu)	<(**O**)?> (**P**)$_{(O)}A[n/x]$ (*n* muss nicht neu sein)

---

[19] Siehe Rahman (1993).

Dialogische Modallogik (für T, B, S4 und S5)

2.2 Modale Tableaux

Für die Modallogik muss noch die folgende strategische Überlegung ergänzt werden:[20] Wenn **O** einen Dialogkontext wählen kann, dann wird er, um die Spielweise von **P** zu erschweren, immer einen neuen eröffnen. **P** dagegen ist es nicht erlaubt, neue Dialogkontexte zu eröffnen, und er wird daher immer schon vorhandene auswählen müssen.[21] **O** kann in den folgenden zwei Fällen einen Dialogkontext wählen, in denen er daher einen neuen Dialogkontext eröffnet:

1. **O** greift eine □-Aussage von **P** an

2. **O** verteidigt sich auf einen Angriff gegen eine ◊-Aussage

Um eine Systematik für die Strategientableaux aufzubauen, ist es nötig, diese Fälle durch eine geeignete Regel einzubauen, die besagt, dass immer wenn **O** die Wahl hat, er sich für einen Dialogkontextwechsel entscheidet.
    Um die modalen Rahmenregeln, die sich auf die Dialogkontext-Wahlen beziehen, für die unterschiedlichen Modallogiken einzufangen, müssen die folgenden Maßnahmen für die Bildung neuer Dialogkontexte in den Strategiesystemen beachtet werden:

a) Die Behauptungen, um die auch im neuen Kontext argumentiert werden darf, werden diesem hinzugefügt.

b) Die Behauptungen, um die im neuen Kontext nicht mehr argumentiert werden darf, werden im neuen Kontext nicht niedergeschrieben.

Dies ergibt folgende Fälle, die die oben beschriebenen Tableaux um die Regeln für die Modaloperatoren ergänzen:

---

[20] Die in der Folge vervollständigten Tableaux-Systeme haben starke Ähnlichkeit mit denen in Fitting (1993).

[21] Diese strategischen Überlegungen zu den Modaloperatoren entsprechen genau denjenigen zu den Quantoren (vergleiche z.B. Fußnote 10), mit dem Unterschied, dass **P** im Falle der Quantoren neue Konstanten einführen darf, im Falle der Modaloperatoren aber keine neuen Dialogkontexte eröffnen kann.

Dialogische Modallogik (für T, B, S4 und S5)

1) Modale Ergänzungen für die Tableaux-Systeme

(O)-Fall	**(P)-Fall**
(**O**)$\Box A$	(**P**)$\Box A$
----------------	----------------
<(**P**)?> (**O**)A	<(**O**)?> (**P**)$^{\#}A$
(**O**)$\Diamond A$	(**P**)$\Diamond A$
----------------	----------------
<(**P**)?> (**O**)$^{\#}A$	<(**O**)?> (**P**)A

Das hochgestellte Zeichen '#' soll auf die Bildung eines neuen Kontextes hinweisen. Wir nennen Formeln der Form (**P**)$\Box A$ und (**O**)$\Diamond A$ *#-Formeln,* ihre Teilformeln A entsprechend auch *#-Teilformeln*. Die anderen Modalformeln, die keine Neubildung eines Kontextes erfordern, nennen wir *normale Modalformeln*.

Die Neubildung von Dialogkontexten muss durch ein geeignetes Verfahren für die Hinzufügung (beziehungsweise Nicht-Hinzufügung) der vorherigen Formeln ergänzt werden. Wir nennen die Regeln, die die genauen Schritte dieses Verfahrens vorschreiben, *#-Regeln*. Nun müssen wir die #-Regel für jedes Modallogik-System gesondert studieren:

2) Die #-Regeln

Die Regelung der Kontextbildung für T

> $T^{\#}$-*Regel:*
> Wenn in einem Kontext eine normale Modalformel (**O**)$\Box A$ (bzw. (**P**)$\Diamond A$) vorkommt, so kann (**O**)A (bzw. (**P**)A) in jeden untergeordneten Kontext erster Stufe übernommen werden. Keine anderen Formeln außer diesen und der Teilformel der #-Formel, die die Neubildung des Kontextes erfordert hat, können im neuen Kontext verwendet werden.

Sehen wir uns Beispiel 5 wieder an, und fügen eine Nummerierung hinzu, die die Runden zählt:

Dialogische Modallogik (für T, B, S4 und S5)

Beispiel 10:

1	O				P	
			0		$\Box(a\to b)\to(\Box a\to\Box b)$	(0)
(1)	$\Box(a\to b)$	0	I		$\Box a\to\Box b$	(2)
(3)	$\Box a$	2	II		$\Box b$	(4)
1.1						
(5)	?	4	III		b	(12)
(7)	$a\to b$		IV	1	?	(6)
(9)	a		V	3	?	(8)
(11)	b		VI	7	a	(10)

P gewinnt

Das entsprechende (effektive symmetrische) Strategientableau sieht so aus:

1	
(0)	(**P**) $\Box(a\to b)\to(\Box a\to\Box b)$
(I.1)	(**O**)$_{(O)}$ $\Box(a\to b)$
(I.2)	(**P**) $\Box a\to\Box b$

Die effektive Löschregel in (1.1) bewirkt, dass die Zeile (0) durchgestrichen wird:

1	
(0)	~~(**P**) $\Box(a\to b)\to(\Box a\to\Box b)$~~
(I.1)	(**O**)$_{(O)}$ $\Box(a\to b)$
(I.2)	(**P**) $\Box a\to\Box b$
(II.1)	(**O**)$_{(O)}$ $\Box a$
(II.2)	(**P**) $\Box b$

Hier wird wiederum die Löschregel wirksam:

1	
(0)	~~(**P**) $\Box(a\to b)\to(\Box a\to\Box b)$~~
(I.1)	(**O**)$_{(O)}$ $\Box(a\to b)$
(I.2)	~~(**P**) $\Box a\to\Box b$~~
(II.1)	(**O**)$_{(O)}$ $\Box a$
(II.2)	(**P**) $\Box b$
(III)	$<$(**O**)?$>$ (**P**)$^{\#}$ b

Dialogische Modallogik (für T, B, S4 und S5)

Jetzt wird die T$^{\#}$-Regel angewendet:

1

(0)	~~(**P**) □(a→b) →(□a →□b)~~	
(I.1)	(**O**)$_{(O)}$ □(a→b)	
(I.2)	~~(**P**) □a →□b~~	
(II.1)	(**O**)$_{(O)}$ □a	
(II.2)	(**P**) □b	
(III)	<(**O**)?> (**P**)$^{\#}$ b	

1.1

(III)	<(**O**)?> (**P**)$^{\#}$ b	
(IV)	<(**P**)?> (**O**) a→b	
(V)	<(**P**)?> (**O**) a	
(VI)	(**P**) a,... | <(**P**)a> (**O**) b	
	Der Baum ist geschlossen	

P hat eine Gewinnstrategie für □(a→b)→(□a→□b), weil in 1.1 die Teilformeln der normalen Modalformeln (**O**)$_{(O)}$ □(a→b) und (**O**)$_{(O)}$ □a aus 1 übernommen werden durften.

Die Regelung der Kontextbildung für S4

S4$^{\#}$-Regel:

Wenn in einem Kontext eine normale Modalformel (**O**)□A (bzw. (**P**)◊A) vorkommt, so kann (**O**)A (bzw. (**P**)A) in jeden untergeordneten Kontext beliebiger Stufe übernommenen werden. Keine anderen Formeln außer diesen und der Teilformel der #-Formel, die die Neubildung des Kontextes erfordert hat, können im neuen Kontext verwendet werden.

Sehen wir das effektive symmetrische Strategientableau für Beispiel 6 an, diesmal ohne Kommentare:

Dialogische Modallogik (für T, B, S4 und S5)

Beispiel 11:

1		
(0)	(P)☐a →☐☐a	
(I.1)	(O)$_{(O)}$☐a	
(I.2)	(P)☐☐a	
1.1		
(II)	<(O)?> (P)$^{\#}$☐a	
1.1.1		
(III)	<(O)?> (P)$^{\#}$a	
(IV)	<(P)?> (O)a	
	Der Baum ist geschlossen	

Die Regelung der Kontextbildung für B

$B^{\#}$-*Regel:*

Wenn in einem Kontext eine normale Modalformel (O)☐A (bzw. (P)◊A) vorkommt, so kann (O)A (bzw. (P)A) in jeden unter- oder übergeordneten Kontext erster Stufe übernommen werden. Keine anderen Formeln außer diesen und der Teilformel der #-Formel, die die Neubildung des Kontextes erfordert hat, können im neuen Kontext verwendet werden.

Sehen wir uns Beispiel 4 als (effektives symmetrisches) Strategientableau an:

Beispiel 12:

1		
(0)	(P)a →☐◊a	
(I.1)	(O)$_{(O)}$a	
(I.2)	(P)☐◊a	
1.1		
(II)	<(O)?> (P)$^{\#}$◊a	
1		
(III)	<(O)?> (P)a	
	Der Baum ist geschlossen	

Dialogische Modallogik (für T, B, S4 und S5)

Die Regelung der Kontextbildung für S5

S5#-Regel:

Wenn in einem Kontext eine normale Modalformel (**O**)$\Box A$ (bzw. (**P**)$\Diamond A$) vorkommt, so kann (**O**)A (bzw. (**P**)A) in jeden beliebigen Kontext übernommen werden. Keine anderen Formeln außer diesen und der Teilformel der #-Formel, die die Neubildung des Kontextes erfordert hat, können im neuen Kontext verwendet werden.

Sehen wir uns das klassische symmetrische Strategientableau für $\Diamond\Diamond a \to \Box\Diamond a$ an:

Beispiel 13:

1

(0)	(**P**)$\Diamond\Diamond a \to \Box\Diamond a$
(I.1)	(**O**)$\Diamond\Diamond a$
(I.2)	(**P**)$\Box\Diamond a$

1.1

(II)	<(**O**)?> (**P**)$^\#\Diamond a$

1.2

(IV)	<(**P**)?> (**O**)$^\#\Diamond a$

1.2.1

(V)	<(**P**)?> (**O**)$^\# a$
(III)	<(**O**)?> (**P**)a

Der Baum ist geschlossen

2.3 Das semantische Entscheidungsverfahren von Hughes und Cresswell und die Dialogische Modallogik

Der Zusammenhang zwischen Kripke-Modellen[22] und der klassischen Dialogischen Modallogik sollte spätestens bei den Strategien-Tableaux klar geworden sein. Hier werden wir ein Übersetzungsverfahren von unserem Strategiensystem in das Entscheidungsverfahren von Hughes/Cresswell (1978) angeben. Dieses Übersetzungsverfahren soll den Zusammenhang zwischen den Strategien für klassische Junktorenmodallogik mit den entsprechenden Kripke-Modellen für *T*, *S4* und *S5* explizit herstellen.[23]

---

[22] Vgl. z.B. Kripke (1963a und 1963b).

[23] Die Übersetzung der Strategien-Verfahren für *B* und für die modale Quantorenlogik in bekannte Tableaux-Systeme sollte aufgrund der gegebenen Hinweise klar sein. Vgl. zu diesem Punkt auch die klassische Literatur über semantische Tableaux für Modallogik:

Dialogische Modallogik (für T, B, S4 und S5)

1) Das Entscheidungsverfahren von Hughes und Cresswell

Dieses semantische Verfahren beruht auf der Methode des indirekten Beweises.[24] Man nimmt an, dass die Hauptformel falsch ist, und versucht danach durch Berechnung der Wahrheitswerte (in der Folge '⊤' für 'wahr' und '⊥' für 'falsch') der Teilformeln einen Widerspruch zu erzeugen. Wenn dies nicht gelingt, ist die Formel gültig. Um diese wohlbekannte Methode auf die Modallogik anwenden zu können, arbeiten Hughes und Cresswell mit Diagrammen, die Kästchen beinhalten, die die möglichen Welten des modelltheoretischen Ansatzes repräsentieren. Die unterschiedlichen Modallogiken werden jeweils durch eine Regel charakterisiert, die angibt, wann ein neues Kästchen gebildet wird, und welche Formeln mit welchen Wahrheitswerten in dem (alten und dem) neuen Kästchen niedergeschrieben werden.[25]

Ein neues Kästchen soll in folgenden zwei Fällen gebildet werden:

1. Eine □-Formel ist mit dem Wahrheitswert ⊥ signiert

2. Eine ◊-Formel ist mit dem Wahrheitswert ⊤ signiert

Wir nennen diese Formeln wiederum #-Formeln. Die anderen Modalformeln, die keine Neubildung von Kästchen erfordern, nennen wir wieder normale Modalformeln. Wenn ein neues Kästchen aufgrund einer #-Formel im Ausgangskasten *w.1* gebildet wird, ist dieses neue Kästchen aus *w.1* zugänglich. Wir übernehmen hier zunächst die Notationsvereinbarung für Dialogkontexte, die jetzt auf die Bildung von Kästchen angewendet wird:

Über- und Unterordnung der Kästchen:

a) Das Ausgangs-Kästchen erhält die Nummer *w.1*.

b) Das erste Kästchen, das aus dem Kästchen mit der Nummer *w.n* eröffnet wird, erhält die Nummer *w.n.1*, das zweite die Nummer *w.n.2*, und entsprechend das *m*-te die Nummer *w.n.m*.

Hintikka (1957, 1961, 1962 und 1963), Guillaume (1958), Kripke (1963a und 1963b). Für einen Überblick siehe Bull/Segerberg (1984).

[24] Vgl. Hughes/Cresswell (1978, Kapitel 5 und 6).

[25] Diese Regeln sollen die Zugänglichkeitsrelation der Kripke-Systeme widerspiegeln.

Dialogische Modallogik (für T, B, S4 und S5)

c) Ein Kästchen *w.n* heiße einem Kästchen *w.n.m* übergeordnet, entsprechend heiße *w.n.m* dem Kästchen *w.n* untergeordnet.

d) Ein Kästchen *w.n* stellt für *w.n.m.l* ein übergeordnetes Kästchen 2. Stufe dar, *w.n.m.l* entsprechend bezüglich *w.n* ein untergeordnetes Kästchen 2. Stufe. Entsprechend seien Über- und Unterordnung für beliebige Stufen definiert.

Diagramme für T

T-Regel:
Wenn in einem Kästchen eine Modalformel $\Box A$ (bzw. $\Diamond A$) mit dem Wahrheitswert $\top$ (bzw. $\bot$) vorkommt, so muss A mit dem selben Wahrheitswert in diesem Kästchen und in jedem untergeordneten Kästchen erster Stufe niedergeschrieben werden.

Beispiel 14:

w.1

$\top\Box\top(\top a \land \top b) \rightarrow \bot\Box\Box\top(\top\Diamond\top a \rightarrow \top\Diamond\top b)$
#

w.1.1

$\top(\top a \land \top b)$
$\bot\Box\top(\top\Diamond\top a \rightarrow \top\Diamond\top b)$
#

w.1.1.1

$\bot(\top\Diamond\top a \rightarrow \bot\Diamond\bot b)$

Erläuterungen: In diesem Diagramm soll das Zeichen '#' die Formeln signalisieren, die die Bildung eines neuen Kästchens erfordern. In *w.1.1* wurde die Teilformel der normalen Modalformel $\top\Box(a \land b)$ mit dem von der T-Regel geforderten Wahrheitswert niedergeschrieben. Die zweite Formel in *w.1.1* ist die Teilformel der #-Formel $\bot\Box\Box(\Diamond a \rightarrow \Diamond b)$. In *w.1.1.1* wurde die Teilformel der #-Formel $\bot\Box(\Diamond a \rightarrow \Diamond b)$ niedergeschrieben.

Nun ist es offensichtlich, dass in diesem Beispiel kein Widerspruch erzeugt werden konnte. Die Formel $\Box(a \land b) \rightarrow \Box\Box(\Diamond a \rightarrow \Diamond b)$ ist also nicht *T*-gültig. Sie wäre gültig, wenn man $\top(\top a \land \top b)$ auch in *w.1.1.1* übertragen dürfte. Also dann, wenn man die Teilformel der modalen Normalformel $\top(a \land b)$ auch in ein untergeordnetes

Dialogische Modallogik (für T, B, S4 und S5)

Kästchen zweiter Stufe übernehmen dürfte. Dies ist der Fall bei dem Entscheidungsverfahren für *S4*:

Diagramme für S4

    S4-Regel:
    Wenn in einem Kästchen eine Modalformel $\Box A$ (bzw. $\Diamond A$) mit dem Wahrheitswert $\top$ (bzw. $\bot$) vorkommt, so muss A mit dem selben Wahrheitswert in diesem Kästchen und in jedem untergeordneten Kästchen beliebiger Stufe niedergeschrieben werden.

Diese Regel ergibt für das oben angegebene Beispiel das folgende Diagramm:

Beispiel 15:

```
                        w.1
┌─────────────────────────────────────────────────┐
│ ⊤□⊤(⊤a∧⊤b)→⊥□□⊤(⊤◊⊤a→⊤◊⊤b)                      │
│                       #                          │
└─────────────────────────────────────────────────┘

                       w.1.1
┌─────────────────────────────────────────────────┐
│              ⊤(⊤a∧⊤b)                            │
│              ⊥□⊤(⊤◊⊤a→⊤◊⊤b)                     │
│                       #                          │
└─────────────────────────────────────────────────┘

                      w.1.1.1
┌─────────────────────────────────────────────────┐
│              ⊤(⊤a∧⊤b)                            │
│              ⊥(⊤◊⊤a→⊥◊⊥b)                       │
└─────────────────────────────────────────────────┘
```

Erläuterungen: In w.1.1.1 kommt ein Widerspruch vor, nämlich $\top b$, $\bot b$ (im Diagramm wurde der Widerspruch durch Unterstreichen hervorgehoben). Die Formel $\Box(a \wedge b) \rightarrow \Box\Box(\Diamond a \rightarrow \Diamond b)$ ist also *S4*-gültig.

Diagramme für S5

    S5-Regel:
    Wenn in einem Kästchen eine Modalformel $\Box A$ (bzw. $\Diamond A$) mit dem Wahrheitswert $\top$ (bzw. $\bot$) vorkommt, so muss A mit dem selben Wahrheitswert in diesem Kästchen und in jedem anderen Kästchen niedergeschrieben werden.

Dialogische Modallogik (für T, B, S4 und S5)

Die Anwendung des Entscheidungsverfahrens auch für *S5* stellt keine zusätzlichen Probleme dar, sodass wir uns hier erlauben, auf ein Beispiel zu verzichten.

2) Die Übersetzung von Strategien in das Entscheidungsverfahren von Hughes und Cresswell

Mit den schon getroffenen Notationsvereinbarungen dürfte der Zusammenhang zwischen dem Entscheidungsverfahren von Hughes und Cresswell und den Strategientableaux offensichtlich geworden sein:

1. **P**-Formeln entsprechen ⊥-Formeln

2. **O**-Formeln entsprechen ⊤-Formeln

3. Kontexte entsprechen Kästchen (einschließlich der dazugehörigen Nummerierung)

Wenn diese Übersetzungen durchführt sind, ergeben sich außerdem die beiden folgenden Zusammenhänge:

4. Die strategischen #-Formeln entsprechen den #-Formeln des Entscheidungsverfahrens

5. Die strategischen #-Regeln entsprechen den #-Regeln des Entscheidungsverfahrens

Betrachten wir dies noch anhand eines Beispiels. Dazu stellen wir das Beispiel 13 in Kästchenform dar:

Dialogische Modallogik (für T, B, S4 und S5)

Beispiel 16:

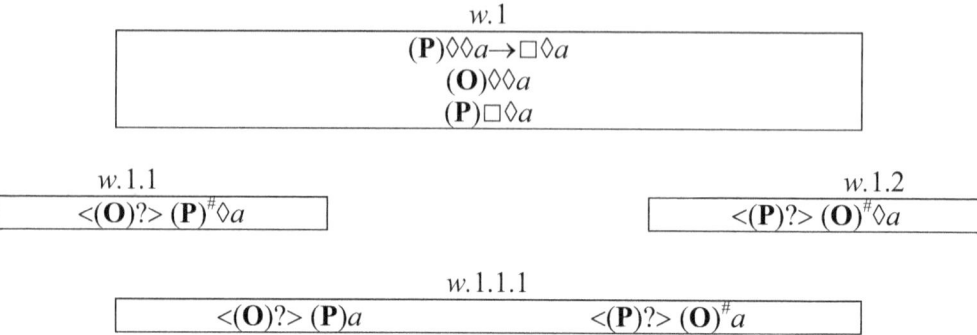

Schlussbemerkungen

In diesem Aufsatz haben wir Vorschläge gemacht, den dialogischen Ansatz in der Logik so zu erweitern, dass in ihm auch Modallogik betrieben werden kann. Dabei haben wir uns auf die gängigsten modallogischen Systeme *T, B, S4* und *S5* beschränkt. Eine dialogische Rekonstruktion auch weiterer der vielen bekannten Modallogiken sollte auf Grundlage dieser Vorschläge möglich sein.

Was ist aber durch eine dialogische Fassung der Modallogik (neben den effektiven Versionen der rekonstruierten Systeme) gewonnen? Wir möchten hier kurze Hinweise geben, wie die im dialogischen Ansatz vorhandenen Differenzierungen, die nun auch für die Modallogik zur Verfügung stehen, ausgenutzt werden können.[26]

1) Die Unterscheidung Partienebene/Strategieebene

Die Unterscheidung zwischen der Ebene der Partien, auf der Sinn- bzw. Bedeutungsfragen angesiedelt werden können, und der Ebene der Strategien, auf der Geltungsfragen angesiedelt werden können, ist in dieser Form in anderen Ansätzen in der Logik nicht verfügbar.[27] In einer früheren Arbeit haben wir gezeigt, wie sie für theoretische Zwecke fruchtbar gemacht werden kann.[28]

---

[26] Eine ausführlichere Diskussion der Besonderheiten und daraus resultierenden Vorteile des dialogischen Ansatzes findet sich in Rückert (2001).

[27] Aus dialogischer Sicht werden diese beiden Ebenen in den meisten anderen Ansätzen vermischt, bzw. es spielt sich alles immer schon auf der Strategieebene ab.

[28] Vgl. Rahman/Rückert (1998/99).

Dialogische Modallogik (für T, B, S4 und S5)

2) Die Unterscheidung Partikelregeln/Rahmenregeln

Das differenzierte Regelwerk der Dialogischen Logik erlaubt es, unterschiedliche Logiken dadurch zu erhalten, dass man unter Beibehaltung der immer gleichen Partikelregeln bestimmte Rahmenregeln abändert oder hinzufügt.[29] So unterscheiden sich z.B. die klassische und die effektive Version einer Logik immer nur in einer bestimmten Rahmenregel, und Arbeiten zur dialogischen parakonsistenten und freien Logik wurden wiederum andere Rahmenregeln hinzugefügt oder geändert, um die Hauptideen dieser Logiken im dialogischen Ansatz umzusetzen.[30] Da die Änderungen an unterschiedlichen Stellen im Regelwerk stattfinden, ist es im dialogischen Ansatz sehr einfach, Logiken zu kombinieren.[31] So können die in den anderen Aufsätzen vorgeschlagenen Rahmenregeländerungen zur hier vorgestellten dialogischen Modallogik hinzugefügt werden, um dadurch sehr einfach zum Beispiel eine parakonsistente oder eine freie Modallogik zu erhalten.

Anhang: Die Nicht-Verzögerungsregel

In diesem Anhang soll die sogenannte Nicht-Verzögerungsregel etwas ausführlicher diskutiert und formuliert werden. Im Haupttext lautet sie folgendermaßen:

> *RR 4 (keine Verzögerungen):*
> X darf ein Argument von Y nur dann ein weiteres Mal angreifen bzw. sich auf einen Angriff ein weiteres Mal verteidigen (letzteres ist nur bei klassischer Rahmenregelung erlaubt), wenn sich dadurch neue Zugmöglichkeiten ergeben.

Die Hauptidee hinter dieser Regel ist, dass in einem Dialog nur Züge gemacht werden dürfen, die die Spielsituation verändern. Dies wäre nur dann nicht der Fall, wenn auch Wiederholungen von Angriffen oder Verteidigungen zugelassen würden, die zu bloßen Wiederholungen von schon gespielten Zugfolgen führen. Zunächst muss definiert werden, was Verteidigungs- und Angriffswiederholungen (im strikten Sinne) sind:

---

[29] Diese Vorgehensweise entspricht dem im Zusammenhang mit der *Display Logic* sogenannten *Došen's Principle* (vgl. Wansing (1994)).

[30] Vergleiche Rahman/Carnielli (2000) und Rahman/Rückert/Fischmann (1997).

[31] Für eine Kombination von freier mit parakonsistenter Logik, u.a. zur Behandlung von Fiktionen, siehe Rahman (1999a und 2001).

Dialogische Modallogik (für T, B, S4 und S5)

Verteidigungswiederholungen

In den folgenden Fällen handelt es sich um Verteidigungswiederholungen (im strikten Sinne):

a) Ein Angriff, der schon verteidigt wurde, wird noch einmal mit derselben Verteidigung beantwortet.

b) Ein Angriff auf einen Existenzquantor, der schon unter Verwendung einer damals neuen Konstante verteidigt wurde, wird noch einmal unter Verwendung einer neuen Konstante verteidigt.

c) Ein Angriff auf einen Möglichkeitsoperator, der schon unter Eröffnung eines neuen Dialogkontextes verteidigt wurde, wird noch einmal unter Eröffnung eines neuen Dialogkontextes verteidigt.

Angriffswiederholungen

In den folgenden Fällen handelt es sich um Angriffswiederholungen (im strikten Sinne):

a) Eine Formel wird angegriffen, obwohl die gleiche Formel (aus demselben Dialogkontext) schon mit dem gleichen Angriff angegriffen wurde.

b) Ein Allquantor wird unter Verwendung einer neuen Konstante angegriffen, obwohl der gleiche Allquantor (aus dem selben Dialogkontext) schon unter Verwendung einer damals neuen Konstante angegriffen wurde.

c) Ein Notwendigkeitsoperator wird unter Eröffnung eines neuen Dialogkontextes angegriffen, obwohl der gleiche Notwendigkeitsoperator (aus demselben Dialogkontext) schon unter Eröffnung eines damals neuen Dialogkontextes angegriffen wurde.

Bei intuitionistischer Rahmenregelung kann sich durch eine Angriffswiederholung die Spielsituation deshalb ändern, weil durch eine Angriffswiederholung ein Angriff zum letzten noch nicht verteidigten Angriff wird, der zuvor nicht der letzte noch nicht verteidigte Angriff war.[32] Dies kann dem Proponenten aber nur dann Vorteile

---

[32] Rahman/Roetti (1999) schlagen eine gegenüber der intuitionistischen duale Rahmenregelung zur Formulierung parakonsistenter Logiken vor. Für diesen Fall müsste auch die Nicht-Verzögerungsregel entsprechend abgeändert werden.

einbringen, wenn seit dem wiederholten Angriff der Opponent in Form von gesetzten Primformeln weitere Zugeständnisse gemacht hat, auf die **P** wegen der formalen Rahmenregel angewiesen ist.[33] Aber auch bei klassischer Rahmenregelung kann der Proponent auf eine Angriffswiederholung angewiesen sein, um eine klassisch gültige Formel (etwa die Peirce'sche Formel $((a \rightarrow b) \rightarrow a) \rightarrow a$) auch gewinnen zu können.[34] Aufgrund dieser Überlegungen gelangen wir zur folgenden Einschränkung bezüglich Angriffs- und Verteidigungswiederholungen:

> *Restriktionen für Angriffs- und Verteidigungswiederholungen:*
> Verteidigungswiederholungen (im strikten Sinne) sind grundsätzlich nicht erlaubt. Angriffswiederholungen (im strikten Sinne) sind nur dem Proponenten erlaubt, und zwar nur dann, wenn der Opponent seit dem zu wiederholenden Angriff eine Primformel gesetzt hat, oder wenn er seit dem zu wiederholenden Angriff einen Dialogkontext als zugelassen ausgewiesen hat, der zuvor noch nicht als zugelassen bekannt war.

Eine Schwierigkeit

In den Modallogiksystemen mit Transitivität der Zugelassenheitsrelation zwischen den Dialogkontexten muss dem Opponenten noch folgender Fall untersagt werden:

> Der Opponent eröffnet einen neuen Dialogkontext, um einen Notwendigkeitsoperator anzugreifen, obwohl der gleiche Notwendigkeitsoperator aus einem übergeordneten Dialogkontext schon unter Eröffnung eines damals neuen Dialogkontextes angegriffen wurde.[35]

---

[33] Für die Formulierung der Nicht-Verzögerungsregel für die in Rahman/Rückert/Fischmann (1997) vorgeschlagenen dialogischen freien Logiken, müsste beachtet werden, dass neben der Einführung neuer Primformeln und Dialogkontexte (mit ihren Zulässigkeitsrelationen) auch die Einführung neuer Konstanten relevant ist.

[34] Wir danken Joao Marcos dafür, dass er uns auf diesen Fall aufmerksam gemacht hat.

[35] Für eine ausführlichere Behandlung dieses Problems im Zusammenhang mit einer dialogischen Fassung des modallogischen Systems *G* vgl. Nortmann (2001).

Dialogische Logik und Relevanz

Shahid Rahman[*] und Helge Rückert

Abstract:
Many of the discussions about conditionals can best be put as follows: Can those conditionals that involve an entailment relation be formulated within a formal system? Now, it is doubtful that anyone conceives of the material implication as representative of entailment – in this case a false statement will entail anything, and a true statement will be entailed by anything. Other, non-classical approaches, such as the modal approach to entailment, were not very successful either. The grounds for the failure of these approaches to entailment have usually been that they ignore the 'meaning connection' between antecedent and consequent in a valid entailment (or to put it in other words, the antecedent must be relevant to the conclusion). In order to consider these claims against the classical understanding of conditionals as sensible, we should have an account of what the concept of "meaning connection" or "relevance" involves.

The dialogical approach to the concept of relevance allows the following semantic idea to be expressed within a semi-formal system: In an argumentation it sometimes makes sense to distinguish between redundant and non-redundant parts of the argument in question. In this approach a valid formula is relevant if and only if every part of it is necessary in order to show the validity of this formula. More technically, we show a new, dialogical way to build relevant systems for propositional and first-order logic with classical and intuitionistic features but without uniform substitution and present their corresponding tableaux.

Rahman, S. und Rückert, H.: 'Dialogische Logik und Relevanz', *FR 5.1 Philosophie, Universität des Saarlandes*, Memo Nr. 27, Dezember 1998

[*] Ich bedanke mich bei der Fritz-Thyssen-Stiftung, die meine Arbeit an diesem Aufsatz durch ein Projekt, das in Zusammenarbeit von den Archives - Centre d'Etudes et de Recherche Henri-Poincaré, Université Nancy 2 (Gerhard Heinzmann) und der FR 5.1 Philosophie, Universität des Saarlandes (Kuno Lorenz) durchgeführt wurde, gefördert hat.

Dialogische Logik und Relevanz

1 Einleitung

Dieser Aufsatz ist Resultat eines von uns im Sommersemester 1998 unter dem Titel „Erweiterungen der Dialogischen Logik" an der Universität des Saarlandes gehaltenen Seminars.[1] Ebenfalls aus dieser Quelle hervorgegangen sind schon veröffentlichte Artikel zur parakonsistenten Logik (Rahman/Carnielli (2000)) zur freien Logik (Rahman/Rückert/Fischmann (1997)) und zur Modallogik (Rahman/Rückert (1999)), ein entsprechender Aufsatz zur konnexen Logik ist in Vorbereitung (Rahman/Rückert (2001b)).

Vor diesem Seminar war der dialogische Ansatz bis auf einige Ausnahmen nur für die klassische und effektive Junktoren- und Quantorenlogik ausgearbeitet, was schon durch Paul Lorenzen und Kuno Lorenz bei der Entwicklung der Dialogischen Logik geleistet worden ist (Lorenzen/Lorenz (1978)). Zu den wenigen Versuchen, diesen Ansatz auch für andere Teilbereiche der Logik fruchtbar zu machen, gehören u.a. die Arbeit von Fuhrmann (1985) zur Relevanzlogik, sowie einige Ausführungen zur Modallogik, die neuerdings in Lorenzen (1987) zu finden sind.

Die Ansätze zu einer dialogischen Relevanzlogik von Fuhrmann stellen so etwas wie einen Vorgänger zu unserem Aufsatz dar. Sie unterscheiden sich allerdings von den von uns in diesem Aufsatz vorgelegten Vorschlägen, Relevanzüberlegungen im dialogischen Ansatz zu erfassen, in einigen prinzipiellen Punkten. Deshalb sei vorab schon auf die wichtigsten hingewiesen:

1) Die dialogische Relevanzlogik soll sich nicht nur auf Wenn-Danns erster Ordnung beschränken (insbesondere sollen auch quantorenlogische Formeln Berücksichtigung finden).

2) Die Idee der Relevanz soll mittels eines Relevanzkriteriums auf der Strategieebene umgesetzt werden (und nicht durch Rahmenregeln auf der Partienebene).

3) Das schon bestehende dialogische Gerüst für die Junktoren- und Quantorenlogik soll erhalten bleiben, die Relevanzlogik soll also eine Erweiterung des bestehenden Ansatzes darstellen.

---

[1] Wir möchten uns bei allen Teilnehmern dieses Seminars recht herzlich bedanken.

1.1 Relevanz und Redundanz

In der philosophischen Diskussion um die kontraintuitiven Konsequenzen einer wahrheitswertdefiniten Fassung des Wenn-Dann kann man zwei komplementäre Positionen erkennen:

Auf der einen Seite stehen die semantischen Klassiker, wie z.B. Quine (1965, S. 16-17), die zu diesen Konsequenzen stehen, sowie die pragmatischen Klassiker, insbesondere Grice (1967 und 1989), die die Verwendung der Sprache von der logischen Semantik trennen. Die Anomalien des wahrheitsdefiniten Wenn-Dann träten demnach nur als solche auf, weil die pragmatische und die logische Ebene verwechselt würden.[2]

Die Relevanzlogiker, wie Anderson/Belnap (1975 und 1992), versuchen dagegen, die Semantik des wahrheitsdefiniten Wenn-Dann mit einer implikativen Deutung zu verbinden, die den Alltagsgebrauch adäquater erfasst als dies in der klassischen Semantik möglich ist, indem sie einen inhaltlichen Zusammenhang zwischen Vorder- und Nachsatz in die Formulierung der Junktorenlogik einführen (vgl. Heydrich (1995, S. 2)).

Um die Problemstellung zu verdeutlichen, möchten wir zunächst zwei Beispiele anführen. Das eine stammt in seinen Grundzügen von Cooper (1968, S. 297) und wurde von Read (1988, S. 23-24) verschärft; das andere wurde in der jüngeren Vergangenheit durch C.I. Lewis bekannt gemacht, stammt aber schon aus dem Mittelalter (eine Version dieses Arguments wurde von Alexander Neckam um 1200 überliefert).

Das Cooper-Read-Beispiel:

Dieses Beispiel soll zeigen, wie die klassische Logik ein Argument als gültig erklärt, obwohl die Prämissen wahr sind, und die Konklusion falsch ist. Nehmen wir an, Jaakko Hintikka habe behauptet, dass Kuno Lorenz in Saarbrücken lehrt, und nehmen wir weiterhin an, dass Wilfried Hinsch dies verneint. Betrachten wir nun die folgende Aussage:

(1) Wenn Lorenz in Saarbrücken lehrt, stimmt Hintikkas Behauptung.

Nun, Aussage (1) ist offensichtlich wahr. Folgende Aussage ist hingegen offensichtlich falsch:

---

[2] Solche Positionen kann man auch in den koginitionswissenschaftlichen Diskussionen um das Wenn-Dann wiederfinden. Eine Darstellung und Kritik der Aufnahme dieser Positionen in den Kognitionswissenschaften findet man in Rahman/Rao (2000).

Dialogische Logik und Relevanz

(2) Wenn Hinschs Behauptung stimmt, dann auch Hintikkas.

Falsch ist auch folgende Aussage:

(3) Wenn Lorenz in Saarbrücken lehrt, stimmt Hinschs Behauptung.

Nun präsentieren wir ein Argument, dessen Prämissen die Aussage (1) und die Negation von (2) sind, und dessen Konklusion die Aussage (3) ist:

$(a \rightarrow b)$ Wenn Lorenz in Saarbrücken lehrt, stimmt Hintikkas Behauptung.

$\neg(c \rightarrow b)$ Es ist nicht der Fall, daß wenn Hinschs Behauptung stimmt, dann auch Hintikkas.

$(a \rightarrow c)$ Also: Wenn Lorenz in Saarbrücken lehrt, stimmt Hinschs Behauptung.

Die Prämissen – nämlich (1) und die Negation von (2) – dieses Arguments sind wahr, und die Konklusion – nämlich (3) – ist falsch. Klassisch betrachtet ist das Argument aber gültig, da die Ableitung

$$(a \rightarrow b), \neg(c \rightarrow b) \vdash (a \rightarrow c)$$

klassisch gültig ist. Der klassische Logiker könnte argumentieren, dass (2) und (3) gemäß der klassischen Logik nicht gleichzeitig falsch sein können – da $(c \rightarrow b) \vee (a \rightarrow c)$ klassisch gilt – und somit das Argument eine unmögliche Situation darstellt. Die Relevanzlogiker könnten erwidern, dass die Situation, wenn man nicht schon die klassische Semantik voraussetzt, die ja eigentlich zur Debatte steht, ganz und gar nicht unmöglich ist.

Dialogische Logik und Relevanz

Das Neckam-Lewis Beispiel:

Dieses Beispiel wurde schon von Alexander Neckam als Argument für das *ex falso sequitur quodlibet* angeführt, wird heutzutage allerdings meist C.I. Lewis zugeschrieben:

1) $a \wedge \neg a$ (Prämisse)

2) a (per Vereinfachung aus 1)

3) $a \vee b$ (per Addition aus 2)

4) $\neg a$ (per Vereinfachung aus 1)

5) b (per disjunktivem Syllogismus aus 3 und 4)[3]

Relevanzlogiker lehnen an diesem Argument meist die uneingeschränkte Verwendung des disjunktiven Syllogismus ab: Wenn man die Disjunktion $a \vee b$ mit Hilfe von a bekommen hat, ergebe es keinen Sinn, den disjunktiven Syllogismus mit $\neg a$ bei gerade dieser Disjunktion anzuwenden.

    Die Kritiken der Relevanzlogiker richten sich im Wesentlichen gegen die Verwendung von logischen Schlüssen, die rein formal und ohne Rücksicht auf inhaltliche Zusammenhänge durchgeführt werden. Das erste Beispiel zeigt, dass die klassische Gültigkeit von den inhaltlichen Deutungen eines Arguments abtrennbar ist. Das zweite Beispiel liefert einen Hinweis auf den Grund einer solchen Trennung: Die Fragen nach dem ob, wie und wofür eine Prämisse

---

[3] „*Ist es nicht so, dass wenn Sokrates (gleichzeitig) ein Mann ist und nicht ein Mann ist, er (eben)* [per Vereinfachung] *ein Mann ist? Wenn aber Sokrates ein Mann ist, dann (gilt)* [per Addition]: *Sokrates ist ein Mann oder ein Stein. D.h., wenn Sokrates (gleichzeitig) ein Mann ist und nicht ein Mann ist, dann ist er ein Mann oder ein Stein. Wenn aber Sokrates (gleichzeitig) ein Mann ist und nicht ein Mann ist, dann ist er (eben) nicht ein Mann. Also, wenn Sokrates (gleichzeitig) ein Mann ist und nicht ein Mann ist, dann ist er ein Stein* [per disjunktivem Syllogismus] *[...]. Seht ihr also nicht ein, dass auf diesem Wege aus der Unmöglichkeit, die darin besteht, dass Sokrates (gleichzeitig) ein Mann ist und nicht ein Mann ist, beliebiges folgt?*"

    Der Originaltext lautet: „Nonne igitur si Sortes est homo, et Sortes non est homo, Sortes est homo? Sed si Sortes est homo, Sortes est homo vel lapis; ergo, si Sortes est homo, et Sortes non est homo, Sortes est homo vel lapis; sed si Sortes est homo, et Sortes non est homo, Sortes non est homo; ergo, si Sortes es homo, et Sortes non est homo, Sortes est lapis [...]. Videsne igitur quonamodo ex hoc impossibili quod est, Sortem esse hominem et Sortem non esse hominem, sequitur quidlibet?" (Neckam (1863, S. 288-89))

verwendet wurde, spielen keine Rolle, während gemäß den Relevanzlogikern gerade dadurch der inhaltliche Bezug eines Argumentationsschemas ermöglicht wird.

Nun hat man nicht sehr viel gewonnen, wenn man den vagen Begriff der Relevanz durch den vagen Begriff der Verwendung (*use*) ersetzt. Die Ironie dabei ist, dass die Relevanzlogiker durchaus einige formale Kalküle vorweisen können, aber keine sonderlich überzeugende Semantik zur Verfügung haben. Diese Mängel wirken bei bestimmten Beispielen ziemlich krass. So ist $a \rightarrow (b \rightarrow b)$ offensichtlich nicht relevant, da die Gültigkeit dieser Formel ohne den Vordersatz bewiesen werden kann. Nun ist aber für Anderson und Belnap die Formel $(a \rightarrow b) \rightarrow ((b \rightarrow a) \rightarrow (b \rightarrow a))$ relevant. Die umständliche Argumentation auf den Seiten 91-92 des Buches *Entailment I* zeigt, dass es den Autoren offensichtlich bewusst ist, dass die Relevanz der Formel $(a \rightarrow b) \rightarrow ((b \rightarrow a) \rightarrow (b \rightarrow a))$ eine unangenehme Nebenerscheinung ihres Kalküls ist.

Die Verknüpfung von inhaltlichem Zusammenhang eines Arguments und der Verwendung einer Prämisse bedarf einiger Erläuterungen: In der Formel $a \rightarrow (a \rightarrow a)$ ist es offensichtlich, dass der Vordersatz für den Nachweis des Hintersatzes nicht benötigt wird, aber man kann nicht ohne Weiteres behaupten, dass der Vordersatz nicht mit dem Hintersatz inhaltlich zusammenhinge (schließlich kommt in beiden Teilen des Wenn-Dann dieselbe Aussagevariable vor).

Eine einsichtige Theorie der Relevanz kann unseres Erachtens aus einigen Ideen von Hugh MacColl gewonnen werden, die von Rahman (1997 und 1998) herausgearbeitet wurden. Im zweiten Aufsatz der Reihe *The Calculus of Equivalent Statements and Integration Limits* von 1878 weist MacColl darauf hin, dass Wenn-Danns mit einem *zero*-Wenn-Teil (d.h. mit einem inkonsistenten Vordersatz) nicht informativ sind – d.h. sie sagen nichts über den Dann-Teil aus.[4] Diese Bemerkung untermauert MacColls Verfahren für die Erkennung von Redundanzen. Eine genaue allgemeine Formulierung des Erkennungsverfahrens für Redundanzen kann mit Hilfe des Begriffs der Wahrheitswertbestimmung erreicht werden:[5]

- Eine nicht-leere Menge von in α vorkommenden Aussagevariablen $\{a, b, c,...\}$ heiße für α wahrheitswertbestimmend, wenn die Wahrheit bzw. Falschheit von $a, b, c,...$ die Wahrheit bzw. Falschheit der Aussage α nach den klassischen Wahrheitstafeln bestimmt.

---

[4] "*Any implication of the form 0:x convey no information, and my therefore be omitted.*" (MacColl (1878, S. 185)

[5] Ein zwar deutlich verschiedener, aber doch in eine ähnliche Richtung abzielender Vorschlag findet sich in Weingartner/Schurz (1986) und Weingartner (2000).

- Es sei Σ die Menge aller Aussagevariablen, die in α vorkommen. Wenn es eine für α wahrheitswertbestimmende Menge gibt, die die Aussagevariable x ($\in \Sigma$) nicht einschließt, sagen wir, dass x eine redundante Aussage (genauer *w-redundante* Aussage) bezüglich α darstellt.

So ist z.B. a in der Aussage $a \to (b \vee \neg b)$ *w*-redundant, da, auch wenn der Wahrheitswert von a unbekannt ist, der Wahrheitswert der Aussage $a \to (b \vee \neg b)$ trotzdem als wahr bestimmt werden kann; in MacColls eigener Notation: $(a^? \to (b \vee \neg b))$[1].

MacColl spricht im Zusammenhang von nicht-informativen Wenn-Danns von Wahrheitswerten für Teilaussagen, die unabhängig von dem Wenn-Dann, in dem sie vorkommen, festgestellt werden. Die Idee besteht darin, dass z.B. in einem Wenn-Dann mit tautologischem Dann-Teil die Wahrheit dieses Dann-Teils unabhängig vom Wenn-Teil festgestellt werden kann, und dies sollte gemäß MacColls Ansicht bei einem starken Wenn-Dann nicht der Fall sein. Dafür ist die Angabe eines genauen Kriteriums erforderlich:

- In einer Aussage besteht eine *w*-Abhängigkeitsrelation, wenn keine ihrer Aussagevariablen *w*-redundant ist. Wir nennen eine solche Aussage in Anlehnung an Rahman (1998) *w-stark*.

- Eine klassische Tautologie ohne *w*-redundante Aussagevariablen nennen wir eine *w-starke Tautologie*.

Daraus ergibt sich folgende Liste von Beispielen:

nicht *w*-starke Tautologien	*w*-starke Tautologien
$((a \to b) \to a) \to a$	$((a \to a) \to a) \to a$
$a \to (b \vee \neg b)$	$a \to (a \vee \neg a)$
$(a \wedge \neg a) \to b$	$(a \wedge \neg a) \to a$
$a \to (b \to a)$	$a \to (a \to a)$
$a \to (a \vee b)$	$a \to (a \vee a)$
$(a \wedge b) \to a$	$(a \wedge a) \to a$

Anzumerken ist, dass obwohl weder $b\to(a\vee\neg a)$ noch $(a\wedge\neg a)\to b$ w-stark sind (b ist jeweils w-redundant), es $a\to(a\vee\neg a)$ und $(a\wedge\neg a)\to a$ dennoch sind. Dies wirkt etwas merkwürdig, wenn man bedenkt, dass es durchaus sein kann, dass für die Bewertung des Hintersatzes von $a\to(a\vee\neg a)$ der Vordersatz a ebenso wenig informativ ist wie b in $b\to(a\vee\neg a)$. Dies gibt dazu Anlass, einen neuen Begriff der Redundanz und der Abhängigkeit zu definieren. Folgende Definitionen sind dazu erforderlich:

- Die singuläre Ersetzung: Wenn ein einzelnes Vorkommnis einer Aussagevariable a in der (komplexen) Aussage α durch einen neuen Buchstaben ersetzt wird, sprechen wir von einer *singulären Ersetzung* des i-ten Vorkommnisses von a in α.[6]

- Wenn ϖ eine dyadische Bewertung und a eine Aussagevariable ist, die in α vorkommt, dann ist das i-te Vorkommnis von a (a_i) genau dann *prim-redundant* (kürzer: *p-redundant*), wenn die Bewertung ϖ von α nicht durch die singuläre Ersetzung von a_i beeinflusst werden kann, d.h. genau dann, wenn die Bewertung von α nach der singulären Ersetzung noch dieselbe ist wie zuvor.[7]

- Eine Aussage, in der keine *p*-redundanten Aussagevariablen vorkommen, nennen wir *p-stark*. Eine klassische Tautologie ohne *p*-redundante Aussagevariablen nennen wir entsprechend eine *p-starke* Tautologie.

---

[6] Die Bezeichnung *singulär* wurde in Anlehnung an MacColl ausgewählt, der in seinem fünften Aufsatz des *Calculus of Equivalent Statements* von *singular statements*, oder einfacher *singulars* spricht. In diesem Aufsatz verwendet MacColl bei der Lösung von Eliminationsaufgaben tiefgestellte Buchstaben, um auf unterschiedliche singuläre Ersetzungen derselben Aussagevariable hinzuweisen (vgl. MacColl (1897, S. 161-163)). Ein demjenigen MacColls sehr nahestehender Gebrauch von singulären Ersetzungen findet sich bei Díaz (1981, S. 70).

[7] Auch der Ausdruck *prim-redundant* wurde in Anlehnung an MacColl ausgewählt, der, wie oben erwähnt, im Zusammenhang mit redundanzfreien Wenn-Danns von *primitive forms* spricht.

Dialogische Logik und Relevanz

Wieder kann man eine Reihe von klassischen Tautologien aufstellen, die nicht *p*-stark sind:

nicht *p*-starke Tautologien

$((a \rightarrow b) \rightarrow a) \rightarrow a$ $\qquad$ $a \rightarrow (b \rightarrow a)$

$((a \rightarrow a) \rightarrow a) \rightarrow a$ $\qquad$ $a \rightarrow (a \rightarrow a)$

$a \rightarrow (b \vee \neg b)$ $\qquad$ $a \rightarrow (a \vee b)$

$a \rightarrow (a \vee \neg a)$ $\qquad$ $a \rightarrow (a \vee a)$

$(a \wedge \neg a) \rightarrow b$ $\qquad$ $(a \wedge b) \rightarrow a$

$(a \wedge \neg a) \rightarrow a$ $\qquad$ $(a \wedge a) \rightarrow a$

Jede *p*-starke Tautologie ist auch eine *w*-starke Tautologie, aber nicht umgekehrt. So ist z.B. das erste Vorkommnis von *a* in der Aussage $a \rightarrow (a \vee \neg a)$ *p*-redundant, da die singuläre Ersetzung $b \rightarrow (a \vee \neg a)$ weiterhin eine klassische Tautologie ist.

Nun stellt der Begriff der *p*-starken-Tautologie unseres Erachtens einen klaren Vorschlag zur Charakterisierung der Relevanz dar. Man kann diesen Begriff sogar verallgemeinern, sodass er nicht unbedingt an den klassischen Ansatz der wahrheitsdefiniten Aussagen gebunden ist. Um die Pointe der Verallgemeinerung zu verdeutlichen zeigen wir, wie eine solche Verallgemeinerung der Definition der Wahrheitswertbestimmung vorgenommen werden soll:

- Eine nicht-leere Menge von in α vorkommenden Aussagevariablen-Vorkommnissen $\{a_i, a_j ..., b_i, b_j ..., c_i, c_j,...\}$ heiße für α *gültigkeitsbestimmend*, wenn es ein Verfahren gibt, mit dem man mit alleiniger Hilfe von $a_i, a_j ..., b_i, b_j,..., c_i, c_j,...$ die Gültigkeit bzw. Ungültigkeit der Aussage α bestimmen kann.

Die Pointe des Vorschlags ist es, den Begriff der Relevanz einzufangen, indem man die Semantik bzw. den Sinn mit Gültigkeit in Verbindung bringt. Die Dialogische Logik verfügt über eine Differenzierung zwischen der Partienebene, auf der die Semantik angesiedelt werden kann, und der Strategie- bzw. Gültigkeitsebene. Wir möchten jetzt eine dialogische Fassung der Relevanzlogik anbieten, die auf diesen Überlegungen beruht. Zunächst sei daher als Ausgangspunkt die Junktoren- und Quantorenlogik im dialogischen Ansatz dargestellt:[8]

1.2 Dialogische Logik

1) *Rahmenregeln*

RR 1 (Ablauf):
Ein Dialog besteht aus einer endlichen Folge von Dialogschritten oder Zügen, in denen zwei Gesprächspartner, der Proponent **P** und der Opponent **O**, abwechselnd Argumente (von **O** bzw. **P** gesetzte Aussagen) gemäß den Partikelregeln und den übrigen Rahmenregeln vorbringen. Der erste Dialogschritt ist das Setzen der These des Dialogs durch **P**. Jeder weitere Dialogschritt oder Zug besteht im Vorbringen eines Arguments durch einen der beiden Dialogpartner. Jedes Argument ist entweder ein Angriff auf eine vorangehende Behauptung des Gegners oder eine Verteidigung auf einen vorhergehenden gegnerischen Angriff gemäß den Partikelregeln, jedoch nicht beides zugleich.

RR 2 (Dialogende):
Ein Dialog ist beendet, wenn dem Spieler am Zug kein nach den Regeln erlaubtes Argument mehr zur Verfügung steht. Einen beendeten Dialog hat derjenige gewonnen, der den letzten Zug gemacht hat, sein Gegner hat den Dialog verloren.

RR 3 (e) (effektive Rahmenregel):
X darf nach eigener Wahl ein beliebiges von Y (X und Y stehen für **O** bzw. **P**, wobei X≠Y) gesetztes Argument angreifen, soweit dies die Partikelregeln und die übrigen Rahmenregeln zulassen, oder sich auf den letzten noch unbeantworteten Angriff von Y verteidigen.

oder

RR 3 (k) (klassische Rahmenregel):
X darf nach eigener Wahl ein beliebiges von Y gesetztes Argument angreifen oder sich auf einen beliebigen Angriff von Y verteidigen, soweit dies die Partikelregeln und die übrigen Rahmenregeln zulassen.

---

[8] Danach werden wir zunächst nur die relevante Aussagenlogik behandeln; der relevanten Quantorenlogik ist ein eigener Abschnitt gewidmet.

RR 4 (keine Verzögerungen):
X darf ein Argument von Y nur dann ein weiteres Mal angreifen bzw. sich auf einen Angriff ein weiteres Mal verteidigen (letzteres ist nur bei klassischer Rahmenregelung möglich), wenn sich dadurch neue Zugmöglichkeiten ergeben.[9]

RR 5 (formale Rahmenregel):
P darf nur solche Primaussagen als Argumente setzen, die **O** bereits zuvor gesetzt hat. **O** darf Primaussagen jederzeit setzen (soweit dies die Partikelregeln und die übrigen Rahmenregeln zulassen). Primaussagen sind (im formalen Dialog) nicht angreifbar.

2) Partikelregeln

$\vee, \wedge, \rightarrow, \neg, \bigwedge, \bigvee$	***Angriff***	***Verteidigung***
$A \vee B$	?	A

		B
		(Der Verteidiger hat die Wahl)
$A \wedge B$	?L(inks)	A
	---	---
	?R(echts)	B
	(Der Angreifer hat die Wahl)	
$A \rightarrow B$	A	B
$\neg A$	A	$\otimes$ (Keine Verteidigung möglich. Nur Gegenangriff spielbar)
$\bigwedge_x A$	$?_n$ (Der Angreifer hat die Wahl)	$A\,[n/x]$
$\bigvee_x A$	?	$A\,[n/x]$ (Der Verteidiger hat die Wahl)

---

[9] Diese Regel, die das Arbeiten mit Angriffsschranken umgeht, sollte künftig noch näher untersucht und formaler formuliert werden. Mit ähnlichem Wortlaut wird sie auch schon in Fuhrmann (1985) verwendet.

Dialogische Logik und Relevanz

Die angegebenen Rahmen- und Partikelregeln definieren die effektiven (bei RR 3(e)) bzw. klassischen (bei RR 3 (k)) formalen Dialogspiele. Logische Gültigkeit wird folgendermaßen definiert:

Def. Gültigkeit:
Eine Formel heiße in einer bestimmten Dialogischen Logik gültig, wenn **P** unter den entsprechenden Regeln eine formale Gewinnstrategie hat. (Eine Gewinnstrategie zu haben, bedeutet, zu allen Zugwahlen des Gegners immer mindestens selbst eine Zugmöglichkeit zur Verfügung zu haben, sodass man schließlich den Gewinn erzwingen kann.)

Es kann gezeigt werden, dass bei effektiver bzw. klassischer Rahmenregelung sich genau die Formeln als gültig erweisen, die auch bei anderen Ansätzen als effektiv bzw. klassisch gültig gelten.[10]

(*Anmerkung:* Bei den Regeln RR 3 (e) und RR 3 (k) haben wir die symmetrische Variante angegeben. Symmetrisch deshalb, da **O** und **P** jeweils gleiche Rechte und Pflichten haben. Es kann gezeigt werden, dass sich die Rechte von **O** einschränken lassen, die Klasse der Formeln, für die **P** eine Gewinnstrategie hat, aber unverändert bleibt.)

Beispiel 1 (bei RR 3 (e) oder RR 3 (k)):

	O			**P**	
				$((a{\rightarrow}b){\wedge}a){\rightarrow}b$	(0)
(1)	$(a{\rightarrow}b){\wedge}a$	0		b	(8)
(3)	$a{\rightarrow}b$		1	?L	(2)
(5)	a		1	?R	(4)
(7)	b		3	a	(6)

P gewinnt

---
[10] Diesbezügliche Beweise finden sich u.a. in Rahman (1993).

Dialogische Logik und Relevanz

Beispiel 2 (bei RR 3 (k)):

	O			P	
				$\bigwedge_x(P_x \vee \neg P_x)$	(0)
(1)	$?_n$	0		$P_n \vee \neg P_n$	(2)
(3)	?	2		$\neg P_n$	(4)
(5)	P_n	4			
(3')	?	2		P_n	(6)

P gewinnt

Anmerkungen zu den Beispielen:
Hier wie in der Folge sind die Beispiele so einfach gewählt, dass man anhand eines Dialoges auch direkt sehen kann, ob **P** eine Gewinnstrategie hat oder nicht. Während für Beispiel 1 kein Unterschied zwischen effektiver und klassischer Rahmenregelung besteht, ist die Formel aus Beispiel 2 nur bei letzterer gewinnbar.

Zur Notation: In der **O**-Spalte sind die Züge von **O** notiert, in der **P**-Spalte diejenigen von **P**. Die Zahlen am linken und rechten Rand geben an, in welcher Reihenfolge die Züge vorgebracht wurden. Zug (0) stellt das uneigentliche Anfangsargument dar, um das in der Folge argumentiert wird. Angriffe sind durch eine Zahl am inneren Rand gekennzeichnet, die angibt, gegen welchen Zug sich der Angriff richtet. Die Verteidigung auf einen Angriff steht immer in derselben Zeile wie dieser. Einen Angriff mit zugehöriger Verteidigung, also eine komplette Zeile, bezeichnet man als Runde.

(Wie in Beispiel 2 ersichtlich kann es bei klassischer Rahmenregelung möglich sein, dass sich **P** auf einen Angriff, auf den er sich zuvor schon verteidigt hat, noch einmal (anders) verteidigt. Um für diese zweite Verteidigung in der Notation Platz zu schaffen, wird der entsprechende Angriff noch einmal notiert. Man beachte aber, dass es sich dabei nicht um einen Zug im Dialog handelt, was durch einen Strich wie in (3') bei Beispiel 2 angedeutet wird.)

2 Relevanz und Dialoge

2.1 Sinn und Geltung

1) Gewinnstrategien

Geltung wird in der Dialogischen Logik über den Begriff der Gewinnstrategie (für den Proponenten) erfasst. Eine Formel ist gültig (Gültigkeit = logische Geltung), wenn der Proponent über eine Gewinnstrategie auch bei formaler Rahmenregelung verfügt. Der Proponent verfügt über eine Gewinnstrategie, wenn er bei bestmöglichem Spiel immer gewinnen kann, egal wie der Opponent agiert. Dies kann folgendermaßen präzisiert werden: Der Proponent besitzt in einer bestimmten Spielstellung eine Gewinnstrategie, wenn diese Stellung eine Gewinnstellung für ihn ist. Der Begriff der Gewinnstellung ist dabei rekursiv definiert: Eine Stellung ist eine Gewinnstellung für den Proponenten, wenn er zu jedem regelgemäßen Zug des Opponenten selbst mindestens eine regelgemäße Entgegnung zur Verfügung hat, die den Dialog mit Gewinn für den Proponenten beendet oder wieder zu einer Gewinnstellung führt. Fragen der Geltung sind also in der Dialogischen Logik auf der Ebene der Strategien angesiedelt, auf der es nicht nur um regelkonformes Spielen, sondern um im Sinne des gewinnen Wollens gutes Spielen geht.

2) Zugmöglichkeiten

Unter der Strategieebene ist in der Dialogischen Logik noch die Ebene der Partien angesiedelt, auf der Fragen des Sinns behandelt werden können. So kann der Sinn einer Aussage dadurch bestimmt werden, welche Zugmöglichkeiten insgesamt in Dialogen um diese Aussage durch die Regeln ermöglicht werden. Dabei sind natürlich strategisch schlechte Züge mit eingeschlossen. Insbesondere kann es so auch passieren, dass der Proponent einen Dialog um eine eigentlich gültige Aussage verliert, da er einen oder mehrere schlechte Züge spielt.

Durch die Form der Partikelregeln ist gewährleistet, dass jedes Teilformel-Vorkommnis in einem möglichen Dialog nur entweder als Zug des Opponenten oder als Zug des Proponenten vorkommen kann. Wenn z.B. $\neg a$ als Zug des Opponenten erscheint, so kann das darin enthaltene Teilformel-Vorkommnis a im weiteren Verlauf nur als Zug des Proponenten erscheinen, und ebenso im umgekehrten Fall (dies schließt natürlich nicht aus, dass die Primformel a nicht doch als Zug des Opponenten bzw. Proponenten erscheinen kann; dann handelt es sich aber um ein anderes Vorkommnis, a ist dann nicht als Angriff auf das obige $\neg a$ gesetzt worden).

Bei einer Subjunktion $a \rightarrow b$ kann das Teilformel-Vorkommnis a nur vom Angreifer und das Teilformel-Vorkommnis b nur vom Verteidiger gesetzt werden. Man beachte wieder, dass bei $a \rightarrow a$ zwar von beiden Spielern a als Zug vorgebracht werden kann, es sich dann aber um verschiedene Vorkommnisse handelt.

Bei Konjunktionen und Disjunktionen können die Konjunkte bzw. Disjunkte jeweils nur vom Verteidiger gesetzt werden. Der Unterschied besteht lediglich darin, dass bei einer Konjunktion der Angreifer entscheiden kann, welches Konjunkt zu setzen ist, bei einer Disjunktion hingegen der Verteidiger wählt, welches Disjunkt er als Verteidigung behauptet. Wiederum ist bei den beiden Formeln $a \wedge a$ und $a \vee a$ zu beachten, dass es bei den beiden a jeweils um unterschiedliche Vorkommnisse handelt.

Dialogische Logik und Relevanz

2.2 Relevante Gültigkeit

Die obigen Überlegungen zeigen, dass alle, und nur die Teilformel-Vorkommnisse einer Formel in einem Dialog um diese Formel als Züge gesetzt werden können, und dass außerdem jedes Vorkommnis nur entweder von **P** oder von **O** gesetzt werden kann. Die Gesamtheit dieser Zugmöglichkeiten, die in Dialogen um sie bestehen, bestimmt also den Sinn einer Aussage.

Dahingegen ist die Gültigkeit einer Aussage auf der Strategieebene durch das Vorhandensein einer Gewinnstrategie für **P** in einem formalen Dialog definiert. Unter den gültigen Formeln lassen sich diejenigen, bei denen die Gültigkeit auf dem gesamten Sinn beruht, von denjenigen unterscheiden, durch deren Sinn Züge möglich sind, die zur Bestimmung der Gültigkeit nicht benötigt werden, und die insofern redundant sind. Gültige Formeln ohne für die Gültigkeitsbestimmung redundante Teilformel-Vorkommnisse heißen relevant-gültig und können durch folgendes Relevanzkriterium eingefangen werden:

Relevanzkriterium:
*Eine Formel ist relevant-gültig, wenn **P** für sie eine Gewinnstrategie hat, und er, um eine Gewinnstrategie zu haben, alle seine Zugmöglichkeiten ausschöpfen muss, d.h. wenn er nicht jede Zugmöglichkeit in mindestens einer Variante benötigt, um gewinnen zu können, ist die Formel nicht relevant-gültig.*[11]

Die Zugmöglichkeiten von **P** lassen sich folgendermaßen unterteilen:

1) Angriffe
Immer wenn **O** eine komplexe Formel als Zug vorbringt, so geben die Partikelregeln **P** die Möglichkeit, diese anzugreifen. Das Relevanzkriterium beinhaltet also, dass **P** jede komplexe Formel von **O** mit jedem Angriff in mindestens einer Variante attackieren muss, um eine Gewinnstrategie zu haben. Dabei hat er nur bei dem Angriff auf Konjunktionen zwei Möglichkeiten, die er auch ausnutzen muss, nämlich ?L und ?R. Man beachte, dass es sich dabei auch um zwei verschiedene Angriffsmöglichkeiten handelt, wenn es um eine Formel wie $a \wedge a$ geht.

---

[11] In der Formulierung des Relevanzkriteriums genügt es, nur auf die Zugmöglichkeiten von **P** einzugehen, da diejenigen von **O** sowieso alle beachtet werden müssen, da **P** ja eine Gewinnstrategie haben soll. Dadurch ist also gewährleistet, dass der gesamte Sinn, d.h. alle Zugmöglichkeiten von **O** und von **P**, in relevant-gültigen Formeln für die Gültigkeit von Bedeutung ist.

2) Verteidigungen
Alle komplexen Formeln, die **P** in einem Dialog als Zug vorbringt, können von **O** angegriffen werden. **P** muss also auch alle Verteidigungsmöglichkeiten ausschöpfen, um eine Gewinnstrategie zu haben. Dabei können Negationen nicht verteidigt werden, während man nur bei Disjunktionen zwei Möglichkeiten hat, nämlich die Verteidigung mit dem linken oder mit dem rechten Disjunkt (auch bei $a \vee a$).

3) Verwendungen
Durch die formale Rahmenregel ist gewährleistet, dass nur **O** Primformeln zum ersten Mal in einem Dialog setzen darf. Wenn er dies aber getan hat, so eröffnet dies **P** neue Zugmöglichkeiten; er kann dann nämlich die von **O** eingeführten Primformeln selbst zu Angriffs- oder Verteidigungszwecken verwenden. Das Relevanzkriterium besagt also außerdem noch, dass **P**, um eine Gewinnstrategie zu haben, in mindestens einer Variante jede von **O** gesetzte Primformel selbst verwenden muss, um eine Gewinnstrategie zu haben. Man beachte wieder, dass es auf die Vorkommnisse ankommt. Wenn also z.B. **O** in einem einzigen Dialog zweimal die Primformel a setzt (z.B. als Angriff auf $a \rightarrow b$ und als Verteidigung von $a \vee b$), müsste **P** theoretisch beide Vorkommnisse verwenden, um eine Gewinnstrategie zu haben, was natürlich nie nötig ist, sodass ein Vorkommnis von a bei **O** redundant ist.

2.3 Beispiele

An einigen einfachen Beispielen soll nun das Relevanzkriterium in seiner Anwendung verständlicher gemacht werden. Der Einfachheit halber behandeln wir nur Formeln, die effektiv gültig sind (das Relevanzkriterium lässt sich genauso auch bei Verwendung der klassischen Rahmenregel anwenden), und beleuchten die Unterschiede zwischen denjenigen, die auch (effektiv) relevant-gültig sind, und denjenigen, bei denen dies nicht der Fall ist.

Dialogische Logik und Relevanz

Beispiel 3:

	O			P	
				$(a \land \neg a) \to b$	(0)
(1)	$a \land \neg a$	0			
(3)	a		1	?L	(2)
(5)	$\neg a$		1	?R	(4)
			5	a	(6)

P gewinnt

In diesem Beispiel (*ex falso sequitur quodlibet*) hat **P** eine Gewinnstrategie, ohne dass er sich in irgendeiner Variante (hier gibt es sogar gar keine Nebenvarianten) auf den Zug (1) von **O** verteidigen muss. Die Formel ist daher nicht relevant-gültig.

Beispiel 4:

	O			P	
				$(a \lor b) \to (a \lor b)$	(0)
(1)	$a \lor b$	0		$a \lor b$	(2)
(3)	?	2		a [b]	(6)
(5)	a [b]		1	?	(4)

P gewinnt

Diese Formel ist relevant-gültig, denn **P** muss alle seine Zugmöglichkeiten ausnutzen, um zu gewinnen. So greift er mit Zug (4) Zug (1) an und verwendet die Primformeln von **O**, um sich auf den Angriff (1) zu verteidigen, indem er auch alle seine Verteidigungsmöglichkeiten ausnutzt (a in der Hauptvariante und b in der in Klammern angegebenen Nebenvariante).

Beispiel 5:

	O			P	
				$(a \land (a \to b)) \to (a \to b)$	(0)
(1)	$a \land (a \to b)$	0		$a \to b$	(2)
(3)	a	2		b	(8)
(5)	$a \to b$		1	?R	(4)
(7)	b		5	a	(6)

P gewinnt

Diese Formel ist wiederum nicht relevant-gültig, da **P** gewinnen kann, ohne seine beiden Angriffsmöglichkeiten auf Zug (1) zu verwenden. Es genügt der Angriff ?R in Zug (4), während ?L nicht benötigt wird.

Beispiel 6:

O				P	
				$((a \vee b) \wedge \neg a)) \to b$	(0)
(1)	$(a \vee b) \wedge \neg a$	0		$[b]$	
(3)	$a \vee b$		1	?L	(2)
(5)	$a \; [b]$		3	?	(4)
(7)	$\neg a$		1	?R	(6)
			7	a	(8)

P gewinnt

Dieses letzte Beispiel ist wiederum relevant-gültig, da **P** alle Zugmöglichkeiten ausschöpfen muss, um zu gewinnen (die Verteidigung der These (0) benötigt er in der Nebenvariante).

3 Relevante Strategientableaux

3.1 Tableaux für Junktoren und Quantoren

In der Dialogischen Logik wird Gültigkeit mit Hilfe der Strategien definiert. Eine Aussage ist demnach in der dialogischen Deutung der Logik genau dann gültig, wenn der Proponent über eine formale Gewinnstrategie für diese Aussage verfügt. Oder anders ausgedrückt: Die Aussage *A* ist dialogisch genau dann gültig, wenn *A* gegen alle Zugwahlen des Opponenten formal verteidigt werden kann.

Es lässt sich eine einfache Notation einführen, die einen Überblick über die Gewinnstrategien verschafft. Um die Gewinnstellungen aufzählen zu können, unterscheiden wir zunächst einmal die Spielstellungen, in denen **P** eine Formel gesetzt hat (**P**-Fälle), von den Fällen, in denen **O** eine Formel gesetzt hat (**O**-Fälle) – dabei wird jeweils ein Angriffs- und der entsprechende Verteidigungszug zu einer Runde zusammengestellt. Wenn, sowohl in den **O**-Fällen als auch in den **P**-Fällen, **P** die Wahl über den weiteren Dialogverlauf hat, reicht es, wenn er bei nur einem Dialogverlauf gewinnen kann. Wenn dagegen **O** die Wahl hat, muss **P** alle möglichen Dialogverläufe gewinnen können. Man kann demgemäß Regeln für den Dialogverlauf aufstellen, die immer nur von Gewinnstellungen zu Gewinnstellungen führen.

Dialogische Logik und Relevanz

O-Regel		P-Regel	
Opponent	**Proponent**	**Opponent**	**Proponent**
...	...	...	...
$A \vee B$			$A \vee B$
$A \mid B$	<?>	<?>	A
		...	...
			$A \vee B$
		<?>	B
Da hier **O** die Wahl hat, gilt: Kennt **P** Gewinnvarianten für beide Verteidigungen, so kann er damit immer gewinnen.		Hier hat **P** die Wahl: Kennt er eine Gewinnvariante für mindestens einen Dialogverlauf, dann kann er immer gewinnen.	

Erläuterung: Angriffe, die selbst keine angreifbaren Formeln darstellen (Anfragen), klammern wir mit Hilfe der Zeichen '<' und '>' ein.

O-Regel		P-Regel	
Opponent	**Proponent**	**Opponent**	**Proponent**
...	...	...	...
$A \rightarrow B$			$A \rightarrow B$
... $\mid B$	$A \mid ...$	A	$[B]$
Wenn **O** die Subjunktion $A \rightarrow B$ als Argument vorgebracht hat, greift **P** mit A an. **O** kann A angreifen oder sich mit B verteidigen. **P** muss also eine Gewinnvariante für beide Wahlen von **O** kennen.		Hier ist B in eckige Klammern gesetzt, da **P** nicht unmittelbar mit B antworten muss. Er kann zunächst die bisherigen Argumente (einschließlich A) von **O** angreifen – er bleibt dabei aber zur Verteidigung von B verpflichtet, es sei denn, der Dialog kommt vorher zu einem Ende.	

Dialogische Logik und Relevanz

Die Möglichkeiten für Gewinnstrategien können im Falle der anderen Junktoren auf ähnliche Weise angegeben werden:

O-Regel		P-Regel	
Opponent	Proponent	Opponent	Proponent
...	...	...	...
$\neg A$			$\neg A$
	A	A	
Opponent	Proponent	Opponent	Proponent
...	...	...	...
$A \wedge B$			$A \wedge B$
A	<?L>	<?L> | <?R>	$A \mid B$
...			
$A \wedge B$			
B	<?R>		

Für die Quantoren[12] müssen noch die folgenden strategischen Überlegungen betrachtet werden: Wenn **O** eine Konstante auswählen kann, dann wird er, um die Spielweise von **P** zu erschweren, der, um eine gewonnene Endstellung mit Primaussagen erreichen zu können, eventuell auf die Züge von **O** angewiesen ist, immer eine neue Konstante auswählen, also eine, die noch nicht im Dialog vorkam. **P** hingegen wird aus analogen Gründen versuchen, keine neuen Konstanten einzuführen.

O wählt, wenn **P** eine Allaussage als Argument vorgebracht hat, und wenn er selbst eine Existenzaussage behauptet hat, die er gegen einen Angriff von **P** verteidigt:

O-Regel		P-Regel	
Opponent	Proponent	Opponent	Proponent
...	...	...	...
$\vee_x A$			$\wedge_x A$
$A\,[n/x]$	<?>	<?$_n$>	$A\,[n/x]$
(n ist neu)		(n ist neu)	

---

[12] Wir führen hier die Strategientableaux schon mit Quantoren ein, da wir später Quantoren auch in unsere Relevanzlogik mit einbeziehen.

Dialogische Logik und Relevanz

P wählt, wenn O eine Allaussage als Argument vorgebracht hat, und wenn er selbst eine Existenzaussage behauptet hat, die er gegen einen Angriff von O verteidigt:

| O-Regel || P-Regel ||
Opponent	Proponent	Opponent	Proponent
...	...	...	...
<?>	$\vee_x A$	$\wedge_x A$	<?$_n$>
	$A\,[n/x]$	$A\,[n/x]$	
	(n muss nicht neu sein)		(n muss nicht neu sein)

Nun bleibt schließlich der Fall der Primaussagen zu betrachten, der die für **P** gewonnenen Endstellungen definiert. **P** hat eine formale Gewinnstrategie um eine von **O** gesetzte Primaussage (**O**-Regel), wenn er selbst diese Primaussage als Argument verwenden kann. **P** hat eine formale Gewinnstrategie um eine von ihm gesetzte Primaussage (**P**-Regel), wenn **O** sie zuvor selbst als Argument vorgebracht hat. Mit anderen Worten, die Gewinnstrategie um eine Primaussage fällt bei der **O**-Regel mit der Strategie bei Anwendung der **P**-Regel zusammen:

Opponent	Proponent
...	...
a	
	a

Von diesen Überlegungen ausgehend lassen sich zwei Tableaux-Systeme – eines für die klassische und eines für die effektive Junktoren- und Quantorenlogik – aufbauen, die den Zusammenhang zwischen Dialogischer Logik und semantischen Tableaux herstellen. (Hier ist aber zu beachten, dass beim dialogischen Ansatz die Tableaux durch die Partienebene begründet werden. Genauer: Die Partikel- und Rahmenregeln der Partienebene legen die pragmatische Semantik fest, die auf der Strategieebene der Tableaux – auf der der Begriff der Gültigkeit angesiedelt ist – vorausgesetzt wird.)

Dialogische Logik und Relevanz

Klassische Tableaux

(O)-Fall	**(P)-Fall**
(**O**)$A \vee B$	(**P**)$A \vee B$
<(**P**)?> (**O**)A | <(**P**)?> (**O**)B	<(**O**)?> (**P**)A, <(**O**)?> (**P**)B
(**O**)$A \wedge B$	(**P**)$A \wedge B$
<(**P**)?L> (**O**)A, <(**P**)?R> (**O**)B	<(**O**)?L> (**P**)A | <(**O**)?R> (**P**)B
(**O**)$A \rightarrow B$	(**P**)$A \rightarrow B$
(**P**)A, ... | <(**P**)A> (**O**)B	(**O**)A, (**P**)B
(**O**)$\neg A$	(**P**)$\neg A$
(**P**)A, $\otimes$	(**O**)A, $\otimes$
(**O**)$\wedge_x A$	(**P**)$\wedge_x A$
<(**P**)?$_n$> (**O**)$A[n/x]$ (n muss nicht neu sein)	<(**O**)?$_n$> (**P**)$A[n/x]$ (n ist neu)
(**O**)$\vee_x A$	(**P**)$\vee_x A$
<(**P**)?> (**O**)$A[n/x]$ (n ist neu)	<(**O**)?> (**P**)$A[n/x]$ (n muss nicht neu sein)

Erläuterungen:
Die Ausdrücke zwischen den Zeichen '<' und '>' stellen Züge dar, genauer Angriffszüge, aber keine Behauptungen, die man angreifen kann.

Die Schließungsregeln sind die üblichen: Ein Baum ist geschlossen, wenn alle Zweige geschlossen sind. Ein Zweig ist genau dann geschlossen, wenn er ein Paar der Form (**O**)a, (**P**)a enthält. In der Sprache der Dialoge: **P** hat genau dann eine Gewinnstrategie für einen möglichen Dialogverlauf (entspricht in etwa einem Zweig), wenn dieser Dialog mit einer Primaussage von **P** endet, die vorher von **O** gesetzt wurde.

Dialogische Logik und Relevanz

Effektive Tableaux

Die Regeln für die effektiven Tableaux enthalten an bestimmten Stellen Formeln mit dem tiefgestellten Suffix '(**O**)' (z.B. (**P**)$_{(O)}$*A*). Die Anwendung solcher Regeln bewirkt, dass sämtliche vorher gesetzten **P**-bezeichneten Formeln, die auf dem selben Zweig vorkommen, ausgestrichen werden. Dadurch wird die effektive Rahmenregel von der Partieebene auf die Strategieebene übertragen. Um diese Übertragung zu leisten, genügt es, wenn man '(**O**)' bei der **P**-Verteidigung allquantifizierter Aussagen sowie bei den Junktoren einsetzt, bei denen **P** das Recht hat, die dazugehörige Angriffsbehauptung von **O** selbst anzugreifen – d.h. bei der Subjunktion und der Negation.

(**O**)-*Fall*	(**P**)-*Fall*
(**O**)*A*∨*B*	(**P**)*A*∨*B*
---	---
<(**P**)?> (**O**)*A* | <(**P**)?> (**O**)*B*	<(**O**)?> (**P**)*A*, <(**O**)?> (**P**)*B*
(**O**)*A*∧*B*	(**P**)*A*∧*B*
---	---
<(**P**)?L> (**O**)*A*, <(**P**)?R>(**O**)*B*	<(**O**)?L> (**P**)*A* | <(**O**)?R> (**P**)*B*
(**O**)*A*→*B*	(**P**)*A*→*B*
---	---
(**P**)*A*,... | <(**P**)*A*> (**O**)*B*	(**O**)$_{(O)}$*A*, (**P**)*B*
(**O**)¬*A*	(**P**)¬*A*
---	---
(**P**)*A*, ⊗	(**O**)$_{(O)}$*A*, ⊗
(**O**)∧$_x$*A*	(**P**)∧$_x$*A*
---	---
<(**P**)?$_n$> (**O**)*A*[*n*/x] (*n* muss nicht neu sein)	<(**O**)?$_n$> (**P**)$_{(O)}$*A*[*n*/x] (*n* ist neu)
(**O**)∨$_x$*A*	(**P**)∨$_x$*A*
---	---
<(**P**)?>(**O**)*A*[*n*/x] (*n* ist neu)	<(**O**)?> (**P**)*A*[*n*/x] (*n* muss nicht neu sein)

Dialogische Logik und Relevanz

3.2 Relevanztableaux für Junktoren

Für die Relevanzlogik muss noch das Relevanzkriterium eingebaut werden:

Relevanzkriterium für Tableaux:
Jedes Vorkommnis einer Aussagevariable soll für das Schließen von mindestens einem Zweig verwendet werden, der nur mit alleiniger Hilfe dieses Vorkommnisses in Form einer Primaussage geschlossen werden kann.

Die Überprüfung, ob das Kriterium erfüllt ist, setzt natürlich voraus, dass man die Strategien ganz bis zu Ende entwickelt. Kann man die Zweige schließen, ohne dass jede komplexe Aussage entwickelt wurde, dann ist die Anfangsaussage zwar gültig aber nicht relevant-gültig. Klar ist auch, dass man die Relevanztableaux effektiv oder klassisch gestalten kann. Betrachten wir als Beispiel ein effektives Relevanztableau:

Beispiel 7:

i)   **(P)** $(a \wedge \neg a) \rightarrow \neg a$
ii)   **(O)**$_{(O)}$ $(a \wedge \neg a)$
iii)   **(P)** $\neg a$

Die Ausstreichungsvorschrift in Zeile ii) bewirkt, dass die Zeile i) ausgestrichen wird:

i)   ~~**(P)** $(a \wedge \neg a) \rightarrow \neg a$~~
ii)   **(O)**$_{(O)}$ $(a \wedge \neg a)$
iii)   ~~**(P)** $\neg a$~~   (diese Zeile wurde ausgestrichen wegen iv)
iv)   **(O)**$_{(O)}$ a
v)   **(O)** a
vi)   **(O)** $\neg a$
vii) **(P)** a

Der Zweig wurde ohne Hilfe des Vorkommnisses der Aussagevariable a in Zeile v) geschlossen, oder anders ausgedrückt: Das Vorkommnis der Aussagevariable a in Zeile v) ist für das Schießen des Tableaus redundant. Um Redundanzen zu erkennen, ist es praktischer, das oben beschriebene Verfahren der singulären Ersetzung anzuwenden:

- Wenn σ ein Strategientableau für A ist und a eine Aussagevariable ist, die in A vorkommt, dann ist das i-te Vorkommnis von a (a_i) genau

Dialogische Logik und Relevanz

dann *prim-redundant* (kürzer: *p*-redundant), wenn das Strategientableau σ für A nicht durch die singuläre Ersetzung von a_i beeinflusst werden kann, d.h. genau dann, wenn die Gültigkeit bzw. Ungültigkeit von A nach der singulären Ersetzung noch dieselbe ist wie zuvor.

- Wenn eine Aussage *relevant-gültig* ist, so schließt ihr Strategientableau und in ihm kommt keine *p*-redundante Aussagevariable vor.

Wenn man in unserem Beispiel das erste Vorkommnis der Variable a auf der ersten Zeile durch c ersetzt, kann das Tableau trotzdem geschlossen werden. Also ist dieses Vorkommnis von a redundant und die Aussage nicht relevant-gültig:

i)   ~~(P) (c∧¬a) → ¬a~~   (singuläre Ersetzung von a durch c)
ii) (O)$_{(O)}$ (c∧¬a)
iii) ~~(P) ¬a~~   (diese Zeile wurde ausgestrichen wegen iv)
iv) (O)$_{(O)}$ a
v)   (O) c
vi) (O) ¬a
vii) (P) a

Das systematische Überprüfungsverfahren, ob eine Formel relevant-gültig ist, verläuft also in zwei Schritten:

1. Überprüfung, ob es ein schließendes Tableau für die Formel gibt. Gibt es keines, ist die Formel nicht gültig und damit auch nicht relevant-gültig.

2. Überprüfung, ob es auch noch ein schließendes Tableau für eine Formel gibt, die aus der Ausgangsformel durch eine singuläre Ersetzung entstanden ist. Gibt es das, dann ist die Formel zwar gültig, aber nicht relevant-gültig. Eine Formel ist nur relevant-gültig, wenn es zwar ein schließendes Tableau für sie gibt, aber keines mehr nach einer singulären Ersetzung.

3.3 Aufgabe der uniformen Substitution

Bevor wir uns der Quantorenlogik zuwenden, sei noch auf eine Besonderheit der hier vorgestellten dialogischen Relevanzlogik aufmerksam gemacht: Die Regel des uniformen Substituierens ist nicht mehr gültig, wie sich leicht an folgendem Beispiel zeigen lässt:

Man kann sich leicht davon überzeugen, dass die Formel $a \rightarrow a$ relevant-gültig ist. Nehmen wir jetzt die uniforme Substitution $b \rightarrow b/a$ vor, so erhalten wir die Formel $(b \rightarrow b) \rightarrow (b \rightarrow b)$, die ebenso offensichtlich nicht relevant-gültig ist.

Die nötige Aufgabe der uniformen Substitution in unserer Form der Relevanzlogik hat Stephen Read in einem Gespräch zu der Bemerkung veranlasst, dass wir keine Logik mehr betreiben würden, wenn uniformes Substituieren nicht mehr gilt, wobei er sich auf Alfred Tarski berief. Ganz so drastisch sehen wir die Lage allerdings nicht und benutzen weiterhin das Wort 'Logik' für das, was wir machen.

Außerdem gilt uniformes Substituieren in einer (sehr) eingeschränkten Form weiterhin, und interessanterweise auch bezüglich Nicht-Gültigkeit. So sind alle von einer nicht relevant-gültigen Formel durch uniformes Substituieren erhaltbaren Formeln ebenfalls nicht relevant-gültig. Ebenso kann uniformes Substituieren bezüglich Gültigkeit aufrecht erhalten werden, wenn man es stark einschränkt. Zunächst nehmen wir folgende Einschränkung vor:

Eingeschränkte uniforme Substitution:
Es dürfen nur noch Primformeln durch Primformeln uniform substituiert werden.

Allerdings ist diese Einschränkung noch nicht ausreichend, wie man an folgendem Beispiel sieht: $(a \vee b) \rightarrow (a \vee b)$ ist relevant-gültig. Nimmt man jetzt die eingeschränkte uniforme Substitution b/a vor, so erhält man das nicht relevant-gültige $(b \vee b) \rightarrow (b \vee b)$. Also muss eine weitere Einschränkung vorgenommen werden:

Stark eingeschränkte uniforme Substitution:
Es dürfen nur noch Primformeln durch Primformeln uniform substituiert werden, und zwar nur durch solche, die in der Ausgangsformel nicht vorkommen.

Jetzt gilt dann wieder: Alle durch stark eingeschränktes uniformes Substituieren aus einer relevant-gültigen Formel gewonnenen Formeln sind selbst wiederum relevant-gültig.[13]

4 Quantorenlogik

4.1 Abhängigkeit von Konstantenwahlen

Beziehen wir nun die Quantoren mit ein. Bezüglich des Relevanzkriteriums, das besagt, dass **P** alle seine Zugmöglichkeiten ausschöpfen muss, um eine Gewinnstrategie zu haben, ergibt sich das Problem, dass die Partikelregeln für die Quantoren beliebig viele Verteidigungsmöglichkeiten eines Existenz- sowie beliebig viele Angriffsmöglichkeiten auf einen Allquantor erlauben, da man in diesen Fällen eine beliebige Konstante auswählen kann. Was soll es dann aber heißen, dass **P** alle diese Möglichkeiten ausschöpfen muss?

Das Problem kann folgendermaßen gelöst werden: Auch **O** hat ja bei diesen Gelegenheiten die Wahl zwischen beliebig vielen Varianten. Das Relevanzkriterium kann auf diese kritischen Fälle so übertragen werden, das man sagt, dass **P** sich bei einer solchen Wahl zwischen beliebig vielen Zugmöglichkeiten nach einer entsprechenden vorhergehenden Wahl von **O** richten muss, um eine Gewinnstrategie zu haben. Sehen wir ein ganz einfaches Beispiel einer relevant-gültigen quantorenlogischen Formel, um dies zu illustrieren:

Beispiel 8:

	O			**P**	
				$\bigwedge_x P_x \to \bigwedge_x P_x$	(0)
(1)	$\bigwedge_x P_x$	0		$\bigwedge_x P_x$	(2)
(3)	$?_n$	2		P_n	(6)
(5)	P_n	4	1	$?_n$	(4)
	P gewinnt				

Dass sich **P** hier immer nach den Konstantenwahlen von **O** richten muss, um zu gewinnen, kann man leicht einsehen: Würde **O** in Zug (3) eine andere Konstante als n auswählen um anzugreifen, z.B. m, so müsste **P** in Zug (4) ebenfalls m verwenden, um gewinnen zu können, und ebenso bei allen anderen Konstanten.

---

[13] Diese sehr eingeschränkte Form des uniformen Substituierens macht auch die Formulierung eines neuen Begriffs der logischen Form erforderlich, die so lauten könnte: Die wohldefinierte aussagenlogische Formel α hat genau dann die logische Form (der Formel) β, wenn es stark eingeschränkte uniforme Substitutionen gibt, sodass man α aus β erhält (vgl. Rahman (1998)).

Beispiel 9:

O			P	
			$\vee_x(P_x \rightarrow P_x)$	(0)
(1)	?	0	$P_n \rightarrow P_n$	(2)
(3)	P_n	2	P_n	(4)
	P gewinnt			

In dem ebenfalls sehr einfachen Beispiel 2 sieht man leicht, dass sich **P** hier nicht nach einer Konstantenwahl von **O** richten muss, um zu gewinnen. Diese Formel ist daher nicht relevant-gültig.

4.2 Zwei Versionen

Jetzt wollen wir noch einen kritischen Fall begutachten, der zu zwei Versionen unserer dialogischen Quantoren-Relevanzlogik Anlass gibt, einer ganz strengen, und einer etwas liberaleren.

Beispiel 10:

O			P		
			$(P_a \wedge (P_a \rightarrow \wedge_x P_x)) \rightarrow \wedge_x P_x)$		(0)
(1)	$P_a \wedge (P_a \rightarrow \wedge_x P_x)$	0	$\wedge_x P_x$		(2)
(3)	$?_n$ [$?_a$]	2	P_n	[P_a]	(12)
(5)	P_a	1	?L		(4)
(7)	$P_a \rightarrow \wedge_x P_x$	1	?R		(6)
(9)	$\wedge_x P_x$	7	P_a		(8)
(11)	P_n	9	$?_n$		(10)
P gewinnt					

In der strengeren Version unserer Relevanzlogik ist dieses Beispiel nicht relevant-gültig, in der etwas liberaleren hingegen schon. In Zug (9) muss sich **P** immer nach der Konstantenwahl von **O** in Zug (3) richten (hier n), um gewinnen zu können, mit einer einzigen Ausnahme: Hätte **O** in Zug (3) nicht, was aus normalen strategischen Überlegungen richtig ist, eine neue Konstante ausgewählt, sondern a, dann hätte **P** schon nach Zug (5) den Angriff aus Zug (3) verteidigen können. Also wird **P** den Allquantor aus Zug (9) nie mit ?a angreifen müssen, um gewinnen zu können. In der ganz strengen Version ist deshalb die Formel nicht relevant-gültig.

In der etwas liberaleren Version ist es erlaubt, dass **P** von den unendlich vielen Angriffsmöglichkeiten auf einen Allquantor bzw. Verteidigungsmöglichkeiten eines Existenzquantors einige nicht braucht, um gewinnen zu können, solange er noch unendlich viele benötigt.

4.3 Relevante Strategientableaux für Quantoren

Das etwas komplizierte Überprüfungsverfahren, ob eine quantorenlogische Formel (im etwas liberaleren Sinne) relevant-gültig ist, soll hier nur in aller Kürze angegeben werden. Es läuft nach folgenden Schritten ab:

1. Schritt:
Es muss ein schließendes Tableau für die Formel geben, wobei folgende Einschränkung gilt: Bei der Anwendung der Regeln (O)∧ und (P)∨ dürfen nur solche Konstanten verwendet werden, die zuvor schon bei einer Anwendung der Regeln (O)∨ und (P)∧ benutzt worden sind.[14]

2. Schritt:
Es darf kein schließendes Tableau für eine Formel geben, die durch eine singuläre Ersetzung entstanden ist.[15]

3. Schritt:
Es darf kein schließendes Tableau geben, wenn die Einschränkung aus Schritt 1 nicht beachtet wird.

---

[14] Mit anderen Worten: Die Formel muss in der freien Logik, die in Fischmann/Rahman/Rückert (1997) vorgestellt wurde, gültig sein. Der Zusammenhang zwischen freier Logik und Relevanzlogik sollte allerdings nicht überbewertet werden, da die Motivation in beiden Fällen eine völlig andere ist.

[15] Der Begriff der singulären Ersetzung muss zu diesem Zweck auf atomare Aussageformen erweitert werden: Atomare Aussageformen werden singulär ersetzt, indem der Prädikatbuchstabe durch einen neuen substituiert wird.

5 Varianten

Wir haben in diesem Aufsatz eine sehr starke Variante einer dialogischen Relevanzlogik vorgestellt, die nur zu sehr wenigen relevant-gültigen Formeln führt. Das Relevanzkriterium kann auf verschiedene Arten abgeschwächt werden, sodass mehr Formeln relevant-gültig werden, z.B.:

1. O-Relevanz:
P muss nur noch alle Zugmöglichkeiten ausnutzen, die sich aus Zügen von **O** ergeben, um eine Gewinnstrategie zu haben. D.h. er muss alle Angriffsmöglichkeiten ausnutzen und alle von **O** gesetzten Primformeln verwenden, aber nicht mehr alle Verteidigungsmöglichkeiten ausschöpfen. In dieser dialogischen Relevanzlogik wären $(a \land \neg a) \to b$ und $a \to (a \lor b)$ wieder relevant-gültig.

2. P-Relevanz:
Bei der inversen Variante muss **P** nur alle seine Verteidigungsmöglichkeiten ausnutzen, um eine Gewinnstrategie zu haben. Dann sind z.B. $b \to (a \to a)$ und $(a \land b) \to a$ wieder relevant-gültig.

3. Interessanteste Variante:
Am interessantesten erscheint uns die Liberalisierung, die besagt, dass **P** zwar alle Primformeln von **O** verwenden muss, sowie alle Züge von **O** angreifen und alle eigenen verteidigen muss, aber nicht mehr unbedingt mit allen Zugmöglichkeiten. So müsste er bei einer Konjunktion nicht mehr unbedingt beide Konjunkte verlangen, und eine Disjunktion eventuell nur mit einem Adjunkt verteidigen, um eine Gewinnstrategie zu haben. Diese Variante der dialogischen Relevanzlogik sollte zu den Standardsystemen von z.B. Anderson und Belnap ähnlicheren Resultaten führen, und ist sicherlich eine eingehendere Untersuchung wert.

In diesem Aufsatz haben wir den für relevant-gültige Formeln geforderten inhaltlichen Zusammenhang zwischen den Teilformeln in der Dialogischen Logik so einzufangen versucht, dass wir der Strategieebene sozusagen noch ein Relevanzkriterium übergestülpt haben. Dies führte schließlich zu recht komplizierten Überprüfungsverfahren. Es wäre allerdings wünschenswert, wenn man inhaltliche Zusammenhänge auch schon auf der Partienebene durch Änderungen bei den Partikel- und Rahmenregeln einbauen könnte. Einen Vorschlag in dieser Richtung machen wir in unserem Aufsatz zur konnexen Logik im dialogischen Ansatz (vgl. Rahman/Rückert (2001b)).

Dialogical Connexive Logic

Shahid Rahman* and Helge Rückert**

Abstract:
Many of the discussions about conditionals can best be put as follows: can those conditionals that involve an entailment relation be formulated within a formal system? The reasons for the failure of the classical approach to entailment have usually been that they ignore the *meaning connection* between antecedent and consequent in a valid entailment. One of the first theories in the history of logic about meaning connection resulted from the stoic discussions on tightening the relation between the If- and the Then-parts of conditionals, which in this context was called συναρτησις (connection). This theory gave a justification for the validity of what we today express through the formulae $\neg(a \to \neg a)$ and $\neg(\neg a \to a)$. Hugh MacColl and, more recently, Storrs McCall (from 1877 to 1906 and from 1963 to 1975 respectively) searched for a formal system in which the validity of these formulae could be expressed. Unfortunately neither of the resulting systems is very satisfactory. In this paper we introduce dialogical games with the help of a new connexive If-Then ($\Rightarrow$), the structural rules of which allow the Proponent to develop (formal) winning strategies not only for the above-mentioned connexive theses but also for $(a \Rightarrow b) \Rightarrow \neg(a \Rightarrow \neg b)$ and $(a \Rightarrow b) \Rightarrow \neg(\neg a \Rightarrow b)$. Further on, we develop the corresponding tableau systems and conclude with some remarks on possible perspectives and consequences of the dialogical approach to connexivity including the loss of uniform substitution leading to a new concept of logical form.

Rahman, S. and Rückert, H.: 'Dialogical Connexive Logic', *Synthese* 127 (2001), p. 105-139

* I would like to thank the Fritz-Thyssen Foundation, for supporting my work on this paper through a project which has been collaboratively realized by the Archives – Centre d'Etudes et de Recherche Henri-Poincaré, Université Nancy 2 (Gerhard Heinzmann) and the FR 5.1 Philosophie, Universität des Saarlandes (Kuno Lorenz). My thanks also go to Jörg Siekmann (DFKI Saarbrücken) and Harald Ganzinger (Max-Planck Institute for Computer Sciences), who a while ago supported preliminary research which led to this paper.

** I would like to thank the Saarland University for a post-graduate research grant which enabled me to study some of the ideas developed in this paper.

1 Introduction

In order to avoid some of the consequences of the lack of meaning connection of the classical conditional we tightened, in a paper on relevance logic (Rahman/Rückert (1998a)), the relation between the *if* and the *then* part of the conditional by filtering the winning strategies. This leads to rather complicated methods for testing the validity of even simple formulae. Actually there is another more direct way of avoiding the counter-intuitive semantics of the classical conditional. This method makes use of tightening conditions at the level of games already, that is, at the level of the particle and the structural rules instead of waiting until the strategy level has been reached. This is the path we want to follow in this paper, a path which takes us to the stoic discussions on the conditional and to one of its contemporary offsprings, namely *connexive logic* (from the stoic concept συναρτησιζ). The present approach is based on a first formulation of a dialogical connexive If-Then introduced by Rahman (1997) in his *Habilitationsschrift*. The new formulation is not only simpler but, as already mentioned, it develops a new game-based approach to the dialogical concept of connexivity. The connexive logic of Rahman's *Habilitationsschrift* was developed exclusively at the level of tableaux, that is at the strategy, not at the game level, leaving an *ad hoc* flavour which we hope we have not inherited here.

1.1 Meaning Connection and Connexive Logic

We will first discuss two examples which should show what the ideas behind connexive logic are. The first example is a variation on one of Stephen Read's, who used it against Grice's defence of material implication (cf. Read (1993)). The second one is based on an idea of Lewis Carroll's (cf. Gardner (1996)).

The Read example

This example shows how a given disjunction of conditional propositions, none of which is true, is, from a classical point of view, nevertheless valid. Imagine the following situation:

Stephen Read asserts that our dialogical relevance logic is not logic any more. Suppose further, that Jacques Dubucs rejects Read's assertion.[1] Now consider the following propositions:

---

[1] The opinion attributed to Jacques Dubucs here is fictional.

(1)   If Read was right, so was Dubucs: $(a \to b)$.

Now (1) is obviously false. The following proposition is also false:

(2)   If Dubucs was right, so was Read: $(b \to a)$.

Thus, the disjunction of (1) and (2) must be false:

(3) $(a \to b) \vee (b \to a)$.

From a classical point of view, however, this disjunction is valid. The Gricean explanation is to say that though one or the other is true, neither is assertible. But as remarked by Read in his book *Thinking About Logic* (cf. Read (1994, p. 74)) neither of the propositions themselves was asserted -what was asserted was their disjunction. Worse, it is the Gricean theory which states that disjunctions are assertible if and only if the speaker has not enough information to assert either of them. The reason why the above disjunction seems to be false is not that, though true, it is not for some communicative reason assertible, but that despite the truth-functional analysis of conditionals it *is* false.

If we reformulate (3) in the following way:

(4) $(a \to \neg a) \vee (\neg a \to a)$

the truth-functional analysis of this disjunction, which regards the disjunction as valid, shows how awkward such a theory can be. The point of connexive logic is precisely that this disjunction is invalid. Thus, in connexive logic the following holds:

(5) $\neg((a \to \neg a) \vee (\neg a \to a))$

or

(6) $\neg(a \to \neg a)$

and

(7) $\neg(\neg a \to a)$

Proposition (6) is known under the name *first Boethian connexive thesis*. Number (7) is the *first Aristotelian connexive thesis*.

Actually we should use another symbol for the connexive conditional:

(8) $\neg(a \Rightarrow \neg a)$ *(first Boethian connexive thesis)*

(9) $\neg(\neg a \Rightarrow a)$ *(first Aristotelian connexive thesis)*[2]

The Lewis Carroll example

In the 19th century Lewis Carroll presented a conditional which John Venn (1881) called *Alice's Problem* and which resulted in several papers and discussions. The conditional is the following:

(10) $((a \to b) \land (c \to (a \to \neg b))) \to \neg c$

If we consider $a \to b$ and $a \to \neg b$ as being incompatible the conditional should be valid. Consider for example the following propositions:

(11)   If Read was right, so was Dubucs: $(a \to b)$

(12)   If Read was right, Dubucs was not: $(a \to \neg b)$

They look very much as if they were incompatible, but once again, the truth-functional analysis does not confirm this intuition: if a is false both conditionals are true. Boethius presupposed this incompatibility on many occasions (cf. Boethius (1969)). This motivated Storrs MacCall to formulate the *second Boethian thesis of connexivity*:

(13) $(a \Rightarrow b) \Rightarrow \neg(a \Rightarrow \neg b)$ *(second Boethian connexive thesis)*

Aristotle used instead proofs corresponding to the formula:

(14) $(a \Rightarrow b) \Rightarrow \neg(\neg a \Rightarrow b)$ *(second Aristotelian connexive thesis)*

which is now called the *second Aristotelian thesis of connexivity*. Aristotle even showed in *Analytica Priora* 57a36-b18 (cf. Aristotle (1928)) how the first and second Aristotelian thesis of connexivity are related. Aristotle first argues against $(a \Rightarrow b) \land (\neg a \Rightarrow b)$ in the following way: from $a \Rightarrow b$ we obtain $\neg b \Rightarrow \neg a$ by

---

[2] At this point it should be mentioned that the connexive theses are given various names in the literature. What we call the first Boethian thesis, is often referred to as the Aristotelian thesis, and what we call the second Boethian thesis is often called simply the Boethian thesis.

contraposition, and from $\neg b \Rightarrow \neg a$ and $\neg a \Rightarrow b$ we then obtain $\neg b \Rightarrow b$ by transitivity, contradicting the thesis $\neg(\neg b \Rightarrow b)$. Thus, he has established $\neg((a \Rightarrow b) \land (\neg a \Rightarrow b))$. And therefore $(a \Rightarrow b) \Rightarrow \neg(\neg a \Rightarrow b)$.

Hugh MacColl was the first to attempt to embed the connexive theses in a formal system. In his papers *The Calculus of Equivalent Statements* he gives the following condition for the second Boethian thesis:

> "Rule 18. If A (assuming it to be a consistent statement) implies B, then A does not imply B' [i.e. not-B]." (MacColl (1878, p. 180))

We see that with this consistency assumption for the Boethian thesis MacColl introduces a metalogical feature of the classical If-Then into the object language. This yields a new connective and not only new axioms. The fact that connexive logic is not simply an extension of classical logic becomes evident as soon as one realizes that $\neg((a \to \neg a) \lor (\neg a \to a))$ is the negation of a classical tautology. In other words, the conjunction of the first Boethian and the first Aristotelian thesis is, from a classical point of view, a contradiction. Thus the addition of these theses makes any classical system trivial.[3]

The question now is how to formulate a connexive logic with an intuitive semantics. Unfortunately, no system developed since Aristotle's times seems to be very satisfactory.[4] Very recently Astroh (1999) and Pizzi/Williamson (1997) presented interesting new approaches. Astroh's system is based on modifications of Gentzen Calculi whereas Pizzi and Williamson develop modal connexive logics.

Our approach follows MacColl's idea of introducing metalogical features into the object language of a new conditional. For this aim we feel that the dialogical approach to logic is more natural and appropriate than the model-theoretic one. Thus we will first, very briefly, introduce dialogical logic.

---

[3] Routley/Montgomery (1968) studied the effects of adding connexive theses to classical logic.

[4] Cf. Angell (1962); McCall (1963, 1964, 1966, 1967, 1975), and Linneweber-Lammerskitten (1988, p. 354-373).

1.2 A brief Introduction to Dialogical Logic

Dialogical logic, suggested by Paul Lorenzen in 1958 and developed by Kuno Lorenz in several papers from 1961 onwards,[5] was introduced as a pragmatic semantics for both classical and intuitionistic logic.

The dialogical approach studies logic as an inherently pragmatic notion using an overtly externalised argumentation formulated as a *dialogue* between two parties taking up the roles of an *Opponent* (**O** in the following) and *a Proponent* (**P**) of the issue at stake, called the principal *thesis* of the dialogue. **P** has to try to defend the thesis against all possible allowed criticism *(attacks)* by **O**, thereby being allowed to use statements that **O** may have made at the outset of the dialogue. The thesis *A* is logically valid if and only if **P** can succeed in defending *A* against all possible allowed criticism by **O**. In the jargon of game theory: **P** has a *winning strategy* for *A*. We will now describe an intuitionistic and a classical dialogical logic.

Suppose the elements and the logical constants of first-order language are given with small italic letters (*a, b, c,*...) for elementary formulae, capital italic letters for formulae that might be complex (*A, B, C,*...), capital italic bold letters (***P, Q, R,***...) for predicators and τ_i for constants. A dialogue is a sequence of formulae of this first-order language that are stated by either **P** or **O**.[6] Every move – with the exception of the first move through which the Proponent states the thesis – is an aggressive or a defensive act. In dialogical logic the meaning in use of the logical particles is given by two types of rules which determine their *local* and their *global* meaning (*particle* and *structural rules* respectively).

The particle rules specify for each particle a pair of moves consisting of an attack and (if possible) the corresponding defence. Each such pair is called a *round*. A round is *opened* by an attack and is *closed* by a defence if one is possible.

---

[5] Cf. Lorenzen/Lorenz (1978). Further work has been done for example by Rahman (1993).

[6] Sometimes, we use X and Y to denote **P** and **O** with X ≠ Y.

Dialogical Connexive Logic

Particle Rules

∨, ∧, →, ¬, ⋀, ⋁	**Attack**	**Defence**
$A \vee B$	?	A --- B (The defender chooses)
$A \wedge B$	?L --- ?R (The attacker chooses)	A --- B
$A \rightarrow B$	A	B
$\neg A$	A	⊗ (No defence, but only counter-attack is allowed)
$\bigwedge_x A$	$?_n$ (The attacker chooses)	$A\,[n/x]$
$\bigvee_x A$	?	$A\,[n/x]$ (The defender chooses)

The first column contains the form of the formula in question, the second one possible attacks against this formula, and the last one possible defences against those attacks. (The symbol '⊗' indicates that no defence is possible.) Note that for example '?L' is a move – more precisely it is an attack but not a formula. Thus if one partner in the dialogue states a conjunction, the other may initiate the attack by asking either for the left-hand side of the conjunction ("show me that the left-hand side of the conjunction holds", or '?L' for short) or the right-hand side ("show me that the right-hand side of the conjunction holds", or '?R'). If, on the other hand, one partner in the dialogue states a disjunction, the other may initiate the attack by asking to be shown *any* side of the disjunction ('?').

Next, we fix the way formulae are sequenced to form dialogues with a set of structural rules (orig. *Rahmenregeln*):

Dialogical Connexive Logic

Structural Rules

R0 (*starting rule*)
Moves are alternately uttered by **P** and **O**. The *initial formula* is uttered by **P**. It provides the topic of argument. Every move below the initial formula is either an attack or a defence against an earlier move stated by the other player.

R1 (*no delaying tactics rule*)
P may repeat an attack or a defence (only allowed when playing classically) if and only if **O** has introduced a new atomic formula (which can now be used by **P**). (No other repetitions are allowed.)

R2 (*formal rule for atomic formulae*)
P may not introduce atomic formulae: any atomic formula must be stated by **O** first.

R3 (*winning rule*)
X wins iff it is Y's turn but he cannot move (whether to attack or defend).

$R_I 4$ (*intuitionistic rule*)
In any move, each player may attack a (complex) formula asserted by his partner or he may defend himself against *the last not already defended* attack. Only the latest open attack may be answered: if it is X's turn at position n and there are two open attacks m, l such that $m < l < n$, then X may not defend against m.[7]

These rules define an intuitionistic logic. To obtain the classical version simply replace $R_I 4$ by the following rule:

$R_C 4$ (*classical rule*)
In any move, each player may attack a (complex) formula asserted by his partner or he may defend himself against *any attack* (including those which have already been defended).

As already mentioned, validity is defined in dialogical logic via winning strategies of **P**:

---

[7] Notice that this does not mean that the last open attack was the last move.

Dialogical Connexive Logic

Definition: Validity
In a certain dialogical system a formula is said to be valid iff **P** has a (formal) winning strategy for it, i.e., **P** can in accordance with the appropriate rules succeed in defending A against all possible allowed criticism by **O**.[8]

Example 1 (either with classical or intuitionistic structural rule; it makes no difference):

	O			**P**	
				$((a \to b) \wedge a) \to b$	(0)
(1)	$(a \to b) \wedge a$	0		b	(8)
(3)	$a \to b$		1	?L	(2)
(5)	a		1	?R	(4)
(7)	b		3	a	(6)
P wins					

Example 2 (classical):

	O			**P**	
				$\wedge_x(P_x \vee \neg P_x)$	(0)
(1)	$?_n$	0		$P_n \vee \neg P_n$	(2)
(3)	?	2		$\neg P_n$	(4)
(5)	P_n	4			
(3')	?	2		P_n	(6)
P wins					

Remarks:
Notation: Moves are labelled in (chronological) order of appearance. They are not listed in the order of utterance, but in such a way that every defence appears on the same level as the corresponding attack. Thus, the order of the moves is labelled by a number between brackets. Numbers without brackets indicate which move is being attacked.

Example 2 shows how the classical structural rule works: the Proponent may, according to the classical structural rule, defend an attack which was not the last one. This allows the Proponent to state *Pn* in move (6). For notational reasons we repeated the attack of the Opponent, but actually this move does not take place. That is why, instead of tagging the attack with a new number, we repeated the number of the first attack and added an apostrophe.

---

[8] See consistency and completeness theorems in Barth/Krabbe (1982), Krabbe (1985) and Rahman (1993).

Dialogical Connexive Logic

The quite simple structure of the dialogue in this and the following examples should make it possible to recognise with the help of only one dialogue whether **P** has a winning strategy or not.

2 Connexivity and Dialogues

2.1 Extending the Particle Rules: The Operators V and F

Our dialogical formulation of the connexive If-Then makes use of the following operators: the *defensibility* operator **V** and the *attackability* operator **F**. The operator **F** is related to the well-known *failure operator* of *Prolog*.[9]

We will first introduce the corresponding particle rules:

1) The Operator **V**

In stating the formula **V**A the argumentation partner X asserts that A can be defended under certain conditions. The other argumentation partner Y challenges **V**A by asserting that there is no condition under which A can be defended, that is, the challenger asserts that attacks on A can be played successfully independent of what the conditions are. Thus, the challenge of Y compels X (who stated **V**A in the so-called *upper section*) to open a *subdialogue* where he (X) states A and Y attacks A. Now, because of the scope of challenge which extends to any condition, *the challenger must play formally*. Graphically:

V	Attack	Defence
VA	?$_V$	
	Subdialogue	*Subdialogue*
		A
	(The challenger must play formally in the subdialogue)	(The defender chooses the subdialogue)

---

[9] Gabbay (1987) used this operator for modal logic. Hoepelman/van Hoof (1988) applied this idea of Gabbay's to non-monotonic logics. Finally Rahman (1997, chapter II(A).4.2) introduced the F-Operator in the formulation of semantic tableaux and dialogical strategies for connexive logic.

Dialogical Connexive Logic

Notice that upper sections and their subdialogues are sections of just one dialogical game where one of the argumentation partners wins or loses.

Notice also that the particle rules of the operator **V** allow a change in the right to introduce atomic formulae, that is, the Proponent is in this version of dialogical logic the argumentation partner who stated the thesis which motivated the whole dialogue game, not the argumentation partner who plays formally. Thus the formal structural rule has to be reformulated. We will do this later; for our present purposes we will introduce a graphic mark that signalises which of the argumentation partners has to argue formally – let us call this restriction the *formal restriction*. We will do this by attaching the symbol '●' to the argumentation partner who plays under the formal restriction (and the symbol '○' to the other). By means of this device both cases of arguing with the operator **V** (with and without changing the formal restriction) can be distinguished. In order to keep track of different sections of the dialogue game we will enumerate them in the following way: The initial dialogue section where the Proponent stated the thesis which motivated the whole dialogue game carries the number 1 and will be called the *initial dialogue*. The m-th subdialogue of the upper section n carries the number $n.m$. For example 1.2.3 is the number of the third subdialogue of the upper section 1.2, which is the second subdialogue of the initial dialogue 1.

Case 1:

n	Y°	$X^{\bullet}$
	...	VA
	$?_V$	
$n.m$	$Y^{\bullet}$	X°
		A
	...	

Case 2:

n	$Y^{\bullet}$	X°
	...	VA
	$?_V$	
$n.m$	$Y^{\bullet}$	X°
		A
	...	

2) The operator **F**

The operator **F** is the dual of **V**. Thus, in stating the formula **F**A the argumentation partner X asserts that A can be attacked successfully under certain conditions. The other argumentation partner Y challenges **F**A by asserting that there is no condition under which A can be attacked successfully. Thus, the challenge of Y compels X to open a *subdialogue* where he (X) states $\neg A$ and Y attacks it. Again, *the challenger must play formally*:

F	**Attack**	**Defence**
FA	$?_F$	
	Subdialogue	*Subdialogue*
		$\neg A$
	(The challenger must play formally in the subdialogue)	(The defender chooses the subdialogue)

Again two cases (with and without changing the formal restriction) should be distinguished here:

Case 1:

n	Y$^{\circ}$	X$^{\bullet}$
	...	**F**A
	$?_F$	
$n.m$	Y$^{\bullet}$	X$^{\circ}$
		$\neg A$
	...	

Case 2:

n	Y$^{\bullet}$	X$^{\circ}$
	...	**F**A
	$?_F$	
$n.m$	Y$^{\bullet}$	X$^{\circ}$
		$\neg A$
	...	

The question is now the following: are the argumentation partners of a subdialogue allowed to use formulae conceded by the other player in the initial dialogue? The answer to this question is given by the formulation of appropriate structural rules in the next section. Since these structural rules fix the global semantics of our connexive If-Then, we will first introduce this new conditional:

3) The Connexive If-Then

As mentioned above, MacColl employed the concept of consistency while stating the second Boethian thesis of connexivity. That the proposition A, explains MacColl in a footnote, is a consistent one, means that A is possibly true. That is, no logical contradiction follows from the assumption of the truth of A:

> "Note. The implication $\alpha:\beta'$ asserts that α and β are inconsistent with each other; the non-implication $\alpha \div \beta'$ asserts that α and β are consistent with each other.
>
> [...] α is a consistent statement - i.e., one which may be true." (MacColl 1878, p. 184)

As we understand it, MacColl's reformulation of the meaning connections implicit in traditional hypotheticals comprises the following conditions for the connexive If-Then:

1. The If-part should be contingent or not inconsistent. In other words, the If-part should not yield a redundant Then-part by producing an inconsistency.

2. The Then-part should not yield a redundant If-part. That is, the Then-part should not be tautological.

These two conditions can be expressed very easily by means of the operators **V** and **F**:

- $A \Rightarrow B$ is not connexively valid if the If-part is not defensible. In other words, it is *disconnexive* if the argumentation partner who states $A \Rightarrow B$ cannot win **V**A.

The idea here is that *ex contradictione nihil sequitur* (nothing follows from contradiction). Similarly:

Dialogical Connexive Logic

- $A \Rightarrow B$ is *disconnexive* if the Then-part is not attackable. Shorter, $A \Rightarrow B$ is disconnexive if the argumentation partner who states $A \Rightarrow B$ cannot win **F**B.

The idea here is that *ex quodlibet verum nequitur* (there is no proposition from which tautological or assumed truth follows).

This amounts to the following formulation of the connexive If-Then: If X states $A \Rightarrow B$, the challenger Y can choose between the following attacks:

1. He can ask for the If-part

2. He can ask for the Then-part

3. He can start a standard attack on the conditional: that is, he will assume A and ask for B

X's defences are the following:

1. He defends the attack on the If-part by stating **V**A

2. He defends the attack on the Then-part by stating **F**B

3. He defends the standard attack by stating B

This yields the following particle rule for the connexive If-Then:

$\Rightarrow$	Attack	Defence
$A \Rightarrow B$	?front	**V**A
	?back	**F**B
	A	B
	(The challenger chooses between these three attacks)	

Now we come to study the relations between a subdialogue and its upper section. The idea of subdialogue is that all If-Thens (but no other formulae) of the upper section are relevant for the subdialogue, but not the other way round:

- Standard attacks on conditionals may be stated not only in the section in which these formulae have been stated but also from a (corresponding) subdialogue.

- Formulae with negations, conjunctions, disjunctions, or quantifiers as principal connective may be attacked and defended only in the section in which these formulae have been stated. The same restriction applies for the attacks '?front' and '?back'.

- Attacks on **V** and **F** formulae may be stated only in the section in which these formulae have been stated. Defences of these formulae have to be stated in subdialogues.

As already mentioned, the dialogical semantics of the connexive If-Then requires a new formulation of the formal structural rule R2 and a new rule stating which attacks are allowed and from which sections.[10] More precisely, these rules should capture the structural features described above.

2.2 Structural Rules for Connexive Logic

R2' (formal rule for connexive logic):

2.1. *Changes of the formal restriction:*
At the start of a dialogue **P** plays under the formal restriction. Changes of the formal restriction are regulated solely by the particle rules of **V** and **F**.

2.2. *Statement of atomic propositions by the argumentation partner who plays without the formal restriction:*
The argumentation partner who does not play under the formal restriction in a determinate section may state an atomic proposition in this section whenever needed.

---

[10] A reformulation of R1 is also necessary: R1': The argumentation partner who plays under the formal restriction may repeat an attack or a defence if and only if the argumentation partner without formal restriction has introduced a new atomic formula (which can now be used by his partner). (No other repetitions are allowed.)

Dialogical Connexive Logic

2.3. *Statement of atomic propositions by the argumentation partner who plays under the formal restriction:*
The argumentation partner who plays under the formal restriction in a determinate section may state in this section only atomic formulae which his argumentation partner has already stated in this section.

R5 (statement of attacks in a section):
The argumentation partner X in a determinate section may attack (in accordance with the particle and other structural rules) any (complex) formula stated by Y in this section. X may also start standard attacks on conditionals stated by Y in the corresponding upper section. (No other formulae may be attacked.)

2.3 Examples

It should be clear that a classical and an intuitionistic version of connexive logic can be obtained. In the following examples it makes no difference:

Example 3:

1		O°				$P^\bullet$	
					$\neg(a \Rightarrow \neg a)$		(0)
(1)	$a \Rightarrow \neg a$		0		$\otimes$		
(3)	$\lor a$		1	?front		(2)
				3	$?_\lor$		(4)
1.1		O°				$P^\bullet$	
(5)	a			1	a		(6)
(7)	$\neg a$			7	a		(8)
	$\otimes$						

P wins

The dialogue for the first Boethian thesis is very simple. The Proponent wins in the subdialogue because the If- and the Then-part of the conditional conceded by the Opponent are incompatible.

Dialogical Connexive Logic

Example 4:

1		O°				$P^{\bullet}$	
						$\neg(\neg a \Rightarrow a)$	(0)
(1)	$\neg a \Rightarrow a$		0			$\otimes$	
(3)	Fa				1	?back	(2)
					3	?$_F$	(4)
1.1		O°				$P^{\bullet}$	
(5)	$\neg a$						
(7)	a				1	a	(6)
	$\otimes$				5	a	(8)

P wins

The dialogue for the first Aristotelian thesis is also very simple and can easily be won by a clever Proponent. It is obvious that it makes no difference if **O** instead of defending himself with move (7) chooses to attack the Proponent's move (6).

Example 5:

1		O°				$P^{\bullet}$	
						$(a \Rightarrow b) \Rightarrow \neg(a \Rightarrow \neg b)$	(0)
(1)	$a \Rightarrow b$		0			$\neg(a \Rightarrow \neg b)$	(2)
(3)	$a \Rightarrow \neg b$		2			$\otimes$	
(5)	Va				1	?front	(4)
					5	?$_V$	(6)
1.1		O°				$P^{\bullet}$	
(7)	a				1	a	(8)
(9)	b				3	a	(10)
(11)	$\neg b$				11	b	(12)
	$\otimes$						

P wins

This shows how to win a dialogue for the second Boethian thesis. It should be clear that if **O** attacks the thesis with '?front' or '?back' this will not lead him to win the dialogue. This can also be observed in the second Aristotelian thesis and in some other formulae in our examples:

Dialogical Connexive Logic

Example 6:

1	**O**°				**P**•	
					$(a{\Rightarrow}b){\Rightarrow}\neg(\neg a{\Rightarrow}b)$	(0)
(1)	$a{\Rightarrow}b$	0			$\neg(\neg a{\Rightarrow}b)$	(2)
(3)	$\neg a{\Rightarrow}b$	2			$\otimes$	
(5)	Fb			1	?back	(4)
				5	?$_F$	(6)
1.1	**O**°				**P**•	
(7)	$\neg b$					
				3	$\neg a$	(8)
(9)	a	8			$\otimes$	
(11)	b			1	a	(10)
	$\otimes$			7	b	(12)
P wins						

It should be easy to see that at the end it makes no difference if **O** defends the attack of move (8). Actually **P** then wins even faster.

These are the dialogues for the connexive theses. We would now like to show the dialogues of dangerous formulae. These are formulae that can be won by the Proponent in a classical logic and that make trivial every classical system which has been extended by the addition of the connexive theses. These formulae are the first difficulties which any connexive system should solve. Our solution is as follows:

Example 7:

1	**O**°				**P**•	
					$\neg(a{\Rightarrow}\neg a){\Rightarrow}a$	(0)
(1)	$\neg(a{\Rightarrow}\neg a)$	0				
	$\otimes$			1	$a{\Rightarrow}\neg a$	(2)
(3)	?front	2			Va	(4)
(5)	?v	4				
1.1	**O**•				**P**°	
					a	(6)
(7)	a	2			$\neg a$	(8)
(9)	a	8			$\otimes$	
O wins						

Notice that it would be a mistake if **O** played a standard attack on the Proponent's move (2) in the initial dialogue: in this case, **P** could defend himself against the attack of move (1) (when playing according to the classical structural rule). Similarly it can be shown that $\neg(\neg a{\Rightarrow}a){\Rightarrow}\neg a$ is not connexively valid.

Now we will show that our connexive logic renders the negation of *ex falso*

Dialogical Connexive Logic

sequitur quodlibet valid. Example 9 shows that the so called *explosive formula* $\neg a \Rightarrow (a \Rightarrow b)$ is also valid. Thus the connexive approach to logic should be distinguished from the paraconsistent one.

Example 8:

1	O°				P•	
					$\neg(a \wedge \neg a) \Rightarrow b$	(0)
(1)	$(a \wedge \neg a) \Rightarrow b$	0			$\otimes$	
(3)	$\mathbf{V}(a \wedge \neg a)$		1		?front	(2)
			3		?v	(4)
1.1	O°				P•	
(5)	$a \wedge \neg a$					
(7)	a		5		?L	(6)
(9)	$\neg a$		5		?R	(8)
	$\otimes$		9		a	(10)

P wins

Example 9:

1	O°				P•	
					$\neg a \Rightarrow (a \Rightarrow b)$	(0)
(1)	$\neg a$	0			$a \Rightarrow b$	(2)
(3)	a	2				
	$\otimes$		1		a	(4)

P wins

It is easy to check that on no occasion could **O** successfully use an attack '?front' or '?back'.

The next example shows that the universal quantification does not present any special problem:

Dialogical Connexive Logic

Example 10:

	O°			**P**•	
1				$\wedge x(Px{\Rightarrow}Qx){\Rightarrow}\wedge x\neg(Px{\Rightarrow}\neg Qx)$	(0)
(1)	$\wedge x(Px{\Rightarrow}Qx)$	0		$\wedge x\neg(Px{\Rightarrow}\neg Qx)$	(2)
(3)	$?_\tau$	2		$\neg(P\tau{\Rightarrow}\neg Q\tau)$	(6)
(5)	$P\tau{\Rightarrow}Q\tau$		1	$?_\tau$	(4)
(7)	$P\tau{\Rightarrow}\neg Q\tau$	6		⊗	
(9)	$VP\tau$		5	?front	(8)
			9	$?_V$	(10)
1.1	**O**°			**P**•	
(11)	$P\tau$				
(13)	$Q\tau$		5	$P\tau$	(12)
(15)	$\neg Q\tau$		7	$P\tau$	(14)
	⊗		15	$Q\tau$	(16)

P wins

It is easy to see that from move (7) onwards the dialogue follows the same moves as the propositional case in the dialogue for the second Boethian thesis of Example 5. The relation between this formula and the second Boethian thesis was historically first remarked by Hugh MacColl in the paper of 1878 already mentioned.

3 Tableaux for Connexive Logic

3.1 Non-Connexive Tableaux

As already mentioned validity is defined in dialogical logic via winning strategies for **P**, i.e. the thesis *A* is logically valid iff **P** can succeed in defending *A* against all possible allowed criticism of **O**. In this case, **P** has a *winning strategy* for *A*.

A systematic description of the winning strategies available can be obtained from the following considerations:

- If **P** shall win against any choice of **O**, we will have to consider two main different situations, namely the dialogical situations in which **O** has stated a complex formula and those in which **P** has stated a complex formula. We call these main situations the **O**-cases and the **P**-cases, respectively.

In both of these situations another distinction has to be examined:

1. **P** wins by *choosing* an attack in the **O**-cases or a defence in the **P**-cases, iff he can win *at least one* of the dialogues he has chosen.

Dialogical Connexive Logic

2. When **O** can *choose* a defence in the **O**-cases or an attack in the **P**-cases, **P** can win iff he can win *all of the* dialogues **O** can choose.

Classical Tableaux

(O)-cases	**(P)**-cases
(O)$A \vee B$	(P)$A \vee B$
<(P)?> (O)A | <(P)?> (O)B	<(O)?> (P)A, <(O)?> (P)B
(O)$A \wedge B$	(P)$A \wedge B$
<(P)?L> (O)A, <(P)?R> (O)B	<(O)?L> (P)A | <(O)?R> (P)B
(O)$A \rightarrow B$	(P)$A \rightarrow B$
(P)A, ... | <(P)A> (O)B	(O)A, (P)B
(O)$\neg A$	(P)$\neg A$
(P)A, $\otimes$	(O)A, $\otimes$
(O)$\wedge_x A$	(P)$\wedge_x A$
<(P)?$_n$> (O)$A[n/x]$ (n does not need to be new)	<(O)?$_n$> (P)$A[n/x]$ (n is new)
(O)$\vee_x A$	(P)$\vee_x A$
<(P)?> (O)$A[n/x]$ (n is new)	<(O)?> (P)$A[n/x]$ (n does not need to be new)

The closing rules for dialogical tableaux are the usual ones: A branch is closed iff it contains two copies of the same formula, one stated by **O** and the other one by **P**. A tree is closed iff each branch is closed. A closed tree for some formula A presents a winning strategy for A.

For the intuitionistic tableaux, the structural rule about the restriction on defences has to be considered. The idea is quite simple: The tableaux system allows all the possible defences (even the atomic ones) to be written down, but as soon as determinate formulae (negations, conditionals, universal quantifiers) of **P** are attacked, all others will be deleted. Those formulae which compel the rest of **P**'s formulae to be deleted will be indicated with the expression '(**O**)$_{(O)}$' (or

Dialogical Connexive Logic

'$(P)_{(O)}$') which reads *save **O**'s formulae and delete all of **P**'s formulae stated before.*

Intuitionistic Tableaux

(O)-cases	**(P)-cases**
(**O**)$A \vee B$	(**P**)$A \vee B$
<(**P**)?> (**O**)A | <(**P**)?> (**O**)B	<(**O**)?> (**P**)A, <(**O**)?> (**P**)B
(**O**)$A \wedge B$	(**P**)$A \wedge B$
<(**P**)?L> (**O**)A, <(**P**)?R>(**O**)B	<(**O**)?L> (**P**)A | <(**O**)?R> (**P**)B
(**O**)$A \rightarrow B$	(**P**)$A \rightarrow B$
(**P**)A,... | <(**P**)A> (**O**)B	(**O**)$_{(O)}A$, (**P**)B
(**O**)$\neg A$	(**P**)$\neg A$
(**P**)A, $\otimes$	(**O**)$_{(O)}A$, $\otimes$
(**O**)$\wedge_x A$	(**P**)$\wedge_x A$
<(**P**)?$_n$> (**O**)$A[n/x]$	<(**O**)?$_n$> (**P**)$_{(O)}A[n/x]$
(*n* does not need to be new)	(*n* is new)
(**O**)$\vee_x A$	(**P**)$\vee_x A$
<(**P**)?>(**O**)$A[n/x]$	<(**O**)?> (**P**)$A[n/x]$
(*n* is new)	(*n* does not need to be new)

Let us look at two examples, namely one for classical logic and one for intuitionistic logic. We use the tree-shape of the tableau made popular by Smullyan (1968):

Dialogical Connexive Logic

Example 11:

> (P) $\wedge_x \neg P_x \to \neg P_\tau$
> (O) $\wedge_x \neg P_x$
> (P) $\neg P_\tau$
> (O) P_τ
> (O) $\neg P_\tau$
> (P) P_τ
> The tableau closes

The following intuitionistic tableau makes use of the deletion rule:

Example 12:

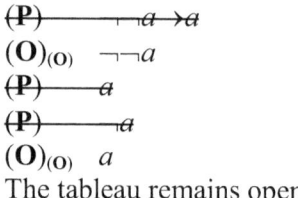

> ~~(P)~~   ~~$a \to a$~~
> (O)$_{(O)}$ $\neg\neg a$
> ~~(P)~~   ~~a~~
> ~~(P)~~   ~~a~~
> (O)$_{(O)}$ a
> The tableau remains open

3.2 Connexive Tableaux[11]

The tableau rules must include all combinations of the two pairs of signs {**O**, **P**} and {●, ○}. For the sake of simplicity the rules will be formulated for X and Y (X ≠ Y), where these letters are slots for **O** and **P**. For the standard logical constants we thus have the following set of rules:

---

[11] The new and improved tableaux system for connexive logic presented here has, with slight modifications, been taken from Rahman/Redmond (2008, section 3.2). The relevant part of the Rahman/Redmond paper has mainly been written by Shahid Rahman. Thanks to Heinrich Wansing (Dresden) for reading an earlier draft of this material and suggesting many and important corrections.

Dialogical Connexive Logic

(Y°)-cases	$(X^\bullet)$-cases
$(Y^\circ)A \vee B$	$(X^\bullet)A \vee B$
---	---
$(Y^\circ)A \mid (Y^\circ)B$	$(X^\bullet)A, (X^\bullet)B$
$(Y^\circ)A \wedge B$	$(X^\bullet)A \wedge B$
---	---
$(Y^\circ)A, (Y^\circ)B$	$(X^\bullet)A \mid (X^\bullet)B$
$(Y^\circ)A \rightarrow B$	$(X^\bullet)A \rightarrow B$
---	---
$(X^\bullet)A \mid (Y^\circ)B$	$(Y^\circ)A, (X^\bullet)B$
$(Y^\circ)\neg A$	$(X^\bullet)\neg A$
---	---
$(X^\bullet)A$	$(Y^\circ)A$

The closing rules are the following:

- A tableau for $(X^\bullet)A$ (i.e. starting with $(X^\bullet)A$) is closed iff each branch (including those of each possible *subtableau*) is closed by means of either the occurrence of a pair of atomic formulae of the form $((Y^\circ)a, (X^\bullet)a)$ or of a *special closing rule*. Otherwise it is said to be open.

The reasons for including clauses on *subtableaux* and on *special closing rules* will be given in the next section.

The Operators V and F

1) The Operator **V**

In the context of a tableau system the intended interpretation of the occurrence of a formula **V**A in a branch is "there is an *open (sub)tableau* for A".

Actually, one could see any tableau for A as a finite sequence of subtableaux such that the first tableau is a single-point one, whose origin is A, and the other members of the sequence are obtained by applications of the tableau rules. We will however, only label explicitly the subtableaux opened by the **V** and **F** operators. To keep track between tableau and subtableaux we will make use of a system of labels: If the branch where one of both operators occurs carries the label i, then its first subtableau has the label $i.1$ and so on.

More generally, the intuitive idea is that a label i names a subtableau and A

Dialogical Connexive Logic

i tells us that *A* is to be evaluated at the subtableau *i* names. Moreover, our labels will be finite sequences of positive integers such as 1.1.1 and 1.1.2.

Definition
A *label* is a finite sequence of positive integers. A *labelled formula* is an expression of the form *A i*, where *i* is the label of the formula *A*.

If the label *i* is a sequence of length > 1 the positive integers of the sequence will be separated by periods. Thus, if *i* is a label and an *n* is a positive integer, then *i.n* is a new label, called *an extension of i*. The label is then an *initial segment* of *i.n*.

Let us assume that the expression (**P**•)V*A* occurs in a branch with the following intended interpretation:

"The proponent who in this branch has the burden of the proof of validity states that there is an open tableau for *A*."

This formula will generate a subtableau for (**P**°)*A* with the following intended interpretation:

"The proponent who in this subtableau does not have the burden of the proof of validity states that there is an open (sub)tableau for *A*."

The tableau rules for the operator **V** must include the combinations of the two pairs of signs {**O**, **P**} and {•, ○}:

(**Y**°)-*case*	(**X**•)-*case*
n (**Y**°)V*A i*	*n* (**X**•)V*A i*
---	---
n+1 (**Y**°)*A i.l*	*n*+1 (**X**°)*A i.l*

Here, '*n*' is the number of the step in the (sub)tableau *i* where V*A* occurs.
 The conditions for the closing of the *whole* branch (the branch which starts with the main formula of the whole tableau and which ends with a subtableau with the label *i.l*) should be clear now:

- The branch of (sub)tableau *i* where V*A* occurs is *open at step n* if the subtableau *i.j* is closed and dually, if the subtableau is open then *i* will *be closed at n*.

Dialogical Connexive Logic

Examples

In the following examples *n* indicates the point in the branch of the tableau *i* where **V** occurs and *i*.1 is the subtableau generated by an application of the rule **V**.

Example 13:

$$\ldots$$
$$n\ (\mathbf{P^\bullet})\mathbf{V}a \wedge \neg a\ i$$
$$(\mathbf{P^\circ})a \wedge \neg a\ i.1$$
$$(\mathbf{P^\circ})a\ i.1$$
$$(\mathbf{P^\circ})\neg a\ i.1$$
$$(\mathbf{O^\bullet})a\ i.1$$

The branch of *i* is *open at n* because the subtableau *i*.1 *closes* with
$\{(\mathbf{P^\circ})a, (\mathbf{O^\bullet})a\}$

Example 14:

$$\ldots$$
$$n\ (\mathbf{P^\circ})\mathbf{V}\neg a\ i$$
$$(\mathbf{P^\circ})\neg a\ i.1$$
$$(\mathbf{O^\bullet})a\ i.1$$

The branch is *closed at n* because the subtableau is *open*

2) The Operator **F**

The operator **F** is the dual of **V**. In the context of a tableau system the intended interpretation of the occurrence of formula **F**A in a branch is "there is *no closed (sub)tableau* for *A*".
  More precisely let us assume that the expression $(\mathbf{P^\bullet})\mathbf{F}A$ occurs in a branch with the following intended interpretation:

> "The proponent who has in this branch the burden of the proof of validity states that there is no closed tableau for *A*."

This formula will generate a subtableau for $(\mathbf{O^\bullet})A$ with the following intended interpretation:

Dialogical Connexive Logic

"The Opponent states that there is a closed (sub)tableau for A where he has the burden of the proof of validity."

The tableau rules are the following:

(Y°)-*Case*	$(X^\bullet)$-*Case*
$n\ (Y^\circ)FA\ i$	$n\ (X^\bullet)FA\ i$
-------------------	---------------------
$n+1\ (X^\bullet)A\ i.l$	$n+1\ (Y^\bullet)A\ i.l$

Notice that this operator produces a change from $X^\bullet$ to $Y^\bullet$ and vice versa.

- The branch of (sub)tableau i where FA occurs is *open at step n* if the subtableau $i.j$ is closed and dually, if the subtableau is open then i is *closed at n*.

Examples

Example 15:

$$\begin{array}{l}\ldots\\ n\ (P^\bullet)Fa\vee\neg a\ i\\ (O^\bullet)a\vee\neg a\ i.l\\ (O^\bullet)a\ i.l\\ (O^\bullet)\neg a\ i.l\\ (P^\circ)a\ i.l\end{array}$$

The branch is *open at n* because the subtableau *closes* with
$\{(P^\circ)a, (O^\bullet)a\}$

Example 16:

$$n\ (\mathbf{P}°)\mathbf{F}\neg a\ i$$
$$(\mathbf{O}^\bullet)\neg a\ i.1$$
$$(\mathbf{P}°)a\ i.1$$

The branch is *closed at n* because
the subtableau is *open*

The Connexive Conditional

1) Tableau Rules for the Connexive Conditional

(Y°)-*Case*	(X•)-*Case*
(Y°) $A \Rightarrow B\ i$	(X•) $A \Rightarrow B\ i$
(Y°)$A \to B\ i$, (Y°)V$A\ i$, (Y°)F$B\ i$	(X•)$A \to B\ i$ | (X•)V$A\ i$ | (X•)F$B\ i$

We will now introduce rules which will have the effect of producing an implicit modal logic in the following sense:

- The subtableaux produced by VA and FA will contain, the subformulae of VA and FA, material implications and no other formula than the subformulae of these implications. Think of the subtableaux as worlds where the only formulae which will be carried from the upper branch are precisely the corresponding material implications. Thus it is as every implication on the upper tableau works as a strict implication.

- The subtableaux produced by V and F are different. That is though the subtableaux have a common ancestor (namely the material implication) one is not accessible to the other.

To implement this we use an idea similar to the deleting device of intuitionistic logic: The formulae VA (or FA) will generate subtableaux which contain no other formulae than the subformula of the V-formula (or F-formula), and the standard conditionals (material implications) of the upper section. For this purpose we use the suffix '$_{[\to]}$' which reads as follows:

$_{[\to]}$-*rule*:
In the subtableau, add a copy of *every* connexive conditional occurring in the upper tableau, replace the main connective by the corresponding material implication, and change the burden of the proof of the material implication(s) according to the rule for the operator at stake if necessary.

In other words each subtableau will at its start only contain either the antecedent or the consequent of the connexive conditional and the corresponding material conditional. The emphasis on *every conditional* will be made clear in example 19.

(**Y**°)-*Cases*	(**X**•)-*Cases*
(**Y**°)VA i	(**X**•)VA i
---	---
(**Y**°)$_{[\to]}A$ $i.n$	(**X**°)$_{[\to]}A$ $i.n$
(**Y**°)FA i	(**X**•)FA i
---	---
(**Y**°)$_{[\to]}A$ $i.m$	(**X**°)$_{[\to]}A$ $i.m$

The main tableau starts for A with (**P**•)A.

Starting rule for strategies for connexive logic:
We assume that a tableau for A starts with (**P**•)A. Thus, a closed tableau (a tableau with all its branches closed) for A proofs that A is valid.

Though the practice of closing branches is straightforward the precise formulation of the adequate closing rules is quite tricky because it must include cases where the branch ends with a subtableau and branches where subtableaux do not occur.

R-C *Closing rules for Ω (Ω is either V or F):*
Let us assume a tableau the origin of which is (**P**•)A. If a branch of such a tableau ends with a subtableau generated by either a (**P**•)Ω-formula or a (**P**°)Ω-formula then the whole branch is closed iff the subtableau does not close. A branch of the same tableau which does

Dialogical Connexive Logic

not end with a subtableau of the form described before[12] is closed iff it ends with a pair of the form $(\mathbf{O}°)a$, $(\mathbf{P}^\bullet)a$. Otherwise it is open.

Notice that we consider that a branch includes the entire sequence of subtableaux generated.

Examples

In the following examples the numeration to the left of the formula indicates the step in the proof while the number to the right labels the tableau and subtableau:

Example 17:

1	$(\mathbf{P}^\bullet)\neg(a \Rightarrow \neg a)$ 1	
2	$(\mathbf{O}°)a \Rightarrow \neg a$ 1	(negation rule on 1)
3	$(\mathbf{O}°)a \rightarrow \neg a$ 1	(left-rule for connexive conditional on 2)
4	$(\mathbf{O}°)Va$ 1	(left-rule for connexive conditional on 2)
5	$(\mathbf{O}°)F \neg a$ 1	(left-rule for connexive conditional on 2)
6	$(\mathbf{O}°)a$ 1.1	(V rule on 4)
7	$(\mathbf{O}°)a \rightarrow \neg a$ 1.1	($_{[\rightarrow]}$-rule on 4)

Now at the subtableau **1.1**, the standard rule on the material implication $(\mathbf{O}°)a \rightarrow \neg a$ applies:

8	$(\mathbf{P}^\bullet)a$ 1.1	|	9	$(\mathbf{O}°)\neg a$ 1.1	
		|	10	$(\mathbf{P}^\bullet)a$ 1.1	

The (unique) branch for the tableau ends with a subtableau generated by a $(\mathbf{O}°)V$-formula. The two branches of the subtableau (**1.1**) close with $(\mathbf{O}°)a$, $(\mathbf{P}^\bullet)a$. Thus, according to **R-C**, the whole branch and tableau *is closed*.

The proof for $\neg(\neg a \Rightarrow \neg a)$ is very similar but makes use of the other operator:

---

[12] That is, if it ends with no subtableau or if it ends with a subtableau generated by a $(\mathbf{O}°)\Omega$-formula, or $(\mathbf{O}^\bullet)\Omega$-formula.

Dialogical Connexive Logic

Example 18:

1	(**P**•)¬(¬a⇒a) **1**	
2	(**O**°)¬a⇒a **1**	(negation rule on 1)
3	(**O**°)¬a→a **1**	(left-rule for connexive conditional on 2)
4	(**O**°)V¬a **1**	(left-rule for connexive conditional on 2)
5	(**O**°)Fa **1**	(left-rule for connexive conditional on 2)
6	(**P**•)a **1.1**	(F-rule on 5)
7	(**O**°)¬a→a **1.1**	([→]-rule on 5)

Now at the subtableau **1.1**, the standard rule on the material implication (**O**°)¬a→a applies:

8	(**P**•)¬a **1.1**		9	(**O**°)a **1.1**
10	(**O**°)a **1.1**			

The two branches of the subtableau **1.1** generated by (**O**°)Fa close with (**O**°)a, (**P**•)a. Thus, according to **R-C**, the whole branch and tableau *is closed*.

In the following example the full strength of the [→]-rule is put into action. This rule allows "carrying" *every connexive conditional* as a material implication into the generated subtableaux

Example 19:

1 (**P**•)(a⇒b)⇒¬(a⇒¬b) **1**
2 (**P**•)(a⇒b)→¬(a⇒¬b **1** | 3 (**P**•)V(a⇒b) **1** | 4 (**P**•)F¬(a⇒¬b) **1**

At this stage it should be clear that the development of the **V** and **F** formulae (3, 4) will produce closed branches, because antecedent and consequent of the connexive conditional are logically contingent.

Let us see what happens in the outmost left branch (2) if we develop the rule of the material implication.

Dialogical Connexive Logic

Left branch:

```
           5 (O°)(a⇒b) 1           (material implication on 2)
           6 (P•)¬(a⇒¬b) 1         (material implication on 2)
           7 (O°)a⇒¬b 1            (negation on 6)
           8 (O°)a→b 1             (left-rule for connexive conditional on 5)
           9 (O°)Va 1              (left-rule for connexive conditional on 5)
          10 (O°)Fb                (left-rule for connexive conditional on 5)
          11 (O°)a 1.1             (V-rule on 9)
          12 (O°)a→b 1.1           ([→]-rule on 5)
          14 (O°)a→¬b 1.1          ([→]-rule on 7)
15 (P•)a ... 1.1     |         16 (O°)b 1.1
                     |  17 (P•)a 1.1  |  18 (O°)¬b 1.1
                     |                |  19 (P•)b 1.1
```

The subtableau closes because of the pair(s) ((O°)a, (P•)a) and ((O°)b, (P•)b). Thus, according to **R-C**, the whole branch *is closed*. As already mentioned the other branches (3, 4) close too, thus the whole tableau closes.

The following example displays the case of a formula that is *dangerous* for connexive logic. It is the formula which indicates that if you add both of the connexive theses the logic will explode into triviality. Indeed if one adds ¬(A→¬A) and ¬(¬A→A) to classical logic, a contradiction results as the following holds:

¬(A→¬A) implies A

¬(¬A→A) implies ¬A

Let us prove that this type of trivialization will not happen in our system. Indeed we show here that a tableau for ¬(a⇒¬a)⇒a does not close. The proof for the dual ¬(¬a⇒a)⇒¬a is very similar.

Dialogical Connexive Logic

Example 20:

$$1\ (\mathbf{P}^\bullet)\neg(a\Rightarrow\neg a)\Rightarrow a\ 1$$
$$2\ (\mathbf{P}^\bullet)\neg(a\Rightarrow\neg a)\rightarrow a\ 1\ |\ 3\ (\mathbf{P}^\bullet)V\neg(a\Rightarrow\neg a)\ 1\ |\ 4\ (\mathbf{P}^\bullet)Fa\ 1\ \text{(right-rule for '}\Rightarrow\text{' on 1)}$$

Branches 3 and 4 yield closed branches. The outmost right branch (4) closes because $(\mathbf{P}^\bullet)Fa$ generates a subtableau which will remain open.

To show that branch 3 closes is a little more complicated. The subtableau which it generates will start with $(\mathbf{P}^\circ)\neg(a\Rightarrow\neg a)$, and follow with $(\mathbf{O}^\bullet)a\Rightarrow\neg a$. The three branches of this subtableau will close and cause the whole branch to close. Indeed, the first branch of the subtableau containing the material implication $(\mathbf{O}^\bullet)a\rightarrow\neg a$ will be open by the standard rules and this will yield the closing of the branch. The second branch of the subtableau containing $(\mathbf{O}^\bullet)Va$, will generate a subsubtableau where the formulae $(\mathbf{O}^\circ)a$, $(\mathbf{O}^\circ)a\rightarrow\neg a$ will yield the closure of the branch with $(\mathbf{O}^\circ)a$, $(\mathbf{P}^\bullet)a$. The case can be shown to be similar for the last branch of the subtableau containing $(\mathbf{O}^\bullet)F\neg a$.

Unfortunately we are not through yet. Moreover, there is a branch which will cause the whole tableau to be open. Let us show this for the branch containing $2\ (\mathbf{P}^\bullet)\neg(a\Rightarrow\neg a)\rightarrow a$:

Left branch:

5 $(\mathbf{O}^\circ)\neg(a\Rightarrow\neg a)$ 1	(material implication on 2)
6 $(\mathbf{P}^\bullet)a$ 1	(material implication on 2)
7 $(\mathbf{P}^\bullet)a\Rightarrow\neg a$ 1	(negation on 6)
8 $(\mathbf{P}^\bullet)a\rightarrow\neg a$ 1 | 9 $(\mathbf{P}^\bullet)Va$ 1 | 10 $(\mathbf{P}^\bullet)F\neg a$ 1	(right-rule for connexive conditional on 7)

The application of the standard tableau rule on 8 yields $(\mathbf{O}^\circ)a$, $(\mathbf{P}^\bullet)\neg a$ which closes with 6 $(\mathbf{P}^\bullet)a$. We will develop the middle branch 9 and open the subtableau **1.1**.

Middle branch:

11 $(\mathbf{P}^\circ)a$ **1.1**	(V-rule on 9)
12 $(\mathbf{P}^\circ)a\rightarrow\neg a$ **1.1**	($_{[\rightarrow]}$-rule on 6)
13 $(\mathbf{O}^\bullet)a$ ... **1.1** | 14 $(\mathbf{P}^\circ)\neg a$ **1.1**	
| 15 $(\mathbf{O}^\bullet)a$ **1.1**	

The subtableau generated by the formula $(\mathbf{P}^\bullet)Va$ closes because of the pair(s) $((\mathbf{P}^\circ)a, (\mathbf{O}^\bullet)a)$. Thus, according to **R-C**, the whole branch and tableau are *open*.

4 Perspectives and Consequences

4.1 The Connexive Disjunction

What we have done until now was produce connexive logic introducing a new connexive conditional.[13] But perhaps the concept of connexivity is also applicable to the other logical constants and we should redefine all connectives and quantifiers in a connexive way. We will now follow this thread:

The job for the If-Then has already been done. Being a monadic connective, the negation does not open the question of how to fix meaning relations between its parts. Thus we are left with the conjunction, the disjunction and the quantifiers. We will leave the quantifiers for a moment and consider the two remaining connectives:

Defending the conjunction $A \wedge B$ compels the defence of both of its subformulae. That is, no part of this conjunction can be redundant. Conjunctions are, so to speak, connexive *per se*.

The crucial case is the disjunction. Suppose that one of the parts of the disjunction $A \vee B$ is a tautology. Thus, this type of disjunctions can produce the same type of lack of meaning connection as the classical conditional does.[14]

This amounts to the following formulation of the connexive disjunction ($A \veebar B$): If X states $A \veebar B$, the challenger Y can choose between the following attacks:

---

[13] It might be worth studying the logics produced by combining the **F** and the **V** operators with all the logical constants independently of the motivations of connexive logic.

[14] It is interesting to observe that the traditional theory of hypotheticals, which was based on reflections about meaning connections, considered only disjunctions and conditionals. It was Boole who extended the denomination *hypothetical* to the other propositional connectives.

Dialogical Connexive Logic

1. He can ask for the front (i.e., left) part

2. He can ask for the back (i.e., right) part

3. He can start a standard attack on the disjunction

X's defences are the following:

1. He defends the attack on the front part by stating **F**A

2. He defends the attack on the back part by stating **F**B

3. He defends the standard attack by stating (at least) one of either A or B

This yields the following particle rule for the connexive disjunction:

$\underline{\vee}$	Attack	Defence
$A \underline{\vee} B$	?front	**F**A
	?back	**F**B
	?	$A \mid B$
	(The challenger chooses between these three attacks)	

The structural rule R5 for connexive logic must also be modified in the following way:

> **R5*** (*statement of attacks in a section*):
> The argumentation partner X in a determinate section can attack any (complex) formula stated by Y in this section, as well as the conditionals *and disjunctions* (only standard attacks allowed) stated by Y in the corresponding upper section. (No other formulae can be attacked.)

Before giving an example we should consider the case of the quantifiers. As with the standard conjunction and for the same reason, the universal quantifier presents no problem. The case of the existential quantifier parallels that of the disjunction. That is, the challenger can, in the context of any instance of the existential quantifier, ask for **F**. We leave it to the reader to work out the details.

Example 21:

1	O			P	
				$\neg((a{\Rightarrow}a)\veebar b)$	(0)
(1)	$(a{\Rightarrow}a)\veebar b$	0		⊗	
(3)	F$a{\Rightarrow}a$		1	?front	(2)
			3	?$_F$	(4)
1.1	O			P	
(5)	$\neg(a{\Rightarrow}a)$				
	⊗		5	$a{\Rightarrow}a$	(6)
(7)	a	6		a	(8)
	P wins				

4.2 The Loss of Uniform Substitution

One important consequence of our approach to connexive logic is that uniform substitution does not hold anymore. Here is one example:

The formula $a{\Rightarrow}a$ clearly holds. Now if we substitute uniformly in the following way $b{\Rightarrow}b/a$ we obtain the inconnexive formula $(b{\Rightarrow}b){\Rightarrow}(b{\Rightarrow}b)$.[15]

But all is not lost: a very restricted form of uniform substitution still holds. We will start with a first restriction:

Restricted uniform substitution
Atomic formulae can be uniformly substituted by atomic formulae. No other uniform substitutions are allowed.

This restriction is still too permissive: the formula $(a{\Rightarrow}b){\Rightarrow}(a{\Rightarrow}b)$ clearly holds. Now if we substitute uniformly with b/a we obtain the not connexively valid formula $(b{\Rightarrow}b){\Rightarrow}(b{\Rightarrow}b)$. Thus a new restriction has to be introduced:

Strong uniform substitution
Atomic formulae can be uniformly substituted by atomic formulae not occurring already in the formula before. No other uniform substitutions are allowed.

---

[15] Rahman (1997) already pointed out the loss of uniform substitution in his *Habilitationsschrift*. We also pointed out the loss of uniform substitution in our paper about relevance logic (Rahman/Rückert 1998a). During a visit to our institute in Saarbrücken, Stephen Read recalled Alfred Tarski's definition of logic which states that a system without uniform substitution is no logic anymore. We do not see things so drastically and continue calling the things we do 'logic'. But, we suppose, this is a matter of choice.

The following holds: any formula obtained by applying strong uniform substitution to a given connexively valid formula is also connexively valid. This allows the formulation of another new concept of logical form:

Definition: Singular logical form
The well-formed propositional formula α has the singular logical form (of the formula) β iff α can be obtained by applying strong uniform substitution to the formula β.[16]

4.3 Connexivity and Modal Logic

The above formulation of the connexive If-Then using the concept of subdialogue seems to be related to modal logics. In Rahman/Rückert (1999) we presented a dialogical formulation of modal logics using the concept of dialogical contexts that corresponds to the concept of subdialogues. Thus, it seems that our connexive If-Then can be formulated in modal logic terms.

The following translation which makes use of the operator θ seems to be promising:

$A \Rightarrow B \quad =_{def} \quad$ Necessary $(A \rightarrow B)$, and
$\qquad\qquad\qquad\qquad \theta A$ (i.e., A *is materially contingent*), and
$\qquad\qquad\qquad\qquad \theta B$ (i.e., B *is materially contingent*).

The first condition indicates that a standard attack is allowed in the section where the conditional was stated as well as in its subsections. The second indicates that the If-part can be won materially[17] but can not be won formally,[18] and the last one indicates the same of the Then-part.[19]

---

[16] See details in Rahman (1997 and 1998). A similar idea can be found in Weingartner (2000) and Weingartner/Schurz (1986).

[17] That is, can be won by the argumentation partner who plays without the formal restriction.

[18] That is, can not be won by the argumentation partner who plays under the formal restriction.

[19] Actually, the operator θ seems to work here in a different way than the usual contingency operators of modal logic: Our contingency operator commits to a new possible dialogical context where the proposition at stake has to be defended materially and not only to the defence of this proposition at the initial context.

Thus, if an argumentation partner Y who plays under the formal restriction states that a given proposition A is contingent, he has to defend the claim that this proposition can be won materially by opening a dialogue context, say $n.m$, where the formal restriction has been changed: That is, it is X now who plays under the formal restriction and must refute the proposition accordingly. Now, if Y has to defend the claim that A can not be won formally, he has to refute in a dialogue context $n.k$ ($n.k \neq n.m$) X's claim that A can be won formally. Notice the difference with stating that a given proposition is possible. Stating that a given proposition is possible does not induce changes of the formal restriction – the reader is reminded that the (possible) change of the formal restriction in subsections is a crucial device of our approach.[20]

If we are seeking a translation of the dialogical connexive logic presented above we should choose the modal logic system T, the accessibility relation of which is reflexive but does not need to be either transitive or symmetric. Reflexivity corresponds to the structural rule that allows standard attacks on conditionals in the same section in which these conditionals have been stated, the fact that the accessibility relation does not need to be transitive reflects the fact that standard attacks on conditionals stated in, say, section (or dialogue context) s_1 may be stated in subsections of s_1 but not from subsections of subsections of s_1, and the fact that the accessibility relation does not need to be symmetric corresponds to the fact that standard attacks on a conditional stated in a given section s_n may not be stated in an upper section s_{n-1}.

Another interesting line for future research might be the development of connexive logic systems that correspond to other modal logic systems than T, for example B, $S4$ or $S5$. This might easily be achieved by regulating the possibility of standard attacks on conditionals in a less stringent way than we have proposed.

5 Concluding Remarks

The aim of this paper was to show how to extend the pragmatic semantics of dialogical logic (cf. Rückert (2001)) in order to capture the intuitions behind traditional and modern connexive logic. We think that this approach has opened some further questions which deserve future research. We would like to finish the paper by mentioning two of these questions:

---

[20] Cf MacColl (1906, p. 7). MacColl uses two contingency operators, namely θ_t (contingently true – corresponds to our **V***)* and θ_f (contingently false – corresponds to our **F**).

1. It seems interesting to consider how to combine this approach to connexive logic with paraconsistent and free logic (cf. Rahman/Carnielli (2000), Rahman/Roetti (1999) and (Rahman 1999b)). Apparently Hugh MacColl attempted such an enterprise in his reflections on the concept of *symbolic existence* (cf. Rahman (1999a, 1999c and 2001)).

2. Deeper research into the consequences of our connexive logic may permit a reconstruction of traditional categorical and modal syllogistics in a way which was already suggested by Hugh MacColl at the end of the 19th century (cf. Rahman (1999a)).[21]

---

[21] We would like to thank Gerhard Heinzmann (Nancy), Erik Krabbe (Groningen), Kuno Lorenz (Saarbrücken), Philippe Nabonnand (Nancy), Ulrich Nortmann (Saarbrücken) and Göran Sundholm (Leiden) for comments on earlier versions of this paper and Mrs. Cheryl Lobb de Rahman for her careful grammatical revision.

Eine neue dialogische Semantik für lineare Logik

Shahid Rahman und Helge Rückert

Zusammenfassung:
Seit der Veröffentlichung von Blass' Aufsatz *A Game Semantics for Linear Logic* (1992) sind mehrere weitere dialogische Systeme für lineare Logik entwickelt worden. Zudem behauptet Girard, der Vater der linearen Logik, in seinen neueren Arbeiten (siehe z.B. Girard (1995, 1998)), dass die Bedeutung der logischen Partikeln über eine dialogische Semantik in den Regeln für diese Partikeln selbst zu finden sei. In der Tat ging die Dialogische Logik aus einem neuen pragmatischen Verständnis der Semantik hervor, das aus der Übertragung von Wittgensteins Sicht der Bedeutung als Gebrauch – eingefangen durch die Formulierung von entsprechenden Gebrauchsregeln – auf das Gebiet der Logik resultierte. Nun ist auf der einen Seite Blass' Spiele-Semantik zwar sehr ansprechend, beschreibt aber tatsächlich affine Logik (in der eine gewisse Art der Vereinfachung bei den Multiplikativa gilt), und nicht lineare Logik. Andererseits ist Girards Spiele-Semantik sehr kompliziert und ihre semantische Motivation nur schwer nachzuvollziehen.

Ziel dieses Aufsatzes ist es, eine neue dialogische Semantik für lineare Logik anzubieten (ohne Vereinfachung für die Multiplikativa), die Ideen der Relevanzlogik aufgreift, und die die für die lineare Logik typische Dynamik einfangen soll. Eine zugrundeliegende Idee lautet dabei, dass Argumente nicht nur bloß Abfolgen von Beweisschritten sind, sondern dass sie auch interaktive Schritte enthalten, in denen Informationen ausgetauscht, zurückgezogen, gesammelt oder getestet werden können. In diesem Zusammenhang ist es daher manchmal sinnvoll, nicht nur zwischen redundanten und nicht-redundanten Teilen eines Arguments zu unterscheiden, sondern auch festzulegen, wie oft eine Information verwendet werden darf. Dies führt zu einer dialogischen Semantik für lineare Logik, in der gefordert wird, dass jeder Teil einer Formel (mit einigen Ausnahmen) genau einmal zu verwenden ist, um die Gültigkeit der Formel nachzuweisen, – wobei verschiedene Vorkommnisse derselben (Teil-)Formel auch als verschiedene Teile angesehen werden. Man beachte, dass es in der Dialogischen Logik einen sehr natürlichen Weg gibt, mehrere Vorkommnisse einer Formel zu unterscheiden: Jedes Vorkommnis einer Formel kann einem anderen Zug im Dialog zugeordnet werden.

Rahman, S. und Rückert, H.: 'Eine neue dialogische Semantik für lineare Logik', zuvor unveröffentlichtes Manuskript (verfasst 2000/01)

Eine neue dialogische Semantik für lineare Logik

1 Motivationen und Ziele

In der jüngeren Vergangenheit ist es offensichtlich geworden, dass es ein stetig wachsendes Interesse an der Erforschung der Dialogischen Logik gibt, das sich von unterschiedlichen Forschungsrichtungen herleitet.[1] Mehrere Faktoren sind für diese neuen Impulse verantwortlich, die einen besonderen Schwerpunkt in den Computerwissenschaften und der Künstlichen Intelligenz aufweisen. Zunächst seien einige dieser Faktoren kurz angerissen, manche eher technischer, andere mehr philosophisch-semantischer Natur.

1) Die technischen Faktoren

Eine neue Nachfrage nach einer Vielfalt von logischen Systemen, die den unterschiedlichsten Anwendungen dienen können, ist von der Künstlichen Intelligenz, den Computerwissenschaften und der Linguistik, sowie von der juristischen Argumentation, der Philosophie und der Psychologie ausgegangen. Diese Nachfrage hat eine intensive Erforschung alter und neuer Logiksysteme hervorgerufen. Die Frage, wie ein gemeinsamer allgemeiner Rahmen zur Erforschung der meisten dieser Logiken formuliert werden könnte, erlangte nun besondere Wichtigkeit. Ein bedeutsamer Schritt in diese Richtung war die Formulierung einer Bedingung, die mitunter als *Došen's Principle* bekannt ist, und die vorschlägt, alternative logische Systeme durch Abänderung von Strukturregeln gegen einen festen Hintergrund von Regeln für die logischen Partikeln zu erhalten (siehe Došen (1988)).[2]

Tatsächlich stellt ein analoges Prinzip ein Charakteristikum der Dialogischen Logik dar. Die Regelmenge ist in der Dialogischen Logik unterteilt in Partikelregeln und Rahmenregeln. Die Partikelregeln bestimmen für jede logische Partikel, wie die entsprechenden Formeln angegriffen und verteidigt werden können, während die Rahmenregeln den generellen Ablauf eines Dialoges festlegen. Es lässt sich sehr leicht einsehen, dass man unterschiedliche logische Systeme erhalten kann, indem man nur die Menge der Rahmenregeln abändert, unter Beibehaltung der immer gleichen Menge an Partikelregeln. So unterscheiden

---

[1] Tatsächlich hatte schon Walton (1985) auf einen Anstieg bei der Erforschung der Dialog-Logik hingewiesen.

[2] Der Ausdruck 'Došen's Principle' stammt von Wansing (1994, S. 128). Dieses Prinzip spielt u.a. eine zentrale Rolle in der *Display Logic*. Die *Display Logic* wurde von Belnap (1982) begründet und vor allem in Wansing (1998) weiter ausgearbeitet. Die Idee der Hervorbringung von Logiken durch das Abändern von Strukturregeln steht auch mit den sogenannten substrukturalen Logiken in engem Zusammenhang (siehe Restall (2000)).

sich etwa die klassische und die intuitionistische Logik in ihrer dialogischen Formulierung nur in einer Rahmenregel. Die umgekehrte Herangehensweise ist ebenfalls möglich: Man kann unterschiedliche Logiken auch dadurch erhalten, dass man neue Partikeln einführt. Ein bekanntes Beispiel für diese Vorgehensweise ist Girards *Linear Logic*. Von daher kann man diese Strategie bei der Entwicklung von Logiken auch *Girard's Principle* nennen.

2) Die philosophisch-semantischen Faktoren

Seit der Veröffentlichung von Blass' Aufsatz *A Game Semantics for Linear Logic* (1992) sind mit der Hilfe von *Girard's Principle* mehrer weitere dialogische Systeme für die lineare Logik entwickelt worden, die unterschiedliche Mengen an linearen Partikeln enthalten (siehe z.B. Abramsky (1997) und Hyland (1997)). Zudem behauptet Girard, der Vater der linearen Logik, in seinen neueren Arbeiten (siehe z.B. Girard (1995, 1998)), dass die Bedeutung der logischen Partikeln über eine dialogische Semantik in den Regeln für diese Partikeln selbst zu finden sei. In der Tat ging die Dialogische Logik aus einem neuen pragmatischen Verständnis der Semantik hervor, das aus der Übertragung von Wittgensteins Sicht der Bedeutung als Gebrauch – eingefangen durch die Formulierung von entsprechenden Gebrauchsregeln – auf das Gebiet der Logik resultierte. Des weiteren kann gemäß Blass und Girard der Vorteil einer dialogischen Semantik für die lineare Logik gegenüber anderen Arten von Semantiken mit Hilfe der folgenden Beobachtung ausgedrückt werden:

„My thesis is that the meaning of logical rules is to be found in the well-hidden geometrical structure of the rules themselves: typically, negation should not be interpreted by NO, but by the exchange between **Player** and **Opponent**." (Girard (1998, S. 1))[3]

Nun ist auf der einen Seite Blass' Spiele-Semantik zwar sehr ansprechend, beschreibt aber tatsächlich affine Logik (in der eine gewisse Art der Vereinfachung bei den Multiplikativa gilt), und nicht lineare Logik. Anderseits ist Girards Spiele-Semantik sehr kompliziert und ihre semantischen Motivation nur schwer nachzuvollziehen.

Ziel dieses Aufsatzes ist es, eine neue dialogische Semantik für lineare Logik anzubieten (ohne Vereinfachung für die Multiplikativa), die Ideen aus der

---

[3] Siehe dazu den Abschnitt über die lineare Negation.

erst kürzlich von uns entwickelten dialogischen Relevanzlogik aufgreift,[4] und die in der Lage ist, die für die lineare Logik typische Dynamik einzufangen, einschließlich des durch die Negation verursachten Rollenwechsels. Eine zugrundeliegende Idee lautet dabei, dass Argumente nicht nur bloß Abfolgen von Beweisschritten sind, sondern dass sie auch interaktive Schritte enthalten, in denen Informationen ausgetauscht, zurückgezogen, gesammelt oder getestet werden können. In diesem Zusammenhang ist es daher manchmal sinnvoll, nicht nur zwischen redundanten und nicht-redundanten Teilen eines Arguments zu unterscheiden, sondern auch festzulegen, wie oft eine Information verwendet werden darf. Dies führt zu einer dialogischen Semantik für lineare Logik, in der gefordert wird, dass jeder Teil einer Formel (mit einigen Ausnahmen) genau einmal zu verwenden ist, um die Gültigkeit der Formel nachzuweisen, – wobei verschiedene Vorkommnisse derselben (Teil-)Formel auch als verschiedene Teile angesehen werden. Man beachte, dass es in der Dialogischen Logik einen sehr natürlichen Weg gibt, mehrere Vorkommnisse einer Formel zu unterscheiden: Jedes Vorkommnis einer Formel kann einem anderen Zug im Dialog zugeordnet werden.

2 Dialoge und die Semantik der linearen Partikeln[5]

Es ist schon oft behauptet worden, dass die lineare Logik diejenige Logik sei, die ein Bewusstsein für beschränkte Ressourcen habe. Dies kann dadurch illustriert werden, dass man die logischen Ausdrücke als Beschreibungen von Übergängen zwischen Handlungen ansieht. So signalisiert z.B. das Konditional 'Wenn A, dann B' (in der Notation der linearen Logik $A \multimap B$), dass man, wenn man eine Handlung des Typs A ausführen kann, auch eine Handlung von Typ B ausführen kann. Um Girards bevorzugtes Beispiel zu verwenden: Wenn man einen Dollar investiert, erhält man ein Päckchen Zigaretten. Nun liegt aber bei jeder neuen Anwendung dieses Konditionals ('einen bestimmten Dollar bezahlen, um ein bestimmtes Päckchen Zigaretten zu bekommen') ein neues *Token* des Handlungs-Typs vor ('einen weiteren Dollar bezahlen, um ein weiteres Päckchen Zigaretten zu bekommen'). Das bedeutet, dass das entsprechende *Token*, sobald eine Handlung des Typs A ausgeführt wurde, nicht mehr verfügbar ist, um den durch das

---

[4] Der Zusammenhang zwischen Relevanzlogik und linearer Logik wurde von Avron (1988) hervorgehoben und von D'Agostino/Gabbay/Broda (1999) für Tableauxsysteme weiterentwickelt.

[5] Lesern, die mit der Dialogischen Logik (und den von uns verwendeten Notationskonventionen) noch nicht vertraut sind, wird empfohlen, sich zunächst den kurzen Anhang durchzulesen.

Eine neue dialogische Semantik für lineare Logik

Konditional ausgedrückten Übergang zu wiederholen (der erste Dollar ist verbraucht, und man muss einen weiteren bezahlen, um ein weiteres Päckchen Zigaretten zu erhalten).

In der Tat kann die lineare Logik als eine Kombination aus Ressourcenbewusstsein und einem Horror vor Irrelevanzen (d.h. einem Horror vor zusätzlichen, unbrauchbaren Annahmen in einem Beweis) aufgefasst werden. Die Relevanzlogik vermeidet die unvorsichtige Einführung von unbrauchbaren Annahmen, die in der klassischen und intuitionistischen Logik möglich ist, dadurch, dass Vereinfachung aufgegeben wird. Die lineare Logik eliminiert den verbleibenden Grad an möglicher Redundanz in der traditionellen Beweistheorie durch die zusätzliche Aufgabe der Kontraktion: Wenn eine Formel n-mal verwendet werden soll, so muss sie auch n-mal als Annahme zur Verfügung stehen. Mit anderen Worten wird in der linearen Logik eine Sequenz $\Gamma \vdash A$, wobei Γ eine endliche Folge von Formeln ist und A eine einzelne Formel, so interpretiert, dass A aus Γ abgeleitet werden kann, wobei jede der in Γ enthaltenen Hypothesen *genau einmal* verwendet wird. Diese Bedingung wird mit Hilfe von *Girard's Principle* eingeführt, d.h. durch die Einführung neuer Partikeln – oder um es anders auszudrücken, durch die Einführung neuer Strukturregeln, die nur lokal wirken, d.h. immer auf bestimmte Partikeln bezogen sind.

Die Partikeln der linearen Logik werden gewöhnlich in multiplikative und additive unterteilt. Die Idee hinter dieser Klassifikation ist leicht einzusehen, wenn man die multiplikative Konjunktion mit der additiven Konjunktion vergleicht. Bei der multiplikativen Konjunktion lautet die Beschränkung, dass jedes Konjunkt genau einmal verwendet werden muss, während bei der additiven Konjunktion die gesamte Konjunktion genau einmal verwendet werden muss (also nur eines der beiden Konjunkte).

Nun kann man sich im dialogischen Ansatz einen Beweis aus Handlungen, dem Setzen (bzw. Vorbringen) von Formeln (bzw. Argumenten), aufgebaut denken. Solche Handlungen werden als Züge bezeichnet. Auf diese Weise ergibt sich ganz natürlich, dass jeder neue Zug als eine neue Handlung angesehen werden kann (auch wenn zweimal die gleiche Formel behauptet wird). Dies erlaubt es, die Semantik für beide Arten von Partikeln der linearen Logik auf natürliche Art und Weise festzulegen. Diese Semantik beschreiben wir ausführlich in den folgenden Kapiteln.

Wir greifen dabei auf einige Ideen der in Rahman/Rückert (1998a) entwickelten dialogischen Relevanzlogik zurück. In der Tat könnten auch andere in dem erwähnten Aufsatz eingeführte Relevanzüberlegungen verwendet werden, um so z.B. eine affine Logik zu erhalten. Wir haben uns für die hier vorgestellte Version entschieden, da sie einem linearen Standpunkt eher zu entsprechen scheint.

Zunächst aber einige Erklärungen und Definitionen, die nötig sind, um die linearen Partikeln einzuführen:

Eine neue dialogische Semantik für lineare Logik

1) Das Aufbrauchen von Zügen und lineare Gültigkeit

Wie schon gesagt, liegen die Hauptideen der linearen Logik in einem Ressourcenbewusstsein und einem Horror vor Redundanzen. Daraus lassen sich zwei Bedingungen ableiten:

1. Jede gesetzte Formel (= Zug) muss verwendet werden, um die Gültigkeit der These nachzuweisen.

2. Kein Zug darf mehr als einmal verwendet werden (mit Ausnahmen für die Exponentiale), um die Gültigkeit der These nachzuweisen. Ist ein Zug verwendet worden, sagen wir auch, dass er aufgebraucht ist.[6]

Zur Überprüfung der Einhaltung beider Bedingungen führen wir mit Hilfe der Zeichen '[' und ']' eine Klammernotation ein: Ist ein Zug eingeklammert worden, bedeutet dies zum einen, dass er verwendet wurde, und zum anderen, dass er in der Folge nicht mehr verwendet werden kann. (Wir geben bei den Regeln für die linearen Partikeln jeweils auch an, wie zu klammern ist.)

Damit lässt sich nun lineare Gültigkeit folgendermaßen definieren:

Def. Lineare Gültigkeit:
Eine Formel heißt gemäß der hier vorgestellten dialogischen Semantik linear genau dann gültig, wenn **P** eine (formale) Gewinnstrategie hat, sodass am Dialogende alle Züge (bis auf die von **P** gesetzten Primformeln) eingeklammert sind und er keine (formale) Gewinnstrategie hat, sodass am Dialogende nicht alle Züge (außer den von **P** gesetzten Primformeln) eingeklammert sind. (D.h. **P** hat dann und nur dann eine (formale) Gewinnstrategie, wenn alle Züge aufgebraucht werden.)

---

[6] Der Ausdruck 'verwenden' bedarf natürlich einer Präzisierung: Eine von **O** gesetzte Primformel wird genau dann verwendet, wenn **P** diese Primformel setzt, um einen Zug von **O** anzugreifen oder sich auf einen Angriff von **O** zu verteidigen. Eine gesetzte komplexe Formel wird verwendet, wenn alle zulässigen Angriffe und Verteidigungen (die ja aufgrund der Subformeleigenschaft immer Setzungen von Teilformeln der anzugreifenden bzw. zu verteidigenden Formel sind) bezüglich dieser Formel gespielt werden (siehe Näheres bei den einzelnen Regeln für die linearen Partikeln).

2) Dialogkontexte und Unterdialoge

Gemäß der hier vorzustellenden dialogischen Semantik finden lineare Dialoge in unterschiedlichen Dialogkontexten statt, d.h. unterschiedliche Züge sind unter unterschiedlichen Bedingungen zu setzen. (Um Girards Bild des Verkaufs von Zigarettenpäckchen aufzugreifen, könnte man sagen, dass unterschiedliche Transaktionen eventuell in unterschiedlichen Geschäften stattfinden.) Welche Dialogkontexte jeweils zum Spielen von Zügen zur Verfügung stehen, wird durch die noch zu formulierenden Partikelregeln angegeben.

Dabei gilt folgendes:

Formale Regel für Dialogkontexte:
Nur **O** darf neue Dialogkontexte eröffnen, **P** darf seine Züge nur in schon vorhandenen Dialogkontexten setzen.

Zur Formulierung der Partikelregeln benötigen wir außerdem den Begriff des Unterdialogs:

Def. Unterdialog:

1. Eröffnet **O** einen neuen Dialogkontext, um einen Zug von **P** anzugreifen oder um einen eigenen Zug zu verteidigen, so heißt dieser neue Dialogkontext ein Unterdialog zu dem Dialogkontext, in dem die angegriffene bzw. verteidigte Formel steht.

2. Jeder Dialogkontext ist ein Unterdialog zu sich selbst (Reflexivität).

3. Ist n ein Unterdialog von m und m ein Unterdialog von l, so ist n auch ein Unterdialog von l (Transitivität).

Da die einzelnen Züge also in unterschiedlichen Dialogkontexten gespielt werden, ist es nötig, dies in der Dialognotation zu berücksichtigen. Zu diesem Zweck führen wir ein Nummerierungssystem für Dialogkontexte ein, indem wir jeweils hinter einem gespielten Zug in Klammern die Nummer des Dialogkontexts notieren, in dem er gesetzt wurde: Z.B. bedeutet 'a <1.1>', dass die Primformel a in Dialogkontext 1.1 gesetzt wurde.

Nummerierungssystem für Dialogkontexte:

1. Der Ausgangsdialog, in dem die These des Dialogs gesetzt wird, erhält die Nummer 1.

2. Der erste Unterdialog, den **O** bezüglich Dialogkontext n eröffnet, erhält die Nummer $n.1$, der zweite die Nummer $n.2$, und entsprechend der m-te die Nummer $n.m$.

3) Die formale Rahmenregel und das Aufbrauchen von Primformeln

Die formale Rahmenregel besagt normalerweise (siehe Anhang), dass **P** eine Primformel nur dann setzen darf, wenn sie zuvor von **O** schon zugestanden wurde, indem dieser sie selbst gesetzt hatte. Da in der linearen Logik das Arbeiten mit Dialogkontexten nötig ist, ist eine Präzisierung dieser Regel erforderlich:

Formale Regel für lineare Logik:
O darf Primformeln jederzeit gemäß den anderen Rahmenregeln und den Partikelregeln setzen. **P** darf in einem Dialogkontext m eine Primformel a nur setzen, wenn a zuvor von **O** in einem Dialogkontext n gesetzt wurde (und noch nicht aufgebraucht ist), wobei m ein Unterdialog von n ist.

Oder graphisch:

O	**P**
a	...
	a
(in Dialogkontext n)	*(in einem Unterdialog m von n nach Wahl von P)*

Klammerkonvention: Sobald eine von **O** zugestandene Primformel a von **P** gesetzt wird, um sich zu verteidigen oder um anzugreifen, so wird der entsprechende Zug von **O** eingeklammert: $[a]$. Von **P** gesetzte Primformeln können prinzipiell nicht eingeklammert werden.

Da aufgrund dieser Regel **P** immer darauf angewiesen ist, von **O** Primformeln (in für ihn günstigen Dialogkontexten) zugestanden zu bekommen, kann man aufgrund einfacher strategischer Überlegungen zu folgendem Ergebnis gelangen: Für **O** kann es nie ein Fehler sein, wenn sich ihm aufgrund der Partikelregeln die Möglichkeit dazu bietet, immer eine Verzweigung in der Dialogkontextstruktur hervorzurufen, während **P** eine dem entgegengesetzte

Eine neue dialogische Semantik für lineare Logik

Strategie verfolgt.[7] Diese Überlegung wird in den später folgenden Dialogbeispielen immer berücksichtigt, so dass trivialerweise schlechte Züge automatisch unterdrückt werden.

2.1 Die Multiplikativa: die multiplikative Konjunktion ('⊗') und die multiplikative Disjunktion ('✶')

Nunmehr können wir die ersten linearen Partikeln einführen. Ein Hauptcharakteristikum der sogenannten multiplikativen Partikeln besteht darin, dass keine der beiden Teilformeln redundant sein darf. Multiplikative Konjunktion und multiplikative Disjunktion unterscheiden sich im Wesentlichen dadurch, dass bei der Konjunktion der Angreifer die Wahl darüber hat, in welchen Unterdialogen die Konjunkte zu setzen sind, während bei der Disjunktion der Verteidiger entscheiden kann, in welchen Unterdialogen er die Disjunkte verteidigen möchte.

1) Die multiplikative Konjunktion ('⊗')

Für die multiplikative Konjunktion '⊗' (engl.: *tensor*) bedeutet dies, dass der Angreifer sowohl das Setzen des linken als auch das Setzen des rechten Konjunktes verlangt, wobei er jeweils wählt, in welchem Unterdialog die Verteidigung stattzufinden hat:

⊗	**Angriff**	**Verteidigung**
$A \otimes B$ (in Dialogkontext n)	¿L (in einem Unterdialog m von n nach Wahl des Angreifers)	A (in m)
	¿R (in einem Unterdialog l von n nach Wahl des Angreifers)	B (in l)

---

[7] Diese Überlegung ist auch für die später noch einzuführenden dialogischen Strategientableaux grundlegend. So ruft z.B. die **O**-Regel für die Disjunktion eine Verzweigung hervor (da hier **O** wählen kann), nicht jedoch die **P**-Regel (und umgekehrt bei der Konjunktion).

157

Eine neue dialogische Semantik für lineare Logik

Klammerkonvention: Sobald der Angriff '¿L' mit A beantwortet wurde, wird das linke Konjunkt eingeklammert: $[A]\otimes B$. Sobald der Angriff '¿R' mit B beantwortet wurde, wird das rechte Konjunkt eingeklammert: $A\otimes[B]$. Die gesamte multiplikative Konjunktion ist genau dann aufgebraucht, wenn beide Konjunkte eingeklammert sind: $[A]\otimes[B]$.

2) *Die multiplikative Disjunktion* ('✶')

Die multiplikative Disjunktion ('✶') wird im Englischen *par* genannt. Auch bei ihr darf keine Teilformel redundant sein. Der Unterschied zur multiplikativen Konjunktion liegt darin, dass hier der Verteidiger wählt, wie (d.h. in welchen Dialogkontexten) er sich verteidigen möchte.

✶	**Angriff**	**Verteidigung**
A✶B (in Dialogkontext n)	¿ (in n)	A (in einem Unterdialog m von n nach Wahl des Verteidigers)
		B (in einem Unterdialog l von n nach Wahl des Verteidigers)

Klammerkonvention: Sobald sich der Verteidiger mit dem linken Disjunkt verteidigt hat, wird dieses eingeklammert: $[A]$✶B. Sobald sich der Verteidiger mit dem rechten Disjunkt verteidigt hat, wird dieses eingeklammert: A✶$[B]$. Die gesamte multiplikative Disjunktion ist genau dann aufgebraucht, wenn beide Disjunkte eingeklammert sind: $[A]$✶$[B]$.

Eine neue dialogische Semantik für lineare Logik

2.2 Die lineare Negation ('⊥') und das lineare Konditional ('—∘')

Bevor wir die ersten linearen Dialoge präsentieren, führen wir zunächst noch die lineare Negation und das lineare Konditional ein, um die Beispiele interessanter gestalten zu können.

1) Die lineare Negation ('⊥')

In der kurzen Einführung in die klassische und intuitionistische Dialogische Logik im Anhang wird hervorgehoben, dass es keine Verteidigung gegen einen Angriff auf eine Negation gibt (durch das Zeichen '/' symbolisiert). Die einzig mögliche Entgegnung ist ein Gegenangriff. Wie von einigen Autoren von semantischen Spielen für lineare Logik angemerkt wurde, ruft ein Gegenangriff einen Wechsel der Rollen hervor. Die Frage ist allerdings, was genau gewechselt wird. Viele der Schwierigkeiten in semantischen Spielen für lineare Logik können durch eine genaue Reflexion auf die Formulierung der Partikelregeln vermieden werden. In den Partikelregeln identifizieren wir nicht (notwendigerweise) immer den Angreifer mit dem Spieler, der als Opponent agiert, und den Verteidiger mit dem Spieler, der als Proponent agiert – dies ist ein häufiger Fehler in Beschreibungen und Anwendungen der Dialogischen Logik. Angriffe und Verteidigungen sind unterschiedliche Züge, die von beiden Spielern vorgebracht werden.[8]

(Zudem muss eine weitere Rollenunterscheidung beachtet werden: Obwohl in der dialogischen klassischen und in der dialogischen intuitionistischen Logik (sowie in vielen weiteren) der Spieler, der den Dialog startet, und derjenige, der unter der formalen Beschränkung spielt (d.h. derjenige für den gilt, dass er gemäß der formalen Rahmenregel Primformeln bzw. Dialogkontexte nur dann selbst verwenden darf, wenn das der andere Spieler schon zuvor getan hat), immer derselbe ist (nämlich der Proponent), ist dies in anderen Logiken nicht notwendigerweise der Fall. So ist es z.B. möglich, eine Art von Negation einzuführen (den **F**-Operator), sodass der Spieler, der den Dialog beginnt, nicht

---

[8] Der Proponent bleibt also nach unserer Auffassung immer der Spieler, der die Anfangsthese hervorgebracht hat, auch wenn er während des Dialoges (lokal) die Angreiferrolle übernimmt, während der Opponent immer der Spieler ist, der gegen die Anfangsthese argumentiert, auch wenn er während des Dialoges (lokal) die Verteidigerrolle übernimmt.

(Es wäre stattdessen auch denkbar, die Bezeichnungen **P** und **O** mit 'Verteidiger' bzw. 'Angreifer' zu identifizieren (was wir nicht für glücklich halten). In diesem Fall müsste man allerdings gesonderte Bezeichnungen für die beiden Spieler einführen (z.B. 'Weiß' und 'Schwarz'), die dann im Laufe des Dialoges beide entsprechend zwischen Proponenten- und Opponentenrolle hin und her wechseln können.)

immer derselbe ist wie derjenige, der unter der formalen Beschränkung spielt (siehe Rahman/Rückert (2001b)) – der Spieler, der eine **F**-Operator-Aussage angreift, muss einen Unterdialog eröffnen, in dem er selbst der formalen Beschränkung unterliegt, und dadurch kann es zu einem Wechsel hinsichtlich der formalen Beschränkung kommen. Diese Art von Rollenwechsel kommt allerdings im Rahmen der linearen Logik nicht vor.)

Die lineare Negation ruft also einen Wechsel in den Angreifer- und Verteidiger-Rollen hervor, keinen Wechsel der Spieler. Dies kann folgendermaßen genauer ausgedrückt werden: Durch Setzen der Formel $A^\perp$ behauptet der Spieler X, dass A unter den gegebenen Dialogbedingungen widerlegt werden kann (deshalb steht der Angriff im selben Dialogkontext wie die angegriffene Formel). Der andere Spieler Y greift $A^\perp$ an, indem er A behauptet, um es in der Folge zu verteidigen und so zu zeigen, dass es unter diesen Bedingungen doch nicht erfolgreich angegriffen werden kann. Dadurch wird der Verteidiger von $A^\perp$ zum Angreifer von A. Graphisch:

$\perp$	**Angriff**	**Verteidigung**
$A^\perp$ *(in Dialogkontext n)*	A *(in n)*	/ *(keine Verteidigung möglich, nur Gegenangriff spielbar)*

Klammerkonvention: Sobald der Angriff mit A gespielt wurde, wird die Negation eingeklammert: $[A^\perp]$.

Es lässt sich leicht einsehen, dass die lineare Negation involutiv ist (zumindest bei klassischer Rahmenregelung), d.h. dass $A^{\perp\perp}$ und A äquivalent sind. Wenn **O** z.B. zeigen will, dass widerlegt werden kann, dass A widerlegt werden kann, wird er nicht umhinkönnen, selbst A zu setzen, das dann von **P** erfolgreich übernommen werden kann.

2) Das lineare Konditional ('—o')

In der linearen Logik wird das Konditional ('—o') gewöhnlich definitorisch unter Zuhilfenahme der multiplikativen Disjunktion und der linearen Negation (analog der bekannten klassischen Äquivalenz) eingeführt:

$$A \multimap B \Leftrightarrow_{\text{def}} A^\perp \bigstar B$$

Damit ist das lineare Konditional den Multiplikativa zuzurechnen. Ein entsprechendes additives Konditional kann zwar problemlos definiert werden (als

Eine neue dialogische Semantik für lineare Logik

$A^\perp \oplus B$), scheint aber relativ uninteressant, da aufgrund der Eigenschaften der Additiva (siehe später) eine Teilaussage immer redundant sein wird, und somit nie ein Zusammenhang zwischen Wenn- und Dann-Teil zustande kommen kann.

Wenn also auch das lineare Konditional nur eine abgeleitete Partikel ist, so wollen wir es in den folgenden Beispielen dennoch verwenden, und geben deshalb eine eigenständige Partikelregel an. (Es dürfte leicht sein einzusehen, wie sich diese ergibt: Es handelt sich um die Spielstellung, zu der man unter Weglassung von zwei Zwischenschritten gelangt, wenn man den Dialog um $A^\perp \star B$ spielt[9]):

—∘	Angriff	Verteidigung
A—∘B (in Dialogkontext n)	A (in Unterdialog m von n nach Wahl des Verteidigers)	B (in Unterdialog l von n nach Wahl des Verteidigers)

Klammerkonvention: Sobald der Angriff A gespielt wurde, klammern wir $[A]$—∘B. Sobald dann der Angriff verteidigt wurde, wird auch noch B eingeklammert, sodass dann das gesamte lineare Konditional aufgebraucht ist: $[A]$—∘$[B]$.

3) Beispiele

Nun zu den ersten Beispieldialogen:

Beispiel 1:

	O			P	
				$[(a$—∘$(a$—∘$b))]$—∘$[(a$—∘$b)]$ <1>	(0)
(1)	$[a]$—∘$[(a$—∘$b)]$ <1>	0		$[a]$—∘b <1>	(2)
(3)	$[a]$ <1>		2		
(5)	a—∘b <1.2>		1	a <1.1>	(4)

O gewinnt

Offensichtlich ist Kontraktion nicht gültig. In Zug (0) behauptet der Proponent die

---

[9] Die Zwischenschritte sind bei Verwendung der klassischen Rahmenregel zwar irrelevant, werden allerdings bei Verwendung der intuitionistischen Rahmenregel in einer denkbaren intuitionistischen Version der linearen Logik bedeutsam, was dazu führt, dass dann das lineare Konditional auch nicht mehr auf die angesprochene Art definitorisch eingeführt werden kann (siehe auch den entsprechenden Abschnitt bei den Schlussbemerkungen).

Eine neue dialogische Semantik für lineare Logik

These des Dialogs, die in Zug (1) durch den Opponenten angegriffen wird, indem er den Wenn-Teil zugesteht und nach dem Dann-Teil fragt. In Zug (2) verteidigt sich der Proponent, indem er den Dann-Teil behauptet. Nun steigert sich das Gefecht: Der nächste Zug des Opponenten greift das Konditional aus Zug (2) an, und der Proponent, da es ihm nicht erlaubt ist, b zu setzen (wegen der formalen Rahmenregel), entscheidet sich dazu, Zug (1) anzugreifen, indem er den atomaren Zug (3) verwendet. Nach der entsprechenden Verteidigung des Opponenten in Zug (5) verliert der Proponent den Dialog. Der Grund dafür ist, dass er nicht Zug (5) angreifen kann, da der atomare Zug (3) schon aufgebraucht ist, und kein entsprechender weiterer atomarer Zug des Opponenten zur Verfügung steht.

Beispiel 2:

	O			P	
				$[(a \star b)^\perp] \multimap [(a^\perp \otimes b^\perp)]$ <1>	(0)
(1)	$[(a \star b)^\perp]$ <1>	0		$[a^\perp] \otimes [b^\perp]$ <1>	(2)
(3)	¿L <1.1>	2		$[a^\perp]$ <1.1>	(4)
(5)	¿R <1.2>	2		$[b^\perp]$ <1.2>	(6)
(7)	$[a]$ <1.1>	4		/	
	/		1	$[a] \star [b]$ <1>	(8)
(9)	¿ <1>	8		a <1.1>	(10)
(11)	$[b]$ <1.2>	6		/	
(9')	¿ <1>	8		b <1.2>	(12)

P *gewinnt*

Es sind auch leicht veränderte Dialogverläufe bezüglich der Reihenfolge der gespielten Züge denkbar, am Ergebnis ändert sich aber letztlich nichts. Auch die anderen bekannten DeMorgan'schen Beziehungen zwischen der multiplikativen Konjunktion und der multiplikativen Disjunktion gelten in der linearen Logik.

Beispiel 3:

	O			P	
				$[((a \star b) \otimes a^\perp)] \multimap [b]$ <1>	(0)
(1)	$[(a \star b)] \otimes [a^\perp]$ <1>	0		b <1.2>	(10)
(3)	$[a] \star [b]$ <1>		1	¿L <1>	(2)
(5)	$[a]$ <1.1>		3	¿ <1>	(4)
(7)	$[a^\perp]$ <1.1>		1	¿R <1.1>	(6)
	/		7	a <1.1>	(8)
(9)	$[b]$ <1.2>		3	¿ <1>	(4')

P *gewinnt*

Auch diese Formel ist linear gültig. **P** hat seine Verteidigungspflicht erfüllen können, und alle Züge sind aufgebraucht, was man daran erkennt, dass lediglich von **P** gesetzte Primformeln nicht eingeklammert sind.

2.3 Die Additiva: die additive Konjunktion ('&') und die additive Disjunktion ('⊕')

Die Additiva unterscheiden sich von den Multiplikativa im Wesentlichen dadurch, dass eine Teilaussage redundant sein kann, da die gesamte additive Formel, sobald ein Angriff verteidigt wurde, schon aufgebraucht ist, sodass bezüglich ihr keine weiteren Angriffe oder Verteidigungen gespielt werden können.

1. Die additive Konjunktion ('&')

Für die additive Konjunktion '&' (engl.: *with*) bedeutet dies, dass der Angreifer zwischen dem Verlangen des linken und dem Verlangen des rechten Konjunktes wählen muss. Er kann also von jedem der beiden Konjunkte verlangen, es gezeigt zu bekommen, aber nicht beide auf einmal in einem Dialog. Damit ergibt sich folgende Partikelregel für die additive Konjunktion:

&	**Angriff**	**Verteidigung**
$A\&B$	¿L	A
	¿R	B
(in Dialogkontext n)	*(in einem Unterdialog m von n nach Wahl des Angreifers; der Angreifer muss zwischen beiden Angriffen wählen)*	*(in m)*

Klammerkonvention: Sobald ein Angriff '¿L' (bzw. '¿R') mit A (bzw. B) beantwortet wurde, wird die additive Konjunktion insgesamt eingeklammert: $[A\&B]$.

Es ist offensichtlich, dass bei der additiven Konjunktion die bei der multiplikativen Konjunktion aufgegebene Vereinfachung wieder gilt: $(A\&B)\multimap A$ bzw. $(A\&B)\multimap B$.

Eine neue dialogische Semantik für lineare Logik

2. Die additive Disjunktion ('⊕')

Die additive Disjunktion ('⊕') wird im Englischen *sum* genannt. Auch bei ihr ist eine Teilformel redundant. Der Unterschied zur additiven Konjunktion liegt hier darin, dass der Verteidiger wählt, wie er sich verteidigen möchte.

⊕	**Angriff**	**Verteidigung**
$A \oplus B$	¿	A
		B
(in Dialogkontext n)	*(in n)*	*(in einem Unterdialog m von n nach Wahl des Verteidigers; der Verteidiger muss zwischen beiden Verteidigungen wählen)*

Klammerkonvention: Sobald die additive Disjunktion durch Setzen eines der Disjunkte verteidigt wurde, wird sie insgesamt eingeklammert: $[A \oplus B]$.

Es ist offensichtlich, dass bei der additiven Disjunktion die bei der multiplikativen Disjunktion aufgegebene Verdünnung wieder gilt: $A \multimap (A \oplus B)$ bzw. $B \multimap (A \oplus B)$.[10]

---

[10] Girard (1995, S. 2) schreibt: „Although „&" has obvious disjunctive features, it would be technically wrong to view it as a disjunction [...] (in the same way „*" [...] is technically a disjunction, but has prominent conjunctive features)."

Wir sind nun in der Lage, dieser Aussage einen klaren Sinn zu geben: Was die multiplikative und die additive Konjunktion beide zu Konjunktionen macht, ist der Umstand, dass hier der Angreifer wählen kann, welches Konjunkt er in welchem Dialogkontext gezeigt bekommen möchte. Die '*disjunctive features*' der additiven Konjunktion bestehen hingegen darin, dass nur eines der beiden Konjunkte in einem Dialog gesetzt werden kann.

Entsprechend sind die multiplikative und die additive Disjunktion beides Disjunktionen, da hier der Verteidiger wählen kann, wie er sich verteidigt. Die '*conjunctive features*' der multiplikativen Disjunktion bestehen darin, dass beide Disjunkte im Dialog zu setzen sind.

Eine neue dialogische Semantik für lineare Logik

3) Beispiele

Beispiel 4:

	O			P	
				$[(a\&b)^\bot]\multimap[(a^\bot\oplus b^\bot)]$ <1> (0)	
(1)	$[(a\&b)^\bot]$ <1>	0		$[a^\bot\oplus b^\bot]$ <1>	(2)
(3)	¿ <1>	2		$[a^\bot]$ <1>	(6)
	/		1	$[a\&b]$ <1>	(4)
(5)	¿L <1.1>	4		a <1.1>	(8)
(7)	$[a]$ <1>	6		/	

P *gewinnt*

Zu diesem Dialog gibt es eine allerdings wenig interessante (da genau analog verlaufende) Nebenvariante: Wenn **O** in Zug (5) nach dem rechten Konjunkt verlangt, dann verteidigt sich **P** in Zug (6) geschickt mit dem rechten Disjunkt und gewinnt ebenso.

Auch bei den Additiva gelten im übrigen alle DeMorgan-Gesetze.

Beispiel 5:

	O			P	
				$[((a\multimap c)\&(b\multimap c))]\multimap[((a\oplus b)\multimap c)]$<1>(0)	
(1)	$[(a\multimap c)\&(b\multimap c)]$ <1>	0		$[(a\oplus b)]\multimap[c]$ <1>	(2)
(3)	$[a\oplus b]$ <1>	2		c <1.1.2>	(10)
(5)	$[a]$ <1.1>	3	¿ <1>	(4)
(7)	$[a]\multimap[c]$ <1.1>	1	¿L <1.1>	(6)
(9)	$[c]$ <1.1.2>	7	a <1.1.1>	(8)

P *gewinnt*

Hätte sich **O** in Zug (5) mit b verteidigt, so hätte **P** in Zug (6) entsprechend nach dem rechten Konjunkt gefragt, und in der Folge auch gewonnen.

Eine neue dialogische Semantik für lineare Logik

Beispiel 6:

	O			P	
				$[((a\otimes b)\&(a\otimes c))]\multimap[(a\otimes(b\&c))]$ <1>	(0)
(1)	$[(a\otimes b)\&(a\otimes c)]$ <1>	0		$[a]\otimes[(b\&c)]$ <1>	(2)
(3)	¿L <1.1>	2		a <1.1>	(8)
(5)	$[a]\otimes[b]$ <1>	1	¿L <1>		(4)
(7)	$[a]$ <1>	5	¿L <1>		(6)
(9)	¿R <1.2>	2		$b\&c$ <1.2>	(10)
(11)	¿R <1.2.1>	10			
(13)	b <1>	5	¿R <1>		(12)
	O *gewinnt*				

Das Dilemma von **P** in diesem Beispiel entsteht dadurch, dass er sich schon in Zug (4) entscheiden muss, welches Konjunkt er von der additiven Konjunktion in Zug (1) verlangt (die anschließend natürlich nicht mehr zur Verfügung steht), zu einem Zeitpunkt also, zu dem er noch nicht weiß, welches der beiden Konjunkte er letztlich benötigt hätte, da dies im weiteren Dialogverlauf in den Händen von **O** liegt (siehe Zug (11)). Deshalb ist es klar, dass **P** auch auf die Verliererstraße gerät, wenn er in Zug (4) nach dem rechten Konjunkt fragt.

2.4 Die Exponentiale ('!' und '?')

Man kann die lineare Logik so auffassen, dass sie keine Logik statischer, bestehen bleibender Situationen darstellt (die man daher auch nicht aufbrauchen kann), sondern eine Logik dynamischer Handlungen, die jeweils nur einmal zur Verfügung stehen, was zur Folge hat, dass die Züge aufgebraucht werden (in diesem Aufsatz notiert mit Hilfe des Einklammerverfahrens).

Nun ist es aber wünschenswert, dass die Ausdrucksstärke der linearen Logik zumindest so groß ist, dass unter bestimmten Umständen Handlungen (bzw. Züge) auch beliebig oft zur Verfügung stehen können, manchmal die Aufbrauchbeschränkung also nicht gilt. Diesem Zwecke dienen besondere lineare Partikeln, die sogenannten Exponentiale '!' und '?', die somit für die Wiederholbarkeit von Handlungen stehen.

Demnach bedeutet !A, dass A beliebig oft (aber mindestens einmal) zur Verfügung steht, und der Angreifer kann daher beliebig oft (aber mindestens einmal) angreifen, und so das Setzen von A verlangen, wenn er es benötigt:

Eine neue dialogische Semantik für lineare Logik

!	Angriff	Verteidigung
!A	¿	A
(in Dialogkontext n)	*(in Unterdialog m von n nach Wahl des Angreifers)*	*(in m)*

Klammerkonvention: Beim ersten Angriff auf !A und erfolgter Verteidigung klammern wir folgendermaßen: ![A]. Dies bedeutet, dass weitere Angriffe nicht mehr verlangt, aber weiterhin möglich sind.

Die zu '!' duale Partikel ist '?'. Sie erlaubt unbeschränkt viele Verteidigungen mit A (aber mindestens eine). Also:

?	Angriff	Verteidigung
?A	¿	A
(in Dialogkontext n)	*(in n)*	*(in Unterdialog m von n nach Wahl des Verteidigers)*

Klammerkonvention: Beim ersten Angriff auf ?A und erfolgter Verteidigung klammern wir folgendermaßen: ?[A]. Dies bedeutet, dass weitere Verteidigungen nicht mehr verlangt, aber weiterhin möglich sind.

Bevor wir zu zwei Beispieldialogen für die Exponentiale kommen, sei darauf hingewiesen, dass die Ausdrucksstärke der linearen Logik durch diese Partikeln dermaßen vergrößert wird, dass sich die klassische und die intuitionistische Logik in ihr reformulieren lassen.[11]

---

[11] Siehe z.B. Girard (1998).

Eine neue dialogische Semantik für lineare Logik

Beispiel 7:

O				P	
				$[!(a^\perp)] \multimap [(?a)^\perp]$ <1>	(0)
(1)	$![(a^\perp)]$ <1>	0		$[(?a)^\perp]$ <1>	(2)
(3)	$?[a]$ <1>	2		/	
(5)	$[a]$ <1.1>		3	¿ <1>	(4)
(7)	$[a^\perp]$ <1.1>		1	¿ <1.1>	(6)
	/		7	a <1.1>	(8)
	P *gewinnt*				

O könnte zwar prinzipiell seinen Zug (3) erneut verteidigen (was allerdings in diesem Fall eine unzulässige Hinauszögerung des Dialogendes wäre), z.B. in Dialogkontext 1.2, doch dann könnte P einfach selbst wiederum in demselben Dialogkontext Zug (1) angreifen usf., und behielte letztlich immer die Überhand.

Neben dem aufgrund der Gültigkeit dieser Formel bestehenden Zusammenhang zwischen '!' und '?' gilt auch die umgekehrte Richtung, sowie die jeweils dualen Beziehungen.

Beispiel 8:

O				P	
				$[!(a\&b)] \multimap [(!a \otimes !b)]$ <1>	(0)
(1)	$![(a\&b)]$ <1>	0		$[!a] \otimes [!b]$ <1>	(2)
(3)	¿L <1.1>	2		$![a]$ <1.1>	(4)
(5)	¿R <1.2>	2		$![b]$ <1.2>	(6)
(7)	¿ <1.1.1>	4		a <1.1.1>	(12)
(9)	$[a\&b]$ <1>		1	¿ <1>	(8)
(11)	$[a]$ <1>		9	¿L <1>	(10)
(13)	¿ <1.2.1>	6		b <1.2.1>	(18)
(15)	$[a\&b]$ <1>		1	¿ <1>	(14)
(17)	$[b]$ <1>		15	¿R <1>	(16)
	P *gewinnt*				

So oft auch O die Züge (4) und (6) erneut angreifen mag, P wird immer das Manöver, das durch einen erneuten Angriff auf (1) eingeleitet wird, und dann mit einem geschickten Angriff auf die richtige Seite der additiven Konjunktion fortgesetzt wird, zur Verfügung haben und somit erfolgreich bleiben.

3 Über Gültigkeit: Gewinnstrategien und dialogische Tableaux für lineare Logik

Bevor wir zu Tableaux für lineare Logik gelangen,[12] präsentieren wir zunächst die üblichen Strategiesysteme für klassische und intuitionistische Logik, um dann durch Abänderungen und Erweiterungen dieser Systeme die Besonderheiten der linearen Logik einzufangen.

3.1 Nicht-lineare Tableaux

Wie schon erwähnt wird Gültigkeit in der Dialogischen Logik über Gewinnstrategien für **P** definiert, d.h. die These A ist genau dann logisch gültig, wenn **P** A gegen alle möglichen erlaubten Angriffe von **O** erfolgreich verteidigen kann. In diesem Falle hat **P** eine *Gewinnstrategie* für A. Eine systematische Beschreibung der Gewinnstrategien kann von den folgenden Überlegungen ausgehen:

> Wenn **P** gewinnen können soll, egal welche Züge **O** wählt, so müssen im Wesentlichen zwei Arten von Situationen betrachtet werden: Nämlich die dialogischen Situationen, in denen **O** eine (komplexe) Formel gesetzt hat, und diejenigen, in denen **P** eine (komplexe) Formel gesetzt hat. Wir nennen diese Situationen entsprechend **O**- und **P**-Fälle.

In beiden Fällen muss eine weitere Unterscheidung untersucht werden:

1. **P** hat beim *Wählen* eines Angriffs in den **O**-Fällen oder einer Verteidigung in den **P**-Fällen genau dann eine Gewinnstrategie, wenn er mindestens einen der ihm zur Wahl stehenden weiteren Dialogverläufe gewinnen kann.

2. Wenn **O** eine Verteidigung in den **O**-Fällen oder einen Angriff in den **P**-Fällen *wählen* kann, hat **P** genau dann eine Gewinnstrategie, wenn er alle weiteren Dialogverläufe, die **O** wählen kann, gewinnen kann.

Die Regeln für das Schließen eines dialogischen Tableaux sind die üblichen: Ein

---

[12] Wir beschränken uns bei der Behandlung der Strategientableaux auf das Fragment der linearen Logik ohne Exponentiale, da ihre Einbeziehung die Tableaux-Systeme erheblich komplexer machen und so den Rahmen dieses Aufsatzes sprengen würde.

Eine neue dialogische Semantik für lineare Logik

Zweig ist genau dann geschlossen, wenn er zwei Kopien einer Primformel enthält, eine von **O** gesetzt, die andere von **P**. Ein Tableau für (**P**)*A* (d.h. für einen Dialog, der mit (**P**)*A* beginnt) ist gnau dann geschlossen, wenn jeder Zweig geschlossen ist. Dies zeigt, dass Strategiesysteme für klassische und intuitionistische Logik nichts anderes sind als die wohlbekannten Tableaux-Systeme für diese Logiken.

Für das intuitionistische Tableaux-System muss noch die Rahmenregel über die Beschränkung der Verteidigungen (*'last duty first'*) berücksichtigt werden. Die Idee ist sehr einfach: Das Tableaux-System erlaubt zunächst das Niederschreiben aller möglichen Verteidigungen (sogar der atomaren), aber sobald bestimmte **P**-Formeln (Negationen und Konditionale) angegriffen werden, werden alle anderen **P**-Formeln ausgestrichen – dies ist eine Umsetzung der Rahmenregel R_I4 für die intuitionistische Logik. Wenn ein Angriff auf eine **P**-Formel verursacht, dass alle anderen **P**-Formeln ausgestrichen werden, ist klar, dass **P** nur den letzten Angriff beantworten kann. Die **P**-Formeln, die ein solches Ausstreichen hervorrufen, werden durch das tiefgestellte Suffix '(**O**)' gekennzeichnet, das folgendermaßen zu lesen ist: Behalte alle **O**-Formeln bei und lösche alle zuvor gesetzten **P**-Formeln.[13]

Klassische Tableaux

(**O**)-*Fälle*	(**P**)-*Fälle*
(**O**)$A \vor B$	(**P**)$A \vor B$
---	---
<(**P**)¿>(**O**)A | <(**P**)¿>(**O**)B	<(**O**)¿>(**P**)A, <(**O**)¿>(**P**)B
(**O**)$A \wedge B$	(**P**)$A \wedge B$
---	---
<(**P**)¿L>(**O**)A, <(**P**)¿R>(**O**)B	<(**O**)¿L>(**P**)A | <(**O**)¿R>(**P**)B
(**O**)$A \to B$	(**P**)$A \to B$
---	---
(**P**)A ... | <(**P**)A>(**O**)B	(**O**)A, (**P**)B
(**O**)$\neg A$	(**P**)$\neg A$
---	---
(**P**)A; /	(**O**)A; /

---

[13] Für Einzelheiten zur Bildung von Tableaux-Systemen ausgehend von Dialogen siehe Rahman (1993) sowie Rahman/Rückert (1998/99). Beweise für Korrektheit und Vollständigkeit der intuitionistischen Strategien-Tableaux finden sich in Rahman (1993). Ein anderer Beweis wurde von Felscher (1986) gegeben.

Eine neue dialogische Semantik für lineare Logik

Unter einer dialogisch bezeichneten Formel verstehen wir (**P**)X oder (**O**)X, wobei X eine Formel ist. Man beachte, dass unter der Linie jeweils Paare von Angriffs- und Verteidigungszügen stehen, also *Runden*. Ausdrücke zwischen den Zeichen '<' und '>', wie z.B. <(**P**)¿> oder <(**O**)¿> sind Züge – genauer gesagt handelt es sich um Angriffe – aber sie sind kein eigentlicher Bestandteil des Tableauxsystems, sondern dienen der besseren Übersichtlichkeit.

Intuitionistische Tableaux

(**O**)-*Fälle*	(**P**)-*Fälle*
(**O**)A∨B	(**P**)A∨B
<(**P**)¿>(**O**)A | <(**P**)¿>(**O**)B	<(**O**)¿>(**P**)A, <(**O**)¿>(**P**)B
(**O**)A∧B	(**P**)A∧B
<(**P**)¿L>(**O**)A, <(**P**)¿R>(**O**)B	<(**O**)¿L>(**P**)A | <(**O**)¿R>(**P**)B
(**O**)A→B	(**P**)A→B
(**P**)A ... | <(**P**)A>(**O**)B	(**O**)$_{(O)}$A, (**P**)B
(**O**)¬A	(**P**)¬A
(**P**)A; /	(**O**)$_{(O)}$A; /

Nachfolgend zwei Beispiele, eines für klassische Logik und eines für intuitionistische Logik. Wir verwenden die von Smullyan (1968) bekannt gemachte *tree-shape*-Notation:

Beispiel 9:

    (**P**)   ((a→b)∧a)→b
    (**O**)   (a→b)∧a
    (**P**)   b
    (**O**)   (a→b)
    (**O**)   a
    (**P**)   a
    (**O**)   b

Das Tableau ist geschlossen

Das folgende intuitionistische Tableau macht Gebrauch von der Ausstreichregel:

Beispiel 10:

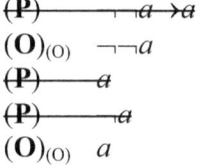

Das Tableau bleibt offen

3.2 Dialogische Tableaux für lineare Logik

Dialogische Tableaux für die lineare Logik sollten Regeln enthalten für:

1. die multiplikativen Partikeln,
2. die additiven Partikeln,
3. das Aufbrauchen der Züge, und
4. das Schließen der Zweige unter Aufbrauchen aller atomaren Züge.

Die Strategietableaux-Regeln für die Multiplikativa (einschließlich der linearen Negation) unterscheiden sich im Wesentlichen nicht von den entsprechenden Regeln im oben vorgestellten Tableaux-System für die klassische Logik. Man beachte, dass das auf der Partienebene nötige Arbeiten mit Dialogkontexten und Unterdialogen hier durch die Strategieverzweigungen eingefangen werden kann:[14]

---

[14] In der Tat ist die in der linearen Logik auf der Partienebene entstehende Unterdialogstruktur im Prinzip nichts anderes als ein Baum möglicher Spielvarianten in einem nicht-linearen Dialog. In der linearen Logik ist es nötig, diese unterschiedlichen Spielvarianten (die ansonsten erst auf der Strategieebene relevant werden) mit Hilfe von Unterdialogen schon auf der Partienebene in einen einzigen Dialog einzubauen, um eine Überprüfung eventueller Redundanzen möglich zu machen. Das Kriterium der linearen Logik, das Redundanzen ausschließt, kann unter dieser Perspektive auch folgendermaßen formuliert werden: Jeder Zug muss in mindestens einer Spielvariante erfolgreich verwendet werden können.

Eine neue dialogische Semantik für lineare Logik

(O)-*Fälle*	(P)-*Fälle*
(O)A✶B	(P)A✶B
----------------------------------	----------------------------
<(P)¿>(O)A | <(P)¿>(O)B	<(O)¿>(P)A, <(O)¿>(P)B
(O)$A \otimes B$	(P)$A \otimes B$
----------------------------------	----------------------------------
<(P)¿L>(O)A, <(P)¿R>(O)B	<(O)¿L>(P)A | <(O)¿R>(P)B
(O)$A \multimap B$	(P)$A \multimap B$
----------------------------------	----------------------
(P)A ... | <(P)A>(O)B	(O)A, (P)B
(O)$A^\perp$	(P)$A^\perp$
------------------	----------------
(P)A; /	(P)A; /

Zur Kontrolle des Aufbrauchens der Züge verwenden wir wieder das schon von der Partieebene bekannte Klammerverfahren:

Aufbrauchen von komplexen Zügen:
Sobald eine Strategieregel bezüglich einer (**O**)- oder (**P**)-bezeichneten komplexen Formel angewendet wurde, so wird diese mit eckigen Klammern eingeklammert. (Man beachte, dass bei den Multiplikativa beim Anwenden einer Strategieregel – sowohl bei den Verzweigungsregeln, als auch bei den Nicht-Verzweigungsregeln – immer beide resultierenden Züge niedergeschrieben werden müssen.)[15]

Um sicherzustellen, dass auch alle Züge verwendet werden, benötigen wir die folgende Regel:

Verwenden aller Züge:
Es sind so lange Strategieregeln anzuwenden, bis alle komplexen (**O**)- oder (**P**)-bezeichneten Formeln eingeklammert sind.

---

[15] Das Aufbrauchen der Primformeln wird später durch die Formulierung der Schließungsregeln für ein Tableau mitbehandelt.

Eine neue dialogische Semantik für lineare Logik

Nach Einhaltung dieser beiden Kriterien sieht das Tableau so aus, dass nur noch atomare Züge uneingeklammert sind. Kommen wir nun zum Aufbrauchen der atomaren Züge:

Aufbrauchen der atomaren Züge:
Wird ein Tableauzweig mit Hilfe eines Paares **(O)**a und **(P)**a geschlossen, so werden beide atomaren Züge eingeklammert.

Schließlich sind wir nun in der Lage anzugeben, wann ein lineares Tableau für **(P)**A geschlossen werden kann, d.h. wann A linear gültig ist:

Schließen eines linearen Tableaus:
Ein lineares Tableau ist geschlossen, wenn (1) alle Zweige geschlossen sind, und (2) alle atomaren Züge zum Schließen verwendet wurden, d.h. jeder atomare Zug eingeklammert ist.

Bevor wir dem hier vorgestellten Strategiensystem für lineare Logik noch Regeln für den Umgang mit Additiva hinzufügen, präsentieren wir zunächst zwei Beispiele für die Multiplikativa:

Beispiel 11:

	(P)	$[(a \multimap (a \multimap b)) \multimap (a \multimap b)]$				
	(O)	$[a \multimap (a \multimap b)]$				
	(P)	$[a \multimap b]$				
	(O)	$[a]$				
	(P)	$[b]$				
(P)	$[a]$			**(O)**	$[a \multimap b]$	
		(P)	a		**(O)**	$[b]$

Das Tableau bleibt offen.

Man beachte, dass das Schließen des Tableaus in der linearen Logik (im Gegensatz zur klassischen Logik) misslingt, da die im Hauptast von **O** gesetzte Primformel a nur zum Schließen eines Zweiges verwendet werden kann, und danach aufgebraucht ist, sodass ein Zweig geöffnet bleibt. Also ist die Formel linear nicht gültig.

Beispiel 12:

> (**P**) $[((a\star b)\otimes a^\perp)\multimap b]$
> (**O**) $[(a\star b)\otimes a^\perp]$
> (**P**) $[b]$
> (**O**) $[a\star b]$
> (**O**) $[a^\perp]$
> (**P**) $[a]$
>
> (**O**) $[a]$ | (**O**) $[b]$

Das Tableau ist geschlossen.

Kommen wir nun zu den Tableauxregeln für die Additiva. Der wesentliche Unterschied zu den Multiplikativa besteht hier darin, dass es sich bei den Strategieverzweigungen sozusagen um echte Verzweigungen auf der Strategieebene handelt, und nicht um eine Aufsplitterung in verschiedene Unterdialoge. Diesen Umstand fangen wir graphisch durch die Verwendung von '||' (im Gegensatz zu '|') ein, sowie inhaltlich durch folgende Regel:

Strategieverzweigungen bei Additiva:
Kommt es zu einer additiven Strategieverzweigung, so werden alle noch nicht aufgebrauchten Züge des Hauptastes (inklusive der multiplikativen Baumstruktur) genau einmal in jeden der beiden entstehenden Zweige übernommen. (Dadurch werden die entsprechenden bezeichneten Formeln im Hauptast aufgebraucht, und sind demgemäß einzuklammern.)

Außerdem ist die Regel für das Aufbrauchen von komplexen Zügen im additiven Fall neu zu formulieren:

Aufbrauchen der Additiva:
Bei additiven Verzweigungsregeln ist die zu analysierende Formel aufgebraucht, wenn beide resultierenden Züge (in verschiedenen Zweigen) niedergeschrieben sind, bei additiven Nicht-Verzweigungsregeln hingegen ist der zu analysierende Zug schon aufgebraucht, wenn eine resultierende Formel niedergeschrieben ist. Man darf also jede der resultierenden Formeln im Tableau niederschreiben, aber nicht beide zusammen (dies soll durch die geschweiften Klammern bei den entsprechenden Regeln angedeutet werden).

Eine neue dialogische Semantik für lineare Logik

Die Strategieregeln für die Additiva sehen damit folgendermaßen aus:

(O)-*Fälle*	(P)-*Fälle*
(O)$A \oplus B$	(P)$A \oplus B$
----------------------------------	--------------------
<(P)¿>(O)A ∥ <(P)¿>(O)B	<(O)¿>(P)A, <(O)¿>(P)B
(O)$A \& B$	(P)$A \& B$
--------------------	-------------------------------
<(P)¿L>(O)A, <(P)¿R>(O)B	<(O)¿L>(P)A ∥ <(O)¿R>(P)B

Zum Abschluss ein Tableau-Beispiel, in dem sowohl Multiplikativa als auch Additiva vorkommen:

Beispiel 13:

				(P)	$[((a \multimap c) \& (b \multimap c)) \multimap ((a \oplus b) \multimap c)]$				
				(O)	$[(a \multimap c) \& (b \multimap c)]$				
				(P)	$[(a \oplus b) \multimap c]$				
				(O)	$[a \oplus b]$				
				(P)	$[c]$				
(O)	$[a]$			∥	(O)	$[b]$			
(O)	$[(a \multimap c) \& (b \multimap c)]$			∥	(O)	$[(a \multimap c) \& (b \multimap c)]$			
(P)	$[c]$			∥	(P)	$[c]$			
(O)	$[a \multimap c]$			∥	(O)	$[b \multimap c]$			
(P)	$[a]$	|	(O)	$[c]$	∥	(P)	$[b]$	|	(O)	$[c]$

Das Tableau ist geschlossen.

4 Schlussbemerkungen

Das Ziel dieses Aufsatzes war es, zu zeigen, wie die pragmatische Semantik der Dialogischen Logik erweitert werden kann, um die Ideen hinter der linearen Logik zu erfassen. Wir denken, dass dieser Ansatz neue Möglichkeiten aufwirft, die der weiteren Erforschung bedürfen. Einige davon seien zum Abschluss angeführt:

1) Lineare Quantoren

In diesem Aufsatz haben wir uns auf die lineare Aussagenlogik ohne Quantoren beschränkt. Üblicherweise werden in der linearen Logik additive Quantoren verwendet, d.h. sowohl der Allquantor als auch der Existenzquantor müssen genau einmal angegriffen und verteidigt werden.

Es sind allerdings noch weitere lineare Quantorenpaare denkbar, z.B. Quantoren, die analog den Exponentialen zwar mindestens einmal angegriffen bzw. verteidigt werden müssen, ansonsten aber bei Bedarf auch beliebig oft zur Verfügung stehen.

Die Formulierung echt multiplikativer Quantoren scheint schwieriger, da es ja nicht möglich ist, alle endlos vielen Angriffe und Verteidigungen zu spielen. Eine Lösung dieses Problems könnte ungefähr folgendermaßen aussehen: Wenn **O** einen Allquantor von **P** angreift oder einen eigenen Existenzquantor verteidigt, so muss er dies mit allen im Dialog schon vorkommenden Konstanten tun, sowie einer neuen, die schematisch für alle weiteren Konstanten verwendet wird. Ist es dagegen an **P**, einen eigenen Existenzquantor zu verteidigen oder einen Allquantor von **O** anzugreifen, so hat er dies ebenfalls mit allen im Dialog vorkommenden Konstanten zu tun, wobei mindestens eine davon durch **O** im Zusammenhang mit Quantoren zuvor eingeführt sein musste. Sollte diese Idee, die noch der Ausarbeitung bedarf, zu einer adäquaten Formulierung von multiplikativen Quantoren führen, so würde das darauf hindeuten, dass ein Zusammenhang mit der dialogischen freien Logik (siehe Rahman/Rückert/Fischmann (1997)) besteht, die auf einer formalen Regel bezüglich der Einführung von Konstanten im Zusammenhang mit Quantoren beruht.

2) Lineare Logik und Modallogik

Das Arbeiten mit Dialogkontexten bzw. Unterdialogen in der dialogischen Semantik für lineare Logik deutet auf einen engen Zusammenhang mit der dialogischen Modallogik (siehe Rahman/Rückert (1999)) hin. Insbesondere scheint folgende Übersetzung der linearen Logik in eine auf bestimmte Weise eingeschränkte S4-Modallogik möglich:

Eine neue dialogische Semantik für lineare Logik

Lineare Logik	*S4-Modallogik*
a	$\square_1 a$
$A^\perp$	$\lozenge_1 \neg_1 A$
$A \otimes B$	$\square_1 A \wedge_2 \square_1 B$
$A \ast B$	$\lozenge_1 A \vee_2 \lozenge_1 B$
$A \& B$	$\square_1 A \wedge_1 \square_1 B$
$A \oplus B$	$\lozenge_1 A \vee_1 \lozenge_1 B$
$!A$	$\square_{1+} A$
$?A$	$\lozenge_{1+} A$

Die Indizes geben dabei an, wie oft die entsprechenden logischen Partikeln anzugreifen bzw. zu verteidigen sind: Index '1' besagt, dass die Formel genau einmal anzugreifen bzw. zu verteidigen ist, Index '2' besagt, dass beide Angriffe bzw. Verteidigungen jeweils genau einmal gespielt werden müssen, und Index '1+' besagt, dass mindestens einmal, ansonsten aber beliebig oft, anzugreifen bzw. zu verteidigen ist.

Sollte diese Übersetzungsvermutung richtig sein, so könnte darin der Schlüssel zu einer Erklärung einiger Eigenschaften der linearen Logik liegen, die diese aufgrund struktureller Zusammenhänge mit der intuitionistischen Logik z.B. für die Programmierung so interessant machen. (Man denke an die wohlbekannten Zusammenhänge zwischen der intuitionistischen Logik und der S4-Modallogik.)

Andererseits würde es aber auch bedeuten, dass nicht nur die klassischen und intuitionistischen Partikeln unter Verwendung der Exponentiale in die lineare Logik übersetzt werden können, sondern die lineare Logik selbst wiederum in die Modallogik (bei genauer Festlegung der Anzahlen von zu spielenden Angriffen und Verteidigungen für die einzelnen Partikeln). Das besondere Neue der linearen Logik bestünde damit nicht mehr in neuen Partikeln, sondern in der prinzipiellen Idee, genau vorzuschreiben, wie oft einzelne Formeln (bzw. Züge) zu verwenden sind.

3) Intuitionistische lineare Logik

In Girard (1995) wird nahegelegt, dass Natürliches Schließen ein Kandidat für die Beantwortung der offenen Frage nach einer intuitionistischen Version der linearen Logik sein könnte:

> „Natural deduction is not equipped to deal with classical symmetry: several hypotheses and one (distinguished) conclusion. To cope with symmetrical

systems one should be able to accept several conclusions at once... But then one immediately loses the tree-like structure of natural deductions, with its obvious advantage: a well-determined last rule. Hence natural deduction cannot answer the question. However it is still a serious candidate for an intuitionistic version of linear logic." (Girard (1995, S. 15))

Die von uns hier vorgeschlagene dialogische Semantik für lineare Logik legt einen anderen Kandidaten für eine intuitionistische Version der linearen Logik nahe: die Verwendung der intuitionistischen Rahmenregel (statt der klassischen) unter sonstiger Beibehaltung der Dialogregeln (allerdings wäre es dann nicht mehr möglich, das lineare Konditional mit Hilfe der multiplikativen Disjunktion und der linearen Negation definitorisch einzuführen).[16]

4) Nicht-kommutative lineare Logik

Inzwischen sind mehrere nicht-kommutative Versionen der linearen Logik bekannt. Der hier vorgestellte dialogische Ansatz bietet einen einfachen Weg, die Idee der Nicht-Kommutativität semantisch einzufangen: Neben der Festlegung der Anzahl von zu spielenden Angriffen und Verteidigungen könnte auch die Reihenfolge, in der bestimmte Züge zu spielen sind, festgelegt werden. Für die multiplikative Konjunktion könnte das so aussehen, dass vor dem Angriff (und der entsprechenden Verteidigung) mit '¿R' zunächst der Angriff '¿L' sowie die entsprechende Verteidigung und alle sich daraus ergebenden Zugmöglichkeiten zu spielen sind. Es ergäbe sich dann unmittelbar, dass $A \otimes B$ und $B \otimes A$ nicht mehr äquivalent wären. Wie die Festlegung der Zugreihenfolgen genau auszusehen hat, um interessante Formen von Nicht-Kommutativität zu erzeugen, bedarf einer genaueren Untersuchung.[17]

---

[16] Es müsste noch näher untersucht werden, inwiefern die Verwendung der intuitionistischen Rahmenregel im Zusammenhang der linearen Logik sinnvoll ist und was sich daraus ergibt.

[17] Wir danken Andreas Blass (Michigan), Dov Gabbay (London), Harry Mairson (Boston) und Sonja Smets (Brüssel) für hilfreiche Kommentare, die zu diesem Aufsatz geführt haben.

Anhang: Eine kurze Einführung in die klassische und intuitionistische dialogische Logik

Die Dialogische Logik, 1958 von Paul Lorenzen angeregt und von Kuno Lorenz in mehreren Aufsätzen ab 1961 ausgearbeitet,[18] wurde als pragmatische Semantik sowohl für die klassische als auch für die intuitionistische Logik eingeführt.

Der dialogische Ansatz untersucht Logik im Wesentlichen mit Hilfe pragmatischer Begriffe und bedient sich dabei einer (standardisierten) offenen Argumentation, die in Form eines *Dialoges* zwischen zwei Parteien stattfindet, die die Rollen des *Proponenten* (**P**) und des *Opponenten* (**O**) der strittigen Aussage, der These des Dialoges, übernehmen. **P** versucht, seine These gegen alle möglichen Kritiken (Angriffe) durch **O** zu verteidigen, wobei er auf Argumente zurückgreifen kann, die **O** zu Beginn oder während des Dialoges zugestanden oder selbst verwendet hat. Die These *A* ist genau dann logisch gültig, wenn **P** sie erfolgreich gegen alle möglichen erlaubten Angriffe durch **O** verteidigen kann. In der Sprache der Spieltheorie: **P** hat eine Gewinnstrategie für *A*. Wir beschreiben nun dialogische Versionen der intuitionistischen und der klassischen Logik.

Es seien die Bausteine und die logischen Konstanten der Prädikatenlogik erster Stufe zusammen mit kleinen kursiven Buchstaben (a, b, c,...) für Primformeln, großen kursiven Buchstaben (A, B, C,...) für Formeln, die komplex sein können, großen fetten kursiven Buchstaben (***P***, ***Q***, ***R***,...) für Prädikatoren und τ_i für Konstanten gegeben. Ein Dialog ist eine Abfolge von Formeln dieser Sprache, die jeweils entweder von **P** oder **O** gesetzt werden.[19] Jeder Zug – mit Ausnahme des uneigentlichen Anfangsarguments – ist entweder eine aggressive (Angriff) oder eine defensive Handlung (Verteidigung). In der Dialogischen Logik ist die Bedeutung (als Gebrauch) der logischen Partikeln durch zwei Arten von Regeln bestimmt, die ihre *lokale* (*Partikelregeln*) und ihre *globale* Bedeutung (*Rahmenregeln*) festlegen.

Die Partikelregeln geben für jede Partikel ein Paar (bzw. mehrere Paare) von Zügen an, bestehend aus einem Angriff und (wenn möglich) der entsprechenden Verteidigung. Jedes solche Paar wird eine *Runde* genannt. Eine Runde wird also durch einen Angriff *eröffnet* und durch eine Verteidigung *geschlossen*.

---

[18] Siehe Lorenzen/Lorenz (1978). Weitere Arbeit wurde u.a. in Rahman (1993) geleistet.

[19] Manchmal verwenden wir X und Y um **P** und **O** zu bezeichnen, mit X ≠Y.

Eine neue dialogische Semantik für lineare Logik

Partikelregeln

¬, ∧, ∨, →, ⋀, ⋁	**Angriff**	**Verteidigung**
¬A	A	/ (Keine Verteidigung, möglich, nur Gegenangriff spielbar)
A∧B	¿L[20] ------- ¿R (Der Angreifer wählt)	A ------- B
A∨B	¿	A ------- B (Der Verteidiger wählt)
A→B	A	B
⋀$_x$A	¿τ (Der Angreifer wählt)	A [τ/x]
⋁$_x$A	¿	A [τ/x] (Der Verteidiger wählt)

Die erste Spalte gibt die Form der in Frage stehenden Formel an, die zweite mögliche Angriffe gegen diese Formel und die letzte mögliche Verteidigungen gegen diese Angriffe. (Das Zeichen '/' zeigt an, dass hier keine Verteidigung möglich ist.[21]) Man beachte, dass z.B. '¿L' zwar ein Zug ist – genauer gesagt handelt es sich um einen Angriff –, aber keine Formel. Also, wenn ein Spielpartner in einem Dialog eine Konjunktion behauptet, so kann sein Gegner einen Angriff starten, indem er entweder nach der linken Seite der Konjunktion fragt ("Zeig mir, dass das linke Konjunkt gilt", oder kürzer '¿L') oder nach der rechten Seite ("Zeig mir, dass das rechte Konjunkt gilt", oder kürzer '¿R'). Wenn andererseits in einem

---

[20] Da das normale Fragezeichen '?' für eine lineare Partikel verwendet wird, haben wir in diesem Aufsatz zur Vermeidung von Konfusionen alle Fragezeichen, die Angriffe in Dialogen kennzeichnen, auf den Kopf gestellt.

[21] In unseren anderen Arbeiten verwenden wir zum Ausüben dieser Funktion das Zeichen '⊗', das aber in diesem Aufsatz nicht zur Verfügung steht, da es ebenfalls schon als Zeichen für eine lineare Partikel dient.

Dialog einer der Spielpartner eine Disjunktion behauptet, so kann der andere seinen Angriff starten, indem er verlangt, irgendein Disjunkt gezeigt zu bekommen ('¿').

Als nächstes legen wir mit Hilfe der *Rahmenregeln* fest, wie Formeln nacheinander vorgebracht werden, um einen Dialog zu bilden.

Rahmenregeln

R0 *(Startregel)*:
Züge werden abwechselnd von **P** und **O** vorgebracht. Die *Anfangsformel* wird von **P** gesetzt. Jeder Zug nach der Anfangsformel ist entweder ein Angriff gegen eine vom anderen Spieler vorgebrachte Formel oder eine Verteidigung gegen einen gegnerischen Angriff.

R1 *(Nicht-Verzögerungsregel)*:
Angriffe und Verteidigungen dürfen nur wiederholt werden, wenn sich dadurch neue Zugmöglichkeiten ergeben.

R2 *(formale Regel für Primformeln)*:
P darf keine Primformeln selbst einführen: jede Primformel muss zuerst von **O** gesetzt werden.

R3 *(Gewinnregel)*:
X gewinnt genau dann, wenn Y am Zuge ist, aber nicht mehr ziehen kann (weder angreifen noch verteidigen).

$R_I 4$ *(intuitionistische Rahmenregel)*:
In jedem Zug kann jeder Spieler eine von seinem Gegner behauptete (komplexe) Formel angreifen oder sich gegen *den letzten noch nicht verteidigten Angriff* verteidigen (*'last duty first'*). Nur der letzte offene Angriff darf beantwortet werden: Wenn in der Position n der Spieler X am Zuge ist, und es offene Angriffe m und l gibt, wobei $m < l < n$, so darf sich X nicht gegen m verteidigen.[22]

Diese Regeln definieren die intuitionistische Logik. Um die klassische Logik zu erhalten muß $R_I 4$ durch die folgende Regel ersetzt werden:

---

[22] Man beachte, dass dies nicht automatisch bedeutet, dass der letzte noch nicht verteidigte Angriff auch der letzte gegnerische Zug ist.

Eine neue dialogische Semantik für lineare Logik

R$_C$4 *(klassische Rahmenregel)*:
In jedem Zug kann man eine vom Gegner behauptete (komplexe) Formel angreifen, oder sich gegen *jeden beliebigen Angriff* (auch gegen solche, die schon verteidigt worden sind) verteidigen.[23]

Wie schon erwähnt, wird Gültigkeit in der Dialogischen Logik über die Existenz von Gewinnstrategien für **P** definiert:

Def. Gültigkeit:
In einem bestimmten dialogischen System ist eine Formel *A* genau dann gültig, wenn **P** eine (formale) Gewinnstrategie für sie hat, d.h. wenn sich **P** gemäß den entsprechenden Regeln *A* gegen alle möglichen erlaubten Angriffe von **O** erfolgreich verteidigen kann.[24]

Beispiel 1 (entweder mit klassischer oder mit intuitionistischer Rahmenregel; es macht keinen Unterschied):

	O			P	
				$((a{\to}b){\wedge}a){\to}b$	(0)
(1)	$(a{\to}b){\wedge}a$	0		b	(8)
(3)	$a{\to}b$	1		¿L	(2)
(5)	a	1		¿R	(4)
(7)	b	3		a	(6)

P *gewinnt*

Beispiel 2 (klassisch):

	O			P	
				$\wedge_x(P_x \vee \neg P_x)$	(0)
(1)	¿τ	0		$P_\tau \vee \neg P_\tau$	(2)
(3)	¿	2		$\neg P_\tau$	(4)
(5)	P_τ	4		/	
(3')	¿	2		P_τ	(6)

P *gewinnt*

---

[23] Im von der dialogischen linearen Logik handelnden Haupttext wird grundsätzlich immer die klassische Rahmenregel verwendet.

[24] Für Konsistenz- und Vollständigkeitstheoreme siehe Barth/Krabbe (1982), Krabbe (1985) und Rahman (1993).

Anmerkungen:
Zur Notation: Die Züge sind in der (zeitlichen) Reihenfolge ihres Auftretens nummeriert. Sie sind aber nicht in dieser Reihenfolge aufgelistet, sondern derart, dass jede Verteidigung in der selben Zeile steht wie der ihr entsprechende Angriff. Die Reihenfolge der Züge wird durch eine Zahl in Klammern wiedergegeben, während Nummern ohne Klammern anzeigen, gegen welchen Zug sich der Angriff richtet.

Beispiel 2 zeigt den Unterschied der klassischen Rahmenregel gegenüber der intuitionistischen: Der Proponent darf gemäß dieser Regel auch einen Angriff verteidigen, der nicht der letzte noch nicht verteidigte ist. Dies gestattet es ihm, in Zug (6) P_τ zu setzen. Aus notationellen Gründen wiederholen wir den entsprechenden Angriff des Opponenten, doch dies ist kein Zug, der tatsächlich stattfindet. Aus diesem Grunde geben wir diesem Angriff keine neue Nummer, sondern wiederholen die Nummer des ersten Angriffs und versehen sie mit einem Apostroph.

Die recht einfache Struktur der Dialoge in diesen sowie in den Beispielen im Haupttext soll es erlauben, meist schon anhand eines Dialoges (mit der eventuellen Angabe von Nebenvarianten) zu überblicken, ob **P** eine Gewinnstrategie hat oder nicht.

Logiques Dialogiques 'Multivalentes'

Helge Rückert

Résumé:
Le but de cet article est de montrer comment les logiques dites multivalentes peuvent être formulées dans le cadre de la logique dialogique. Pour formuler les règles de particule pour ces logiques on introduit l'idée de différents modes d'assertion. En donnant ensuite les règles de particule et les règles structurelles appropriées, on peut reconstruire dialogiquement les systèmes standards de logiques multivalentes. Cela est fait explicitement pour la logique à trois valeurs de Lukasiewicz (L_{3c}). En remplaçant la règle structurelle classique par sa contrepartie intuitionniste on obtient des versions intuitionnistes de systèmes multivalents (par exemple L_{3i}). Les systèmes dialogiques multivalents L_{3c} et L_{3i} sont illustrés par quelques exemples et pour conclure on formule les tableaux stratégiques correspondants.

Abstract:
Aim of this paper is to show how so-called multi-valued logics can be formulated within the framework of Dialogical Logic. In order to formulate the particle rules for multi-valued logics the concept of different assertion modes is introduced. Then, by giving appropriate particle and structural rules standard systems of multi-valued logics can be reconstructed dialogically. This is done explicitly for Lukasiewicz' logic with three values (L_{3c}). By replacing the classical structural rule by its intuitionistic counterpart one obtains intuitionistic versions of the multi-valued systems (for example L_{3i}). The dialogical multi-valued systems L_{3c} and L_{3i} are illustrated with some examples and finally strategic tableaux for them are formulated.

Rückert, H.: 'Logiques Dialogiques 'Multivalentes'', dans Rebuschi, M. et Tulenheimo, T. (eds.): *Logique & Théorie des Jeux*, *Philosophia Scientiae* 8 (2) (2004), p. 59-87

Logiques Dialogiques 'Multivalentes'

1 Introduction

La logique dialogique fut suggérée à la fin des années 1950 par Paul Lorenzen, puis élaborée par Kuno Lorenz.[1] Dans le contexte de *l'Ecole d'Erlangen* il était habituel d'essayer de justifier la logique intuitionniste et de défendre le constructivisme. Pendant longtemps l'approche dialogique fut ainsi étudiée uniquement pour les logiques classique et intuitionniste du premier ordre, à quelques exceptions près.[2] Mais plus récemment il a été montré que la logique dialogique fournissait aussi un cadre très souple permettant de donner une sémantique pragmatique claire pour plusieurs autres logiques non classiques.[3]

Un trait intéressant de la logique dialogique est que les systèmes logiques y sont caractérisés par certains ensembles de règles, à savoir les règles structurelles et les règles de particule.[4] Et parfois deux systèmes logiques ne se différencient que par une seule règle. En particulier, les formulations dialogiques de la logique classique du premier ordre standard et de la logique intuitionniste du premier ordre standard diffèrent seulement sur une règle structurelle. (Les règles de particule sont les mêmes. On pourrait dire que les deux logiques classique et intuitionniste traitent des mêmes particules.) Ensuite quand on formule par exemple des systèmes dialogiques pour une logique non classique en modifiant ou en introduisant de nouvelles règles de particules, c'est dans la plupart des cas compatible avec l'usage de la règle structurelle classique ou de la règle structurelle intuitionniste. On

---

[1] Quelques-uns des premiers textes les plus importants sur la logique dialogique sont rassemblés dans Lorenzen/Lorenz (1978).

[2] Une de ces exceptions est Fuhrmann (1985) qui présente un système dialogique de logique de pertinence.

[3] Ont été publiés entre autres des articles comportant des formulations dialogiques pour la logique modale (Rahman/Rückert (1999)), les logiques modales non-normales (Rahman (2006)), la logique hybride (Blackburn (2001)), la logique libre (Rahman/Rückert/Fischmann (1997)), la logique connexe (Rahman/Rückert (2001b)) et la logique paraconsistante (Rahman/Carnielli (2000), Van Bendegem (2001)). Rückert (2001) est un tour d'horizon et une courte introduction générale à la logique dialogique. (Voir aussi Rahman/Keiff (2004) pour une présentation et une défense générales de la logique dialogique.) Pour un aperçu de l'arrière-plan historique et de quelques développements plus récents concernant la logique dialogique et des approches liées comme la GTS de Hintikka, voir Rahman/Rückert (2001c).

[4] Une conséquence intéressante de cet aspect est que dans l'approche dialogique il est relativement facile de combiner les idées sous-jacentes à différentes logiques non classiques et de les intégrer dans un nouveau système dialogique. Pour une combinaison des logiques intuitionniste, libre et paraconsistante, voir Rahman (2001).

obtient donc automatiquement une version classique et une version intuitionniste du système.

Venons-en aux logiques multivalentes. D'un côté l'idée de formuler des systèmes dialogiques de logiques multivalentes est très naturelle: Comme des formulations dialogiques ont été données pour de nombreuses autres logiques non classiques, pourquoi ne pas en donner une également pour les logiques multivalentes? Mais d'un autre côté, cette idée paraît aussi un peu étrange puisque dans l'approche dialogique il n'y a pas place pour les valeurs de vérité. Il ne s'agit pas d'assigner des valeurs de vérité aux formules, mais de jouer des jeux d'argumentation idéalisée avec ces formules. Cependant cette objection n'est pas sérieuse: De même qu'il y a des formulations dialogiques pour la logique bivalente on en peut donner pour les logiques multivalentes. Et de même que dans la formulation dialogique de la logique à deux valeurs les valeurs de vérité 'vrai' et 'faux' ne jouent aucun rôle, les multiples valeurs de vérité des logiques multivalentes ne jouent aucun rôle dans leur formulation dialogique.[5] Mais ce dont on a besoin est quelque chose dans le cadre dialogique qui corresponde aux valeurs de vérité dans d'autres cadres. Les modes d'assertion feront l'affaire. Avec leur aide, il sera possible de formuler les règles de particule appropriées de manière à reconstruire les systèmes bien connus de logiques multivalentes. Mais ce n'est pas tout. Il sera ensuite possible de remplacer la règle structurelle classique par la règle structurelle intuitionniste pour obtenir une version intuitionniste de la logique multivalente en question.

Cet article est organisé comme suit. Premièrement l'approche dialogique est présentée en donnant les formulations dialogiques habituelles pour les logiques classique et intuitionniste du premier ordre standard. En donnant les règles de particule, on les comparera aux définitions vérifonctionnelles bien connues des connecteurs. Cela sera utile pour pouvoir trouver plus tard les règles de particules adéquates pour les connecteurs multivalents. Ensuite, en introduisant le concept de mode d'assertion il sera possible de donner les règles de particule pour les connecteurs des logiques multivalentes. On le fera explicitement pour la logique à trois valeurs de Lukasiewicz, mais la procédure pour d'autres systèmes devrait apparaître clairement aussi. Après ajustement des règles structurelles nous aurons les systèmes dialogiques L_{3c} et L_{3i}. On les illustrera par quelques exemples de dialogues. Finalement, un traitement plus systématique des stratégies gagnantes sera donné, résultant de la formulation de tableaux stratégiques pour L_{3c} et L_{3i}.

---

[5] C'est pourquoi le titre de cet article est *Logiques Dialogiques 'Multivalentes'* et non pas *Logiques Dialogiques Multivalentes*.

2 La Logique Dialogique: Rapide Aperçu

Dans un dialogue deux parties argumentent à propos d'une thèse en respectant certaines règles données. Le défenseur de la thèse est appelé Proposant (**P**), son adversaire qui attaque la thèse est appelé Opposant (**O**). Chaque dialogue se termine après un nombre fini de coups, avec un joueur qui gagne tandis que l'autre perd. Les règles sont divisées en règles structurelles et règles de particule. Les règles structurelles déterminent le cours général d'un jeu dialogique, tandis que les règles de particule indiquent quels coups sont autorisés pour attaquer les coups de l'autre joueur ou pour défendre ses propres coups.

2.1 Les Règles Structurelles

SR 0 (règle de commencement):
La formule initiale est énoncée par **P**. Elle fournit le sujet de l'argumentation. Les coups sont alternativements énoncés par **P** et **O**. Chaque coup suivant la formule initiale est soit une attaque, soit une défense.

SR 1 (règle contre les tactiques dilatoires):
P et **O** doivent chacun jouer exclusivement des coups qui modifient la situation.[6]

SR 2 (règle formelle):
P ne peut pas introduire de formule atomique, toutes les formules atomiques doivent être préalablement posées par **O**.

SR 3 (règle de victoire):
X gagne ssi c'est le tour de Y mais que celui-ci ne peut pas jouer (ni attaquer ni se défendre).

---

[6] Cette règle remplace les *Angriffsschranken* de Lorenz. Il faut encore la clarifier sur une base formelle.

SR 4i (règle intuitionniste):
A chaque coup, chaque joueur peut attaquer une formule complexe assertée par son adversaire ou se défendre contre la dernière attaque à laquelle il n'a pas encore répondu.

ou

SR 4c (règle classique):
A chaque coup, chaque joueur peut attaquer une formule complexe assertée par son adversaire ou se défendre contre n'importe quelle attaque (y compris celles qui ont déjà été défendues).[7]

2.2 Les Règles de Particule

Maintenant nous pouvons aborder les règles de particule. Pour chaque connecteur nous allons comparer la règle de particule à la définition vérifonctionnelle correspondante. Cela nous aidera à voir certaines connexions qui seront utiles plus tard pour la formulation des règles de particule pour les connecteurs multivalents.

Règle de particule pour la disjonction:

	Attaque	**Défense**
$A \vee B$	?	A -------------- B (Le défenseur choisit)

De même qu'une disjonction (en logique classique) est vraie ssi au moins l'un de ses termes est vrai, dans un dialogue un joueur qui a asserté une disjonction est capable de la défendre ssi il est capable de défendre au moins l'un des deux termes. Ainsi l'attaquant attaque en demandant 'Lequel?' (ou '?' pour abréger) et on doit s'en défendre en assertant l'un des termes (le défenseur a le droit de choisir lequel).

---

[7] Dans SR 4i comme dans SR 4c, nous avons donné la version dite symétrique des règles. Il est possible de diminuer les droits de **O** sans aucun changement au niveau des stratégies de la manière suivante: Pour **P** la règle reste inchangée mais **O** est seulement autorisé soit à se défendre contre le dernier coup de **P**, soit à attaquer ce coup. Ces versions des règles SR 4i et SR 4c sont appelées asymétriques, puisque maintenant **P** a plus de droits que **O**.

Logiques Dialogiques 'Multivalentes'

Règle de particule pour la conjonction:

	Attaque	Défense
$A \wedge B$	? L(eft) [à gauche]	A
	? R(ight) [à droite] (L'attaquant choisit)	B

De même qu'une conjonction (en logique classique) est vraie ssi les deux termes sont vrais, dans un dialogue un joueur qui a asserté une conjonction est capable de la défendre ssi il est capable de défendre les deux termes. Ainsi l'attaquant attaque en demandant l'un (celui de gauche) ou l'autre (celui de droite) des deux termes (il choisit lequel) et le défenseur doit asserter le(s) terme(s) correspondant(s).

Règle de particule pour la subjonction:

	Attaque	Défense
$A \to B$	A	B

De même qu'une subjonction (en logique classique) est fausse ssi l'antécédent est vrai et le conséquent est faux, dans un dialogque un joueur qui a asserté une subjonction ne peut être attaqué que si l'attaquant concède l'antécédent en l'assertant. C'est alors au défenseur de se défendre en assertant le conséquent (ou bien il peut bien entendu contre-attaquer l'antécédent qui vient d'être affirmé par l'attaquant).

Règle de particule pour la négation:

	Attaque	Défense
$\neg A$	A	$\otimes$ (Pas de défense, seule la contre-attaque est possible)

De même qu'une négation (en logique classique) est fausse ssi la formule niée est vraie, dans un dialogue un joueur qui a asserté une négation ne peut être attaqué que si l'attaquant concède la formule niée en l'assertant. Ensuite d'autre part, le défenseur ne peut pas se défendre. (La seule chose qu'il lui reste à faire est d'engager une contre-attaque contre la formule niée qui vient d'être assertée par l'attaquant.)

    Comme cet article se concentre sur le fragment propositionnel de la logique du premier ordre, nous ne discuterons pas ici du traitement des quantificateurs.

2.3 Validité

Les règles structurelles et de particules que nous venons de donner définissent les jeux dialogiques intuitionnistes (avec SR 4i) et classiques (avec SR 4c). La validité logique est définie comme suit:

> **Définition 1** *Validité logique:*
> Une formule est logiquement valide dans un système dialogique donné ssi **P** a une stratégie gagnante formelle pour cette formule. (Avoir une stratégie gagnante formelle signifie que pour n'importe quel coup choisi par votre opposant vous avez au moins un coup possible à votre disposition tel que finalement vous puissiez gagner.)

On peut montrer qu'avec ces règles et cette définition de la validité logique les formules valides obtenues sont les mêmes que celles obtenues par les approches standard de la logique. (Pour obtenir la logique intuitionniste employez la règle intuitionniste, et pour obtenir la logique classique utilisez la règle classique.[8])

2.4 Exemples

Exemple 1 (avec SR 4i ou SR 4c):

	O			P	
				$((a{\to}b){\wedge}a){\to}b$	(0)
(1)	$(a{\to}b){\wedge}a$	0		b	(8)
(3)	$a{\to}b$		1	? L	(2)
(5)	a		1	? R	(4)
(7)	b		3	a	(6)

P gagne.

---

[8] On peut trouver de telles preuves par exemple dans Barth/Krabbe (1982), dans Krabbe (1985), et dans Rahman (1993).

Exemple 2 (avec SR 4c):

	O		P	
			$a \vee \neg a$	(0)
(1)	?	0	$\neg a$	(2)
(3)	a	2	$\otimes$	
(1')	?	0	a	(4)

P gagne.

Remarques concernant les exemples:
Pour l'exemple 1, le fait d'utiliser SR 4i ou SR 4c ne fait pas de différence, mais l'exemple 2 n'est valide qu'en logique classique.

Explication de la notation:
Les coups de **O** sont écrits dans la colonne de **O**, et de manière équivalente pour **P**. Les nombres entre parenthèses dans les marges à gauche et à droite indiquent l'ordre dans lequel les coups sont exécutés. Le coup numéro (0) est la thèse sur laquelle on argumente dans le dialogue. Les attaques sont caractérisées par des nombres sans parenthèses qui montrent quel coup de l'adversaire est attaqué. Les défenses sont toujours écrites sur la ligne de l'attaque correspondante.

(Comme vous pouvez le voir dans l'exemple 2, quand on joue suivant la règle classique il est possible pour **P** de se défendre à nouveau contre une attaque à laquelle il avait déjà répondu auparavant. Pour noter cette défense renouvelée nous répétons l'attaque correspondante, et il faut garder à l'esprit que ce n'est pas un coup dans le dialogue mais seulement une convention de notation qui est indiquée par une apostrophe comme dans (1') de l'exemple 2.)

3 Dialogues pour Logiques 'Multivalentes': Règles de Particule

D'un point de vue technique les systèmes de base de logiques multivalentes sont de simples généralisations des logiques bivalentes. Au lieu des deux valeurs de vérité 'vrai' (ou '1') et 'faux' (ou '0'), on utilise trois valeurs ou plus. Alors bien entendu, il y a plus de fonctions de valeurs de vérité, et donc plus de connecteurs logiques.

Ainsi si nous voulons donner une formulation dialogique des systèmes de base de logiques multivalentes nous devons demander quel type de généralisations doivent être faites dans ce cadre pragmatique où les valeurs de vérité ne jouent pas un rôle essentiel. Une première suggestion naturelle pourrait être qu'au lieu de deux partenaires pour l'argumentation (**P** et **O**), il nous en faut trois pour formuler les logiques trivalentes, quatre pour les logiques quadrivalentes, et ainsi de suite. Mais dans ce qui suit je vais proposer une autre généralisation pour reformuler les logiques multivalentes dans le cadre dialogique.[9]

Pour motiver ma solution nous allons tout d'abord observer les dialogues dits matériels. En général, la logique dialogique n'est pas basée sur l'hypothèse que toutes les formules ont une valeur de vérité définie, soit vrai soit faux. Mais si nous pouvons supposer cela, alors il y a une autre manière de reformuler la logique classique dans le cadre dialogique. Pour les dialogues matériels, nous remplaçons la règle structurelle formelle par la suivante:

> *Règle structurelle pour les dialogues matériels:*
> Les formules atomiques vraies peuvent être assertées (que ce soit par **P** ou **O**), mais il ne faut pas asserter de formule atomique fausse.

Ensuite on peut définir la validité logique comme étant l'existence de stratégies gagnantes dans les dialogues matériels pour toutes les possibilités d'assignations de valeurs de vérité aux formules atomiques. Nous avons donc trouvé un lien entre le concept de valeur de vérité et un authentique concept dialogique, celui d'assertion. A partir de ce lien, la généralisation qui suit est relativement directe: La transition de l'ensemble de deux valeurs de vérité {1, 0} à des ensembles à trois valeurs ou plus dans le cadre dialogique correspond à la transition de l'ensemble {assertable, non assertable} vers des ensembles à plus de deux modes d'assertion.

Dans les dialogues pour logiques multivalentes les formules ne sont donc pas assertées *simpliciter* mais de différentes manières. Dans ce qui suit nous allons noter cela en préfixant les formules par le signe d'assertion de Frege[10] et en utilisant des indices pour différencier les différents modes d'assertion. Ainsi pour les logiques trivalents la table suivante montre les correspondances entre l'approche dénotationnelle avec ses valeurs de vérité, et l'approche dialogique avec sa notion pragmatique de mode d'assertion:

---

[9] Bien sûr je ne peux pas exclure qu'il soit aussi possible de donner des formulations dialogiques de logiques multivalentes basées sur l'idée qui vient d'être mentionnée, à savoir en introduisant plus de deux joueurs dans les dialogues.

[10] Frege a introduit le signe d'assertion '⊢' dans sa *Begriffsschrift* (voir Frege (1964)). Même si nous employons le symbole de Frege cela ne signifie pas nécessairement que nous acceptions tout ce qu'il en a dit. C'est pour nous un simple moyen de notation.

Logiques Dialogiques 'Multivalentes'

Valeurs de vérité		Modes d'assertion
1	≈	$\vdash_1$
½	≈	$\vdash_{½}$
0	≈	non assertable

En général nous aurons besoin de n signes d'assertion différents pour formuler la reconstruction dialogique d'une logique à $n+1$ valeurs de vérité (parce que la valeur de vérité 0 correspond toujours au fait que la formule n'est pas du tout assertable dans un dialogue).

A partir de ces considérations nous sommes maintenant capables de formuler des règles de particule adéquates pour les connecteurs des logiques multivalentes. Dans ce qui suit nous le ferons explicitement pour une logique de Lukasiewicz à trois valeurs de vérité, mais cela devrait faire clairement apparaître comment obtenir également des règles dialogiques pour d'autres logiques multivalentes.

La Disjonction

Table de vérité pour la disjonction de L_3:

A	B	$A \vee_{L3} B$
1	1	1
1	½	1
1	0	1
½	1	1
½	½	½
½	0	½
0	1	1
0	½	½
0	0	0

Logiques Dialogiques 'Multivalentes'

Règles de particule pour la disjonction de L_3:

	Attaque	Défense
$\vdash_1 A \vee_{L3} B$	?	$\vdash_1 A$ ---------------- $\vdash_1 B$ (Le défenseur choisit)

Cette règle correspond exactement à la règle de particule pour la disjonction standard, et ne nécessite pas d'explication supplémentaire. Mais comme dans L_3 on peut aussi asserter une disjonction suivant le mode $\vdash_{1/2}$, nous devons aussi déterminer comment de tels coups peuvent être attaqués et défendus:

	Attaque	Défense
$\vdash_{1/2} A \vee_{L3} B$	?	$\vdash_{1/2} A$ ---------------- $\vdash_{1/2} B$ (Le défenseur choisit)
	$\vdash_1 A$	$\otimes$
	$\vdash_1 B$	$\otimes$
	(L'attaquant choisit entre les trois attaques à sa disposition)	

Du fait que (dans l'approche dénotationnelle) une disjonction n'a la valeur de vérité ½ que si au moins l'un de ses termes a cette valeur, une disjonction ne peut être assertée suivant le mode $\vdash_{1/2}$ que si le défenseur est capable d'asserter au moins un des termes de la disjonction suivant ce mode d'assertion. Comme d'autre part (dans l'approche dénotationnelle) une disjonction ne peut pas avoir la valeur de vérité ½ si au moins un de ses termes est vrai, une disjonction assertée suivant le mode $\vdash_{1/2}$ pourra également être attaquée en assertant l'un de ses termes suivant le mode d'assertion $\vdash_1$. Il n'y a alors pas de défense possible, mais seulement une contre-attaque.

Généralisation des règles pour la disjonction: Supposons qu'au lieu d'une logique de Lukasiewicz à trois valeurs nous ayons une logique à *n* valeurs de vérité $0, 1/(n-1), 2/(n-1), \ldots, 1$. La disjonction est définie par la clause suivante:

$$V(A \vee_{Ln} B) = \max(V(A), V(B))$$

Ce qui signifie que la valeur de vérité de la disjonction est la valeur de vérité maximale de ses deux termes. Maintenant, à quoi ressemblent les règles de particule pour $\vee_{Ln}$? Si $A \vee_{Ln} B$ est établie suivant un mode d'assertion donné $\vdash_x$, l'attaquant a le choix suivant:

1. Il attaque en demandant '?'. Alors le défenseur doit établir l'un des termes de la disjonction suivant le mode d'assertion $\vdash_x$, ou bien

2. Il attaque en affirmant l'un des termes de la disjonction suivant le mode d'assertion $\vdash_y$ avec $y > x$. Il n'y a alors pas de défense pour contrer cette attaque.

La Conjonction

Table de vérité pour la conjonction de L_3:

A	B	$A \wedge_{L3} B$
1	1	1
1	½	½
1	0	0
½	1	½
½	½	½
½	0	0
0	1	0
0	½	0
0	0	0

Règle de particule pour la conjonction de L_3:

	Attaque	**Défense**
$\vdash_1 A \wedge_{L3} B$	?L(eft) [à gauche] ---------------- ?R(ight) [à droite] (L'attaquant choisit entre les deux attaques à sa disposition)	$\vdash_1 A$ ---------------- $\vdash_1 B$

Cette règle correspond parfaitement à la règle de particule pour la conjonction standard et n'exige pas plus d'explication.

Logiques Dialogiques 'Multivalentes'

	Attaque	**Défense**
$\vdash_{1/2} A \wedge_{L3} B$	?	$\vdash_{1/2} A$ --------------- $\vdash_{1/2} B$ (Le défenseur choisit)
	?L(eft)	$\vdash_{1} A$ --------------- $\vdash_{1/2} A$ (Le défenseur choisit)
	?R(ight)	$\vdash_{1} B$ --------------- $\vdash_{1/2} B$ (Le défenseur choisit)
	(L'attaquant choisit entre les trois attaques à sa disposition)	

Comme (dans l'approche dénotationnelle) une conjonction n'a la valeur de vérité ½ que si au moins l'un de ses termes a cette valeur de vérité, une conjonction ne peut être assertée suivant le mode $\vdash_{1/2}$ que si le défenseur est capable d'asserter au moins l'un de ses termes suivant ce mode. D'autre part, du fait que (dans l'approche dénotationnelle) une conjonction n'a la valeur de vérité ½ que si chacun de ses termes a au moins la valeur ½, une conjonction assertée suivant le mode $\vdash_{1/2}$ peut aussi être attaquée en lui demandant chacun de ses termes. La défense consiste alors à asserter le terme demandé suivant le mode $\vdash_{1/2}$ ou $\vdash_{1}$.[11]

Généralisation des règles pour la conjonction: Supposons qu'au lieu d'une logique de Lukasiewicz à trois valeurs nous ayons une logique à n valeurs de vérité $0, 1/(n-1), 2/(n-1),..., 1$. La conjonction est définie par la clause suivante:

$$V(A \wedge_{Ln} B) = \min (V(A), V(B))$$

Ce qui signifie que la valeur de vérité de la conjonction est la valeur de vérité minimale de ses deux termes. A quoi ressemblent alors les règles de particule pour $\wedge_{Ln}$? Si $A \wedge_{Ln} B$ est établie suivant un mode d'assertion donné $\vdash_{x}$, l'attaquant a le

---

[11] Même s'il est permis au défenseur de se défendre contre l'attaque '?L(eft)' avec $\vdash_{1} A$ et contre '?R(ight)' avec $\vdash_{1} B$, il ne doit pas le faire car il perdrait alors contre l'attaque '?'. Donc, s'il se défend en affirmant l'un des termes de la conjonction suivant le mode $\vdash_{1}$, il faut toujours qu'il se défende en affirmant l'autre terme suivant le mode $\vdash_{1/2}$.

Logiques Dialogiques 'Multivalentes'

choix suivant:

1. Il attaque en demandant '?'. Alors le défenseur doit établir l'un des termes de la conjonction suivant le mode d'assertion $\vdash_x$, ou bien

2. Il attaque en demandant le terme de gauche par '?L(eft)'. La défense consiste alors à affirmer le terme de gauche suivant le mode d'assertion $\vdash_y$ avec $y \geq x$.

3. Il attaque en demandant le terme de droite par '?R(ight)'. La défense consiste alors à affirmer le terme de droite suivant le mode d'assertion $\vdash_y$ avec $y \geq x$.

La Subjonction

Table de vérité pour la subjonction de L_3:

A	B	$A \rightarrow_{L3} B$
1	1	1
1	½	½
1	0	0
½	1	1
½	½	1
½	0	½
0	1	1
0	½	1
0	0	1

Logiques Dialogiques 'Multivalentes'

Règle de particule pour la subjonction de L3:

	Attaque	Défense
$\vdash_1 A \rightarrow_{L3} B$	$\vdash_1 A$	$\vdash_1 B$
	$\vdash_{\frac{1}{2}} A$	$\vdash_1 B$ -------------- $\vdash_{\frac{1}{2}} B$ (Le défenseur choisit)
	(L'attaquant choisit entre les deux attaques à sa disposition)	

La première paire d'attaque et défense correspond parfaitement à la règle de particule pour la subjonction standard et ne nécessite pas plus d'explication. Mais il y a une autre possibilité d'attaque: Du fait que (dans l'approche dénotationnelle) si l'antécédent a la valeur de vérité ½, une subjonction est vraie ssi le conséquent est vrai ou a la valeur ½, une subjonction assertée suivant le mode d'assertion $\vdash_1$ peut aussi être attaquée en assertant l'antécédent suivant le mode $\vdash_{\frac{1}{2}}$. La défense consiste alors à asserter le conséquent soit suivant le mode $\vdash_{\frac{1}{2}}$, soit suivant le mode $\vdash_1$.

	Attaque	Défense
$\vdash_{\frac{1}{2}} A \rightarrow_{L3} B$	$?_A$	$\vdash_1 A$ -------------- $\vdash_{\frac{1}{2}} A$ (Le défenseur choisit)
	$\vdash_1 A$	$\vdash_{\frac{1}{2}} B$
	$\vdash_1 B$	$\otimes$
	$\vdash_{\frac{1}{2}} B$	$\vdash_1 A$
	(L'attaquant choisit entre les quatre attaques à sa disposition)	

Comme (dans l'approche dénotationnelle) une subjonction ne peut pas avoir la valeur ½ si l'antécédent a la valeur 0, une subjonction assertée suivant le mode $\vdash_{\frac{1}{2}}$ peut être attaquée par la demande '?$_A$' de l'antécédent, le défenseur devant alors concéder que l'antécédent est assertable en l'affirmant suivant le mode

Logiques Dialogiques 'Multivalentes'

d'assertion $\vdash_1$ ou $\vdash_{½}$. Ensuite, comme (dans l'approche dénotationnelle) quand l'antécédent d'une subjonction a la valeur 1 cette subjonction n'a elle-même la valeur de vérité ½ que si le conséquent a la valeur ½, une subjonction assertée suivant le mode $\vdash_{½}$ pourra aussi être attaquée par l'assertion de l'antécédent suivant le mode d'assertion $\vdash_1$. La défense consiste alors à asserter le conséquent suivant le mode d'assertion $\vdash_{½}$. D'autre part, du fait que (dans l'approche dénotationnelle) si le conséquent d'une subjonction a la valeur de vérité 1, la subjonction elle-même ne peut pas avoir la valeur ½, une subjonction avancée suivant le mode $\vdash_{½}$ peut aussi être attaquée en affirmant le conséquent suivant le mode $\vdash_1$. Il n'y a alors pas de défense. Pour finir, comme (dans l'approche dénotationnelle) quand le conséquent d'une subjonction a la valeur ½ cette subjonction n'a elle-même la valeur de vérité ½ que si l'antécédent a la valeur 1, une subjonction assertée suivant le mode $\vdash_{½}$ pourra aussi être attaquée par l'assertion du conséquent suivant le mode d'assertion $\vdash_{½}$. La défense consiste alors à asserter l'antécédent suivant le mode d'assertion $\vdash_1$.

Généralisation des règles pour la subjonction: Supposons qu'au lieu d'une logique de Lukasiewicz à trois valeurs nous ayons une logique à n valeurs de vérité $0, 1/(n-1), 2/(n-1),..., 1$. La subjonction est définie par la clause suivante:

$$V(A \to_{Ln} B) = \min(1, 1 - V(A) + V(B))$$

Ce qui signifie que la valeur de vérité de la subjonction est 1 si la valeur de vérité du conséquent est supérieure ou égale à celle de l'antécédent; et si la valeur de l'antécédent est supérieure à celle du conséquent, la valeur de vérité de la subjonction équivaut à un moins la différence des deux valeurs.

A quoi ressemblent alors les règles de particule pour $\to_{Ln}$? Si $A \to_{Ln} B$ est établie suivant un mode d'assertion donné $\vdash_x$, nous devons distinguer les cas suivants:

1. Si $x = 1$, l'attaquant attaque en affirmant l'antécédent suivant le mode d'assertion $\vdash_y$ qu'il souhaite, et le défenseur doit affirmer le conséquent suivant le mode d'assertion $\vdash_z$ avec $z \geq y$.

2. Si $x < 1$, l'attaquant peut attaquer:

   a. Soit en demandant '$?_A$'. On peut se défendre contre cette attaque en affirmant l'antécédent suivant le mode $\vdash_y$, avec $y \geq 1 - x$.

   b. Soit en affirmant l'antécédent suivant le mode $\vdash_y$ qu'il souhaite, avec $y \neq 1 - x$. Pour la défense, il nous faut considérer deux cas:

      i. Si $x + y > 1$, alors le défenseur doit affirmer le conséquent suivant le mode $\vdash_z$, avec $z = y + x - 1$.

ii. Si $x + y < 1$, il n'y a alors pas de défense (seule une contre-attaque est possible).

c. Soit en affirmant le conséquent suivant le mode $\vdash_y$ qu'il souhaite. Pour la défense, il nous faut à nouveau considérer deux cas:

i. Si $y \leq x$, alors le défenseur doit affirmer l'antécédent suivant le mode $\vdash_z$, avec $z = y + 1 - x$.

ii. Si $y > x$, il n'y a alors pas de défense (seule une contre-attaque est possible).

La Négation

Table de vérité pour la négation de L_3:

A	$\neg A$
1	0
½	½
0	1

Règles de particule pour la négation de L_3:

	Attaque	Défense
$\vdash_1 \neg_{L3} A$	$\vdash_1 A$	$\otimes$
	$\vdash_{½} A$ (L'attaquant choisit entre les deux attaques à sa disposition)	$\otimes$

Du fait que (dans l'approche dénotationnelle) une négation est vraie ssi la formule niée n'est ni vraie ni n'a la valeur ½, une négation assertée suivant le mode $\vdash_1$ peut être attaquée par l'assertion de la formule niée soit suivant le mode d'assertion $\vdash_1$, soit suivant le mode $\vdash_{½}$. Dans les deux cas, aucune défense n'est possible, seule une contre-attaque est possible.

	Attaque	Défense
$\vdash_{1/2} \neg_{L3} A$	?	$\vdash_{1/2} A$

Comme (dans l'approche dénotationnelle) une négation a la valeur de vérité ½ ssi la formule niée a la valeur ½, une négation assertée suivant le mode d'assertion $\vdash_{1/2}$ ne peut être défendue que si l'on est capable d'asserter la formule niée suivant le mode d'assertion $\vdash_{1/2}$.

Généralisation des règles pour la négation: Supposons qu'au lieu d'une logique de Lukasiewicz à trois valeurs nous ayons une logique à n valeurs de vérité $0, 1/_{(n-1)}, 2/_{(n-1)}, ..., 1$. La négation est définie par la clause suivante:

$$V(\neg_{Ln} A) = 1 - V(A)$$

Ce qui signifie que la valeur de vérité de la négation est 1 moins la valeur de vérité de la formule niée.

A quoi ressemblent alors les règles de particule pour $\neg_{Ln}$? Si $\neg_{Ln} A$ est avancée suivant un mode d'assertion donné $\vdash_x$, nous devons distinguer les deux cas suivants:

1. Si $x = 1$, l'attaquant attaque en affirmant la formule niée dans le mode d'assertion qu'il souhaite, et il n'y a pas de défense (seule la contre-attaque est possible).

2. Si $x < 1$, l'attaquant demande '?' et le défenseur doit affirmer la formule niée suivant le mode $\vdash_y$, avec $y = 1 - x$.

4 Dialogues pour Logiques 'Multivalentes': Validité et Règles Structurelles

Dans la section précédente nous avons donné les règles de particule pour L_3. Pour pouvoir jouer les jeux dialogiques on a encore besoin de formuler les règles structurelles pour L_3. Celles-ci ne sont pas très différentes des règles structurelles correspondante pour la logique du premier ordre standard, classique et intuitionniste. Mais avant d'ajuster ces règles structurelles en fonction des besoins des logiques multivalentes, nous devons tout d'abord traiter le concept de validité dans les logiques multivalentes.

Logiques Dialogiques 'Multivalentes'

Dans l'approche dénotationnelle standard la validité pour les logiques multivalentes est définie à l'aide des valeurs de vérité dites désignées (*designated truth-values*). Ces valeurs de vérité désignées forment un sous-ensemble de l'ensemble de toutes les valeurs de vérité d'une logique multivalente donnée.[12] Ensuite, dans la définition de la validité dans le cadre dénotationnel standard les valeurs de vérité désignées remplacent la valeur de vérité '1' de la logique bivalente:

> **Définition 2** *Validité pour les logiques multivalentes (définition standard):*
> Une formule A est logiquement valide ssi pour toute fonction de valuation V: V(A) est une valeur de vérité désignée. Une inférence de B_1, B_2, B_3,... à A est logiquement valide ssi pour toute fonction de valuation V telle que V(B_1), V(B_2), V(B_3),... sont des valeurs de vérité désignées: V(A) est une valeur de vérité désignée.

Dans L_3 il y a seulement une valeur de vérité désignée, à savoir '1', mais dans d'autres systèmes de logiques multivalentes il pourrait y avoir plus d'une valeur de vérité désignée.

La manière de procéder pour définir la validité pour les logiques multivalentes dans le cadre dialogique est claire: En correspondance avec le concept de valeur de vérité désignée nous avons évidemment besoin du concept de mode d'assertion désigné. L'ensemble des modes d'assertion désignés pour L_3 est $\{\vdash_1\}$, mais il pourrait y avoir des systèmes dialogiques de logiques multivalentes avec plus d'un mode d'assertion désigné.

Afin de préparer la définition dialogique de la validité pour les logiques multivalentes nous introduisons tout d'abord un nouveau moyen. Dans un dialogue de recherche de la validité **P** doit soutenir qu'il y a au moins un mode d'assertion désigné suivant lequel il est capable d'asserter et donc de défendre sa thèse principale A. Ce premier coup d'un dialogue de vérification de la validité sera donné par la notation suivante: $\vdash_{desig} A$. Une expression de cette forme peut alors être attaquée par '?' et doit être défendue en remplaçant $\vdash_{desig}$ par un mode d'assertion désigné spécifique du système de logique multivalente considéré. Dans un dialogue avec des hypothèses, quand la validité d'une inférence est en jeu, les hypothèses qui doivent être concédées par **O** au commencement du dialogue sont: $\vdash_{desig} B_1$, $\vdash_{desig} B_2$, $\vdash_{desig} B_3$,...

Maintenant nous sommes prêts pour formuler les règles structurelles et la notion de validité pour notre système dialogique L_3.

---

[12] Voir par exemple Gottwald (1989, p. 19-20) et Rosser/Turquette (1952).

SR 0-L_3 (règle de commencement):
Le dialogue débute par l'affirmation de $\vdash_{desig} A$ par **P**, A étant ainsi sa thèse. Cela fournit le sujet de l'argumentation. Les coups sont alternativement joués par **P** et **O**. Chaque coup qui suit l'affirmation initiale est soit une attaque, soit une défense. (Dans les dialogues avec des hypothèses **P** n'affirme sa thèse qu'après que **O** a concédé certaines hypothèses par $\vdash_{desig} B_1$, $\vdash_{desig} B_2$, $\vdash_{desig} B_3$,... au début du dialogue.)

La règle de commencement a été ajustée en fonction des considérations que nous venons de faire. Elle est ici formulée en toute généralité, mais comme dans L_3 il n'y a qu'un seul mode d'assertion $\vdash_{desig}$ peut toujours être immédiatement remplacé par $\vdash_1$. Dans les exemples donnés plus bas les dialogues débuteront donc directement avec l'assertion de la thèse (et des hypothèses) suivant le mode $\vdash_1$.

SR 1-L_3 (règle contre les tactiques dilatoires):
P et **O** doivent chacun jouer exclusivement des coups qui modifient la situation.

Il n'y a aucun besoin de changer cette règle.

SR 2-L_3 (règle formelle):
P ne peut pas introduire de formule atomique suivant un certain mode d'assertion. Il peut uniquement le faire après que **O** a asserté la même formule atomique suivant le même mode d'assertion. **O** ne doit pas affirmer une formule atomique suivant plus d'un mode d'assertion.[13]

La règle structurelle formelle doit être légèrement adaptée parce qu'ici les formules atomiques ne sont plus assertées *simpliciter*, mais toujours suivant un certain mode d'assertion.

SR 3-L_3 (règle de victoire):
X gagne ssi c'est le tour de Y mais que celui-ci ne peut pas jouer (ni attaquer ni se défendre).

---

[13] Cette règle dit seulement que **O** n'est pas habilité à établir des formules atomiques suivant plus d'un mode d'assertion. **O** pourrait ainsi théoriquement décider d'affirmer une formule complexe suivant plusieurs modes d'assertion pendant un jeu dialogique. Mais il est clair que cela ne serait pas très sage car il perdrait alors le jeu.

Pas de changement ici.

> *SR 4-L_{3i} (règle intuitionniste):*
> A chaque coup, chaque joueur peut attaquer une formule (complexe) assertée suivant un certain mode d'assertion par son adversaire ou se défendre contre la dernière attaque à laquelle il n'a pas encore répondu.

ou

> *SR 4-L_{3c} (règle classique):*
> A chaque coup, chaque joueur peut attaquer une formule (complexe) assertée suivant un certain mode d'assertion par son adversaire ou se défendre contre n'importe quelle attaque (y compris celles qui ont déjà été défendues).

Les dialogues peuvent être joués avec l'une ou l'autre des deux règles structurelles, la règle intuitionniste ou la règle classique. Quand on utilise cette dernière on obtient une version dialogique du système standard de logique trivalente de Lukasiewicz. Avec la première règle, on en obtient une version intuitionniste.[14]

(Conjecture: De même que l'ensemble des formules valides de L_{3c} est un sous-ensemble propre de l'ensemble des formules valides de la logique classique bivalente, l'ensemble des formules valides de L_{3i} est un sous-ensemble propre de l'ensemble des formules valides de la logique intuitionniste standard du premier ordre.)

> **Définition 3** *Validité logique pour les logiques dialogiques 'multivalentes':*
> Une formule *A* est logiquement valide dans un système dialogique de logique multivalente donné ssi **P** a une stratégie formelle gagnante pour $\vdash_{desig} A$.
> Une inférence de B_1, B_2, B_3,…à *A* est logiquement valide dans un système dialogique de logique multivalente donné ssi **P** a une stratégie formelle gagnante pour $\vdash_{desig} A$ dans un dialogue où les hypothèses B_1, B_2, B_3,…ont été concédées par **O** en assertant $\vdash_{desig} B_1$, $\vdash_{desig} B_2$, $\vdash_{desig} B_3$,… au début du dialogue.

Nous allons maintenant illustrer les systèmes dialogiques L_{3c} et L_{3i} à l'aide de

---

[14] Il faut ici faire attention: nous parlons de la version intuitionniste d'une logique trivalente. Cela ne doit pas être confondu avec le fait qu'il y a des reconstructions de la logique intuitionniste du premier ordre dans un cadre à trois valeurs!

quelques exemples de dialogues.

5 Dialogues pour Logiques 'Multivalentes': Exemples

Commençons par un dialogue avec la formule que nous connaissons déjà par l'exemple 1.

Exemple 3 (dans L_{3c} et L_{3i}):

	O			P	
				$\vdash_1 ((a \rightarrow_{L3} b) \wedge_{L3} a) \rightarrow_{L3} b$	(0)
(1)	$\vdash_{½} (a \rightarrow_{L3} b) \wedge_{L3} a$	0	1	?	(2)
(3)	$\vdash_{½} a$		1	?L	(4)
(5)	$\vdash_{½} a \rightarrow_{L3} b$		5	$?_a$	(6)
(7)	$\vdash_{½} a$				

O gagne.

Comme ce dialogue le montre, **P** n'a pas de stratégie gagnante pour $\vdash_1 ((a \rightarrow_{L3} b) \wedge_{L3} a) \rightarrow_{L3} b$ et donc, cette formule n'est pas valide. Dans le cas où **O** se serait défendu en (1) avec $\vdash_1 (a \rightarrow_{L3} b) \wedge_{L3} a$, le dialogue aurait suivi le cours de l'exemple 1 et **P** aurait pu gagner. Au coup (3), cela n'aurait pas été très différent si **O** s'était défendu avec $\vdash_{½} a \rightarrow_{L3} b$ pour commencer. A la fin du dialogue, **P** perd parce qu'il n'est pas autorisé à introduire de formules atomiques et ne peut par conséquent ni se défendre contre l'attaque de **O** au coup (1), ni attaquer le coup (5).

Attention: Le fait que cette formule n'est pas valide ne signifie pas que la règle d'inférence du *modus ponens* n'est pas valide dans L_3, car $a \rightarrow_{L3} b$ et a impliquent toujours b.[15]

Exemple 4 (dans L_{3c} et L_{3i}):

	O			P	
(H)	$\vdash_1 a \rightarrow_{L3} b$			$\vdash_1 \neg_{L3} a \vee_{L3} b$	(0)
(1)	?	0		$\vdash_1 \neg_{L3} a$	(2)
(3)	$\vdash_{½} a$	2		$\otimes$	
(5)	$\vdash_{½} b$		H	$\vdash_{½} a$	(4)

O gagne.

---

[15] **P** a une stratégie gagnante pour $\vdash_1 b$ sous l'hypothèse que **O** ait concédé $\vdash_1 a \rightarrow_{L3} b$ aussi bien que $\vdash_1 a$ dès le début du dialogue.

Logiques Dialogiques 'Multivalentes'

Ce dialogue montre que $a \to_{L3} b$ et $\neg_{L3} a \vee_{L3} b$ ne sont pas équivalentes dans L_3. La seconde formule implique la première, mais la réciproque ne tient pas.

Remarque: Dans la logique trivalente de Kleene K_3,[16] la subjonction et la disjonction sont encore interdéfinissables de la manière habituelle car $a \to_{K3} b$ et $\neg_{K3} a \vee_{K3} b$ sont équivalentes. C'est la principale différence entre le système de Lukasiewicz et celui de Kleene. Dans la table de vérité standard pour la subjonction de K_3, la seule différence avec L_3 provient de la ligne où A et B ont toutes deux la valeur ½: $a \to_{K3} b$ vaut alors ½, tandis que $a \to_{L3} b$ vaut 1. Voici les règles de particule qui en résultent:

	Attaque	**Défense**
$\vdash_1 A \to_{K3} B$	$\vdash_1 A$ $\vdash_{½} A$ (L'attaquant choisit entre les deux attaques à sa disposition)	$\vdash_1 B$ $\vdash_1 B$
$\vdash_{½} A \to_{K3} B$	$?_A$	$\vdash_1 A$ -------------- $\vdash_{½} A$ (Le défenseur choisit)
	$\vdash_1 A$ $\vdash_1 B$ (L'attaquant choisit entre les trois attaques à sa disposition)	$\vdash_{½} B$ $\otimes$

---

[16] Voir Kleene (1952, § 64).

Logiques Dialogiques 'Multivalentes'

Exemple 5 (dans L_{3c} et L_{3i}):

O				P	
				$\vdash_{1}\neg_{L3}(a \wedge_{L3} \neg_{L3}a)$	(0)
(1)	$\vdash_{\frac{1}{2}} a \wedge_{L3} \neg_{L3}a$	0		$\otimes$	
(3)	$\vdash_{\frac{1}{2}} a$		1	?	(2)
(5)	$\vdash_{\frac{1}{2}} \neg_{L3}a$		1	?R(ight)	(4)
(7)	$\vdash_{\frac{1}{2}} a$		5	?	(6)

O gagne.

Ce dialogue montre que **P** n'a pas de stratégie gagnante pour la négation de la contradiction.

Voici finalement un exemple qui illustre la différence entre le jeu avec la règle structurelle classique et le jeu avec la règle structurelle intuitionniste:

Exemple 6 (dans L_{3c}):

Variante a:

O				P	
(H)	$\vdash_{1} \neg_{L3}b \rightarrow_{L3} \neg_{L3}a$			$\vdash_{1} a \rightarrow_{L3} b$	(0)
(1)	$\vdash_{1} a$	0		$\vdash_{1} b$	(4)
			H	$\vdash_{1} \neg_{L3}b$	(2)
(3)	$\vdash_{1} b$	2		$\otimes$	

P gagne.

Ce dialogue reflète parfaitement celui de la logique dialogique classique 'bivalente' standard. **P** gagne en se défendant avec le coup (4), un coup qui ne serait pas possible en jouant avec la règle structurelle intuitionniste. (Je laisse ici le lecteur se convaincre qu'attaquer avec $\vdash_{\frac{1}{2}} a$ au coup (1) n'aiderait pas **O**.) Par conséquent, **P** n'a pas de stratégie gagnante dans L_{3i}, mais il semble en avoir une dans L_{3c}. Mais il nous faut encore regarder ce qui arrive quand au coup (3), **O** attaque avec $\vdash_{\frac{1}{2}} b$ plutôt qu'avec $\vdash_{1} b$:

Logiques Dialogiques 'Multivalentes'

Variante b:

	O			P	
(H)	$\vdash_1 \neg_{L3} b \rightarrow_{L3} \neg_{L3} a$			$\vdash_1 a \rightarrow_{L3} b$	(0)
(1)	$\vdash_1 a$	0		⊗	
			H	$\vdash_1 \neg_{L3} b$	(2)
(3)	$\vdash_{\frac{1}{2}} b$	2		⊗	
(7)	$\vdash_{\frac{1}{2}} \neg_{L3} a \, [\vdash_1 \neg_{L3} a]$		H	$\vdash_{\frac{1}{2}} \neg_{L3} b$	(4)
(5)	?	4		$\vdash_{\frac{1}{2}} b$	(6)
			7	$? \, [\vdash_1 a]$	(8)

P gagne.

O ne peut pas se défendre contre l'attaque contre coup (7) avec $\vdash_{\frac{1}{2}} a$ puisqu'il a déjà concédé $\vdash_1 a$ (voir la règle structurelle formelle).

6 Systèmes de Tableaux Stratégiques pour L$_{3c}$ et L$_{3i}$

Dans cette section, nous présentons des systèmes de tableaux stratégiques dialogiques pour L$_{3c}$ et L$_{3i}$. Les tableaux stratégiques permettent d'examiner systématiquement s'il y a ou non une stratégie gagnante pour **P** dans un jeu dialogique donné. Voici les idées principales sous-jacentes à ces tableaux stratégiques:[17]

Un arbre stratégique débute avec **P** $\vdash_{\frac{1}{2}} \alpha$, α étant la thèse du dialogue. (Si on s'intéresse à un dialogue avec des hypothèses $\beta_1, \beta_2,...$ il faut ajouter **O** $\vdash_1 \beta_1$, **O** $\vdash_1 \beta_2$...) Les règles de tableaux ci-dessous sont telles qu'elles conduisent toujours de certaines positions gagnantes pour **P** à d'autres positions gagnantes pour **P**. Aussi la considération stratégique suivante est-elle très importante: Si dans une position donnée **O** a plusieurs coups à sa disposition, **P** n'a de stratégie gagnante que s'il peut gagner quelle que soit la manière dont **O** joue. Cela signifie que nous devons considérer tous les choix de **O** comme des possibilités de déroulement du dialogue, et que **P** doit être capable de gagner contre toutes ces variantes. Certaines règles vont ainsi conduire à un embranchement de l'arbre stratégique.[18] D'autre

---

[17] Pour une présentation plus complète des systèmes de tableaux stratégiques dialogiques avec plus d'explications, voir par exemple Rahman (1993), Rahman/Rückert (1998/99) ou Rahman/Rückert (1999). Pour une présentation générale des systèmes de tableaux non dialogiques pour les logiques multivalentes, voir Hähnle (1999).

part, il n'y aura pas d'embranchement aux positions où **P** a le choix entre différents coups car pour avoir une stratégie gagnante, il suffit qu'un seul des coups à sa disposition conduise à une position gagnante.

P a une stratégie gagnante pour α ssi l'arbre stratégique qui débute avec **P** $\vdash_1 \alpha$ est clos. Un arbre stratégique est clos ssi toutes ses branches sont closes. Une branche est close ssi elle contient une expression de la forme **O** $\vdash_x \chi$ et une autre de la forme **P** $\vdash_x \chi$, χ étant une formule atomique.[19]

---

[18] Les expressions qui appartiennent à différentes branches sont séparées par le symbole '|', tandis que les expressions qui appartiennent à la même branche sont séparées par le symbole ','.

[19] Cette règle pour la clôture d'une branche est la contrepartie stratégique de la règle structurelle formelle.

Logiques Dialogiques 'Multivalentes'

6.1 Tableaux Stratégiques pour L_{3c}

O-règles	P-règles
$O \vdash_1 A \vee_{L3} B$	$P \vdash_1 A \vee_{L3} B$
$O \vdash_1 A \mid O \vdash_1 B$	$P \vdash_1 A, P \vdash_1 B$
$O \vdash_{½} A \vee_{L3} B$	$P \vdash_{½} A \vee_{L3} B$
$P \vdash_1 A, P \vdash_1 B, O \vdash_{½} A \mid P \vdash_1 A, P \vdash_1 B, O \vdash_{½} B$	$P \vdash_{½} A, P \vdash_{½} B \mid O \vdash_1 A \mid O \vdash_1 B$
$O \vdash_1 A \wedge_{L3} B$	$P \vdash_1 A \wedge_{L3} B$
$O \vdash_1 A, O \vdash_1 B$	$P \vdash_1 A \mid P \vdash_1 B$
$O \vdash_{½} A \wedge_{L3} B$	$P \vdash_{½} A \wedge_{L3} B$
$O \vdash_{½} A, O \vdash_{½} B \mid O \vdash_1 A, O \vdash_{½} B \mid O \vdash_{½} A, O \vdash_1 B$	$P \vdash_{½} A, P \vdash_{½} B \mid P \vdash_1 A, P \vdash_{½} B \mid P \vdash_{½} A, P \vdash_1 B$
$O \vdash_1 A \rightarrow_{L3} B$	$P \vdash_1 A \rightarrow_{L3} B$
$P \vdash_1 A, P \vdash_{½} A \mid P \vdash_1 A, O \vdash_{½} B \mid O \vdash_1 B$	$O \vdash_1 A, P \vdash_1 B \mid P \vdash_1 B, O \vdash_{½} A, P \vdash_{½} B$
$O \vdash_{½} A \rightarrow_{L3} B$	$P \vdash_{½} A \rightarrow_{L3} B$
$O \vdash_1 A, P \vdash_1 B \mid O \vdash_{½} A, P \vdash_1 B, P \vdash_{½} B$	$P \vdash_1 A, P \vdash_{½} A \mid O \vdash_1 B \mid P \vdash_1 A, O \vdash_{½} B$
$O \vdash_1 \neg_{L3} A$	$P \vdash_1 \neg_{L3} A$
$P \vdash_1 A, P \vdash_{½} A$	$O \vdash_1 A \mid O \vdash_{½} A$
$O \vdash_{½} \neg_{L3} A$	$P \vdash_{½} \neg_{L3} A$
$O \vdash_{½} A$	$P \vdash_{½} A$

Logiques Dialogiques 'Multivalentes'

6.2 Tableaux Stratégiques pour L$_{3i}$

La seule différence entre les règles de tableaux pour L$_{3i}$ et celles pour L$_{3c}$ réside dans le fait que les **P**-règles contiennent deux notations supplémentaires:

- Si une formule a une occurrence avec le suffixe '(**O**)', cela signifie que toutes les autres **P**-expressions qui appartiennent à la même branche doivent être supprimées.[20]

- Si deux formules sont séparées par '*ou*' cela signifie que seulement l'une des deux (n'importe laquelle) résulte de l'application de la **P**-règle correspondante.[21]

Ces modes de notation reflètent les spécificités de la règle structurelle intuitionniste au niveau stratégique.

---

[20] Il faut être prudent avec les **P**-expressions au-dessus des embranchements: comme elles appartiennent à plusieurs branches il peut se produire qu'elles doivent être supprimées seulement pour une branche mais pas pour une autre.

[21] En d'autres termes, c'est une seconde sorte d'embranchements. Ici, une branche seulement doit être close pour que **P** ait une stratégie gagnante.

Logiques Dialogiques 'Multivalentes'

O-règles	P-règles
$\mathbf{O} \vdash_1 A \vee_{L3} B$	$\mathbf{P} \vdash_1 A \vee_{L3} B$
---------------	---------------
$\mathbf{O} \vdash_1 A \mid \mathbf{O} \vdash_1 B$	$\mathbf{P}_{(O)} \vdash_1 A$ ou $\mathbf{P}_{(O)} \vdash_1 B$
$\mathbf{O} \vdash_{\frac{1}{2}} A \vee_{L3} B$	$\mathbf{P} \vdash_{\frac{1}{2}} A \vee_{L3} B$
---------------	---------------
$\mathbf{P} \vdash_1 A, \mathbf{P} \vdash_1 B, \mathbf{O} \vdash_{\frac{1}{2}} A \mid \mathbf{P} \vdash_1 A, \mathbf{P} \vdash_1 B, \mathbf{O} \vdash_{\frac{1}{2}} B$	$\mathbf{P}_{(O)} \vdash_{\frac{1}{2}} A$ ou $\mathbf{P}_{(O)} \vdash_{\frac{1}{2}} B \mid \mathbf{O}_{(O)} \vdash_1 A \mid \mathbf{O}_{(O)} \vdash_1 B$
$\mathbf{O} \vdash_1 A \wedge_{L3} B$	$\mathbf{P} \vdash_1 A \wedge_{L3} B$
---------------	---------------
$\mathbf{O} \vdash_1 A, \mathbf{O} \vdash_1 B$	$\mathbf{P} \vdash_1 A \mid \mathbf{P} \vdash_1 B$
$\mathbf{O} \vdash_{\frac{1}{2}} A \wedge_{L3} B$	$\mathbf{P} \vdash_{\frac{1}{2}} A \wedge_{L3} B$
---------------	---------------
$\mathbf{O} \vdash_{\frac{1}{2}} A, \mathbf{O} \vdash_{\frac{1}{2}} B \mid \mathbf{O} \vdash_1 A, \mathbf{O} \vdash_{\frac{1}{2}} B \mid \mathbf{O} \vdash_{\frac{1}{2}} A, \mathbf{O} \vdash_1 B$	$\mathbf{P}_{(O)} \vdash_{\frac{1}{2}} A$ ou $\mathbf{P}_{(O)} \vdash_{\frac{1}{2}} B \mid \mathbf{P}_{(O)} \vdash_1 A$ ou $\mathbf{P}_{(O)} \vdash_{\frac{1}{2}} B$ $\mid \mathbf{P}_{(O)} \vdash_{\frac{1}{2}} A$ ou $\mathbf{P}_{(O)} \vdash_1 B$
$\mathbf{O} \vdash_1 A \rightarrow_{L3} B$	$\mathbf{P} \vdash_1 A \rightarrow_{L3} B$
---------------	---------------
$\mathbf{P} \vdash_1 A, \mathbf{P} \vdash_{\frac{1}{2}} A \mid \mathbf{P} \vdash_1 A, \mathbf{O} \vdash_{\frac{1}{2}} B \mid \mathbf{O} \vdash_1 B$	$\mathbf{O} \vdash_1 A, \mathbf{P}_{(O)} \vdash_1 B \mid \mathbf{O} \vdash_{\frac{1}{2}} A, \mathbf{P}_{(O)} \vdash_1 B$ ou $\mathbf{P}_{(O)} \vdash_{\frac{1}{2}} B$
$\mathbf{O} \vdash_{\frac{1}{2}} A \rightarrow_{L3} B$	$\mathbf{P} \vdash_{\frac{1}{2}} A \rightarrow_{L3} B$
---------------	---------------
$\mathbf{O} \vdash_1 A, \mathbf{P} \vdash_1 B \mid \mathbf{O} \vdash_{\frac{1}{2}} A, \mathbf{P} \vdash_1 B, \mathbf{P} \vdash_{\frac{1}{2}} B$	$\mathbf{P}_{(O)} \vdash_1 A$ ou $\mathbf{P}_{(O)} \vdash_{\frac{1}{2}} A \mid \mathbf{O}_{(O)} \vdash_1 B \mid \mathbf{P}_{(O)} \vdash_1 A, \mathbf{O} \vdash_{\frac{1}{2}} B$
$\mathbf{O} \vdash_1 \neg_{L3} A$	$\mathbf{P} \vdash_1 \neg_{L3} A$
---------------	---------------
$\mathbf{P} \vdash_1 A, \mathbf{P} \vdash_{\frac{1}{2}} A$	$\mathbf{O}_{(O)} \vdash_1 A \mid \mathbf{O}_{(O)} \vdash_{\frac{1}{2}} A$
$\mathbf{O} \vdash_{\frac{1}{2}} \neg_{L3} A$	$\mathbf{P} \vdash_{\frac{1}{2}} \neg_{L3} A$
---------------	---------------
$\mathbf{O} \vdash_{\frac{1}{2}} A$	$\mathbf{P} \vdash_{\frac{1}{2}} A$

7 Conclusion

Les logiques multivalentes constituent un sujet très large et en développement toujours rapide, avec beaucoup de résultats techniques et d'applications intéressantes. Le but de cet article était d'ouvrir la porte au dialogicien pour qu'il commence à explorer ce champ logique. L'addition cruciale au cadre dialogique a été l'introduction du concept de différents modes d'assertion. Grâce à cela on a montré comment un système de logique multivalente très basique, à savoir une logique de Lukasiewicz à trois valeurs, peut être reconstruit avec des moyens dialogiques (en gagnant du même coup une version intuitionniste de ce système). Rien n'a encore été dit des logiques avec une infinité de valeurs, des *product logics*, etc. Mais je pense qu'une première étape a été réalisée et que les recherches futures pourront conduire à d'intéressants résultats. En particulier, il sera dorénavant possible de combiner les idées sous-jacentes aux logiques multivalentes avec celles d'autres logiques dans le cadre flexible de la logique dialogique.

Cet article peut aussi apporter un éclairage nouveau sur une discussion en cours à propos des différences essentielles entre différentes logiques non classiques. Une réponse, qui dérive de la tradition polonaise des logiques multivalentes (cf. Malinowski (1993)), consiste à dire que différents systèmes logiques mettent en œuvre différentes particules logiques tandis qu'ils ne diffèrent pas dans leur conception de la notion de relation de conséquence. D'un autre côté, des substructuralistes comme Restall (2000) par exemple affirment que différents systèmes logiques résultent de différences structurelles qui conduisent à différentes conceptions de la notion de relation de conséquence. Cet article montre que du point de vue de la logique dialogique, on devrait adopter une position intermédiaire: Différents systèmes logiques résultent toujours de l'interaction des particules logiques (les règles de particule) et des propriétés structurelles (les règles structurelles). Chacun des trois cas suivants est possible:

(1) Différents systèmes logiques peuvent résulter de différentes règles de particule même s'il n'y a pas de différences entre eux liées aux règles structurelles (par exemple L_{3c} et K_{3c})

(2) Deux systèmes logiques distincts ont leurs règles de particule en commun mais ont différents ensembles de règles structurelles (par exemple L_{3c} et L_{3i})

(3) Des systèmes logiques distincts diffèrent à la fois sur leurs règles de particule et sur leurs règles structurelles (par exemple L_{3i} et K_{3c}).[22]

---

[22] Je dois remercier Shahid Rahman (Lille) pour de nombreuses discussions, critiques, suggestions et propositions, et Manuel Rebuschi (Nancy), non seulement pour son effort éditorial et son aide pour la langue française, mais aussi pour avoir suggéré plusieurs améliorations à cet article.

Bibliography

Abramsky, S. (1997): 'Semantics of Interaction: an Introduction to Game Semantics', in Pitts, A. und Dybjer, P. (eds.): *Semantics and Logic of Computation*, Cambridge, p. 1-31

Anderson, A. and Belnap, N. (1975): *Entailment. The Logic of Relevance and Necessity I*, Princeton

Anderson, A. and Belnap, N. (1992): *Entailment II*, Princeton

Angell, R. (1962): 'A Propositional Logic with Subjunctive Conditionals', *Journal of Symbolic Logic* 27, p. 327-343

Aristotle (1928): *The Works of Aristotle Translated into English* (edited by Ross, W.), Vol. I, Oxford

Astroh, M. (1999): 'Connexive Logic', *Nordic Journal of Philosophical Logic* 4, p. 31-71

Avron, A. (1988): 'The Semantics and Proof Theory of Linear Logic', *Theoretical Computer Science* 57, p. 161-184

Barcan, R. (1962): 'Interpreting Quantification' *Inquiry* 5, p. 252-259

Barth, E. and Krabbe, E. (1982): *From Axiom to Dialogue: A Philosophical Study of Logics and Argumentation*, Berlin, New York

Belnap, N. (1982): 'Display Logic', *Journal of Philosophical Logic* 11, p. 375-417

Bencivenga, E. (1978): 'Free Semantics for Indefinite Descriptions', *Journal of Philosophical Logic* 7, p. 389-405

Bencivenga, E. (1980): 'Free Semantics for Definite Descriptions', *Logique et Analyse* 23, p. 393-405

Bencivenga, E. (1981): 'Free Semantics', *Boston Studies in the Philosophy of Science* 47, p. 31-48

Bencivenga, E. (1986): 'Free logics', in Gabbay, D. and Guenthner, F. (eds.): *Handbook of Philosophical Logic*, Vol. III, Dordrecht, p. 373-426

Beth, E. (1955): 'Semantic Entailment and Formal Derivability', *Mededelingen van de Koninklijke Nederlandse Akademie van Wetenschappen, Afdeling Letterkunde* 18, p. 309-342

Blackburn, P. (2001): 'Modal Logic as Dialogical Logic', in Rahman, S. and Rückert, H. (eds.): *New Perspectives in Dialogical Logic*, *Synthese* 127 (1/2), p. 57-93

Blass, A. (1992): 'A Game Semantics for Linear Logic', *Annals of Pure and Applied Logic* 5, p. 487-503

Boethius, A. (1969): *De Hypotheticis Syllogismis* (edited by Obertello, L.), Brescia

Bull, A. and Segerberg, K. (1984): 'Basic Modal Logic', in Gabbay, D. and Guenthner, F. (eds.): *Handbook of Philosophical Logic*, Vol. II, Dordrecht, p. 1-88

Castaneda, H. (1974): 'Thinking and the Structure of the World', *Philosophia* 4 (1), p 2-40

Bibliography

Church, A. (1965): 'Review of Lambert: 'Existential Import Revisited'', *Journal of Symbolic Logic* 30, p. 103-104

Ciabattoni, A., Fermüller, C. and Metcalfe G. (2004): 'Uniform Rules and Dialogue Games for Fuzzy Logics', *LPAR 2004*, p. 496-510

Cooper, W. (1968): 'The Propositional Logic of Ordinary Discourse', *Inquiry* 11, p. 280-297

D'Agostino, M., Gabbay, D. and Broda, K. (1999): 'Tableau Methods for Substructural Logics', in D'Agostino, M., Gabbay, D., Hähnle, R. and Posegga, J. (eds.): *Handbook of Tableau Methods*, Dordrecht, p. 397-467

Degremont, C. and Rahman, S. (2007): 'The Beetle in the Box: Exploring IF-Dialogues', in Pietarinen, A. (ed.): *Truth and Games. Essays in Honour of Gabriel Sandu, Societas Philosophica Fennica* (to appear)

Diamond, C. (ed.) (1976): *Wittgenstein's Lectures on the Foundations of Mathematics*, Hassocks, Sussex

Diaz, R. (1981): *Topics in the Logic of Relevance*, München

Došen, K. (1988): 'Sequent Systems and Groupoid Models I', *Studia Logica* 47, p. 353-389

Felscher, W. (1985): 'Dialogues, Strategies and Intuitionistic Provability', *Annals of Pure and Applied Logic* 28, p. 217-254

Felscher, W. (1986): 'Dialogues as a Foundation for Intuitionistic Logic', in Gabbay, D. and Guenthner, F. (eds.): *Handbook of Philosophical Logic*, Vol. III, Dordrecht, p. 341-372

Fitting, M. (1993): 'Basic Modal Logic', in Gabbay, D., Hogger, C. and Robinson, J. (eds.): *Handbook of Logic in Artificial Intelligence and Logic Programming, Vol. 1: Logical Foundations*, Oxford, p. 365-448

Frege, G. (1964): *Begriffsschrift und andere Aufsätze* (edited by Angelelli, I.), Darmstadt

Fuhrmann, A. (1985): 'Ein relevanzlogischer Dialogkalkül erster Stufe', *Conceptus* XIX 48, p. 51-65

Gabbay, D. (1987): *Modal Provability Foundations for Negation by Failure*, ESPRIT, Technical Report TI 8, Project 393, ACORD

Gardner, M. (1996): *The Universe in a Handkerchief. Lewis Carroll's Mathematical Recreations, Games, Puzzles and Word Plays*, New York

Gethmann, C. (1979): *Protologik. Untersuchungen zur formalen Semantik von Begründungsdiskursen*, Frankfurt a.M.

Giles, R. (1974): 'A Non-Classical Logic for Physics', *Studia Logica* 33 (4), p. 399-417

Girard, J. (1995): 'Linear Logic: Its Syntax and Semantics', in Girard, J., Lafont, Y. and Regnier, L. (eds.): *Advances in Linear Logic*, Cambridge, p. 1-42

Girard, J. (1998): 'On the Meaning of Logical Rules', unpublished manuscript

Bibliography

Gottwald, S. (1989): *Mehrwertige Logik. Eine Einführung in Theorie und Anwendungen*, Berlin
Grice, H. (1967): *Conditionals. Privately circulated notes*, Berkeley
Grice, H. (1989): *Studies in the Way of Words*, Cambridge
Guillaume, M. (1958): 'Rapports entre Calculs Propositionnels Modaux et Topologie impliques par certaines Extensions de la Méthode de Tableaux Sémantiques', *Comptes Rendus Hebdomadaires des Séances de l'Académie des Sciences* 246, p. 1140-1142, p. 2207-2210 and 247, p. 1281-1283
Haas, G. (1984): *Konstruktive Einführung in die formale Logik*, Mannheim, Wien, Zürich
Hähnle, R. (1999): 'Tableaux for Many-Valued Logics', in D'Agostino, M., Gabbay, D., Hähnle, R. and Posegga, J. (eds.): *Handbook of Tableaux Methods*, Dordrecht, p. 529-580
Hamblin, C. (1970): *Fallacies*, London
Hartmann, D. (1998): 'Kulturalistische Logikbegründung', in Hartmann, D. and Janich, P. (eds.): *Die Kulturalistische Wende*, Frankfurt a. M., p. 57-128
Heydrich, W. (1995): *Relevanzlogik und Situationssemantik*, Berlin, New York
Hintikka, J. (1957): *Quantifiers in Deontic Logic*, Helsingfors
Hintikka, J. (1958): 'Towards a Theory of Definite Descriptions', *Analysis* 19, p. 79-85
Hintikka, J. (1961): 'Modality and Quantification', *Theoria* 27, p. 119-128
Hintikka, J. (1962): *Knowledge and Belief: An Introduction to the Logic of the Two Notions*, Dordrecht
Hintikka, J. (1963): 'The Modes of modality', *Acta Philosophica Fennica* 16, p. 65-82
Hintikka, J. (1996): *The Principles of Mathematics Revisited*, Cambridge
Hintikka, J. (1996-98): *Selected Papers*, Vols. I-IV, Dordrecht, Boston, London
Hintikka, J. (1998): 'What is Elementary Logic? Independence-Friendly Logic as the True Core Area of Logic', in Hintikka, J.: *Selected Papers, Vol. 3: Language, Truth and Logic in Mathematics*, Dordrecht, Boston, London, p. 1-27
Hintikka, J. and Sandu, G. (1996): 'A Revolution in Logic?', *Nordic Journal of Philosophical Logic* 1, p. 169-183
Hoepelman, J.. and van Hoof, A. (1988): 'The Success of Failure', *Proceedings of COLING*, Budapest, p. 250-254
Hughes, G. and Cresswell, M. (1978): *Einführung in die Modallogik*, Berlin, New York
Hyland, M. (1997): 'Game Semantics', in Pitts, A. und Dybjer, P. (eds.): *Semantics and Logic of Computation*, Cambridge, p. 131-182
Inhetveen, R. (1982): 'Ein konstruktiver Weg zur Semantik der „möglichen Welten"', in Barth, E. and Martens, L. (eds.): *Argumentation: Approaches to Theory Formation*, Amsterdam, p. 133-141

Johnson, R. (1999): 'The Relation between Formal and Informal Logic', *Argumentation* 13, p. 265-274
Kamlah, W. and Lorenzen, P. (1967): *Logische Propädeutik*, Mannheim
Kleene, S. (1952): *Introduction to Metamathematics*, Amsterdam, Groningen, Princeton
Krabbe, E. (1985): 'Formal Systems of Dialogue Rules', *Synthese* 63 (3), p. 295-328
Krabbe, E. (1986): 'A Theory of Modal Dialectics', *Journal of Philosophical Logic* 15, p. 191-217
Kripke, S. (1963a): 'Semantical Analysis of Modal Logic I. Normal Propositional Calculi', *Zeitschrift für mathematische Logik und Grundlagen der Mathematik* 9, p. 67-96
Kripke, S. (1963b): 'Semantical Considerations on Modal Logic', *Acta Philosophica Fennica* 19, p. 83-94
Lambert, K. (1962): 'Notes on E!: A Theory of Descriptions, *Philosophical Studies* 13, p. 51-59
Lambert, K. (1963): 'Existential Import Revisited', *Notre Dame Journal for Formal Logic* 4, p. 288-292
Leblanc, H. and Thomason, R. (1968): 'Completeness Theorems for some Presupposition-Free Logics', *Fundamenta Mathematica* 62, p. 125-164
Leonard, H. (1956): 'The Logic of Existence', *Philosophical Studies* 7, p. 49-64
Linneweber-Lammerskitten, H. (1988): *Untersuchungen zur Theorie des hypothetischen Urteils*, Cambridge, London, New York, Melbourne
Lorenz, K. (1978): 'Dialogspiele als semantische Grundlage von Logikkalkülen', in Lorenzen, P. and Lorenz, K.: *Dialogische Logik*, Darmstadt, p. 96-162
Lorenz, K. (1981): 'Dialogical Logic', in Marciszewski, W. (ed.): *Dictionary of Logic as Applied in the Study of Language. Concepts/Methods/Theories*, The Hague, Boston, London, p. 117-125
Lorenz, K. (1995): 'Modallogik', in Mittelstraß (ed.): *Enzyklopädie Philosophie und Wissenschaftstheorie* 2, p. 907-911
Lorenzen, P. (1987): *Lehrbuch der konstruktiven Wissenschaftstheorie*, Mannheim, Wien, Zürich
Lorenzen, P. and Lorenz, K. (1978): *Dialogische Logik*, Darmstadt
Martin-Löf, P. (1984): *Intuitionistic Type Theory*, Napoli
MacColl, H. (1878): 'The Calculus of Equivalent Statements (II)', *Proceedings of the London Mathematical Society* 9, p. 177-186
MacColl, H. (1897): 'The Calculus of Equivalent Statements (V)', *Proceedings of the London Mathematical Society* 28, p. 156-183
MacColl, H. (1906): *Symbolic Logic and its Applications*, London, New York, Bombay
Malinowski, G. (1993): *Many-Valued Logics*, Oxford
McCall, S. (1963): *Aristotle's Modal Syllogisms*, Amsterdam

McCall, S. (1964): 'A New Variety of Implication', *Journal of Symbolic Logic* 29, p. 151-152
McCall, S. (1966): 'Connexive Implication', *Journal of Symbolic Logic* 31, p. 415-432
McCall, S. (1967): 'Connexive Implication and the Syllogism', *Mind* 76, p. 346-356
McCall, S. (1975): 'MacColl', in Edwards, P. (ed.) (1975): *Encyclopedia of Philosophy*, Vol IV, London, p. 545-546
McCullough, D. (1971): 'Logical Connectives for Intuitionistic Propositional Logic', *The Journal of Symbolic Logic* 36 (1), p. 15-20
Naess, A. (1966): *Communication and Argument. Elements of Applied Semantics*, Oslo, London
Neckam, A. (1863): *De Naturis Rerum* (edited by Wright, T.), London
Nortmann, U. (2001): 'How to Extend the Dialogical Approach to Provability Logic', in Rahman, S. and Rückert, H. (eds.): *New Perspectives in Dialogical Logic, Synthese* 127 (1/2), p. 95-103
Perelman, C. and Olbrechts-Tyteca, L. (1958): *La Nouvelle Rhétorique*, Paris
Pizzi, C. and Williamson, T. (1997): 'Strong Boethius' Thesis and Consequential Implication', *Journal of Philosophical Logic* 26, p. 569-588
Prawitz, D. (1978): 'Proofs and the Meaning and Completeness of the Logical Constants', in Hintikka, J., Niiniluoto, I. and Saarinen, E. (eds.): *Essays on Mathematical and Philosophical Logic*, Dordrecht, p. 25-40
Priest, G. (1999): 'Negation as Cancellation and Connexive Logic', *Topoi* 18 (1999), p. 141-148
Quine, W. (1965): *Mathematical Logic*, Cambridge
Quine, W. (1976): 'Carnap and Logical Truth', in Quine, W.: *The Ways of Paradox and Other Essays* (revised and enlarged edition), Cambridge, p. 107-132
Quine, W. (1980): 'On What there Is', in Quine, W.: *From a Logical Point of View*, Cambridge, p. 1-19
Rahman, S. (1993): *Über Dialoge, Protologische Kategorien und andere Seltenheiten*, Frankfurt a.M.
Rahman, S. (1997): *Die Logik der zusammenhängenden Behauptungen im frühen Werk von Hugh MacColl* (Habilitationsschrift), Universität des Saarlandes
Rahman, S. (1998): 'Redundanz und Wahrheitswertbestimmung bei Hugh MacColl'. *FR 5.1 Philosophie, Universität des Saarlandes*, Memo Nr. 23, September 1998
Rahman, S. (1999a): 'Ways of Understanding Hugh MacColl's Concept of Symbolic Existence', in Astroh, M. and Read, S. (eds.): *Proceedings of the Conference "Hugh MacColl and the Tradition of Logic" at Greifswald (1998), The Nordic Journal of Philosophical Logic* 3 (1), p. 35-58
Rahman, S. (1999b): 'Argumentieren mit Widersprüchen und Fiktionen', in Buchholz, K., Rahman, S. and Weber, I. (eds.): *Wege zur Vernunft – Philosophieren zwischen Tätigkeit und Reflexion*, Frankfurt a.M., p. 131-145

Bibliography

Rahman, S. (1999c): 'Fictions and Contradictions in the Symbolic Universe of Hugh MacColl', in Mittelstraß, J. (ed.): *Die Zukunft des Wissens*, Konstanz, p. 614-620

Rahman, S. (2001): 'On Frege's Nightmare. A Combination of Intuitionistic, Free and Paraconsistent Logics', in Wansing, H. (ed.): *Essays on Non-Classical Logic* (Advances in Logic – Vol. 1), New Jersey, London, Singapore, Hong Kong, p. 55-80

Rahman, S. (2006): 'Non-Normal Dialogics for a Wonderful World and more', in van Bentham, J., Heinzmann, G., Rebuschi, M. and Visser, H. (eds.): *The Age of Alternative Logics*, Dordrecht, p. 311-334

Rahman, S. (2007): 'The Dialogic of just being Different. Hintikka's new Approach to the Notion of *episteme* and its Impact on "Second Generation" Dialogics', in Kolak, D. and Symons, J. (eds.): *Quantifiers, Questions and Quantum Physics. Essays in Honour of Jaakko Hintikka* (to appear)

Rahman, S. and Carnielli, W. (2000): 'The Dialogical Approach to Paraconsistency', *Synthese* 125 (1/2), p. 201-232

Rahman, S. and Keiff, L. (2004): 'On how to be a Dialogician', in Vanderveken, D. (ed.): *Logic, Thought and Action*, Dordrecht, p. 359-408

Rahman, S. and Rao, N. (2000): ‚Die logische Kompetenz und die Theorie der mentalen Modelle', *Philosophia Scientiae* 4 (2), p. 133-146

Rahman, S. and Redmond, J. (2008): 'Hugh MacColl and the Birth of Logical Pluralism', in Gabbay, D. and Woods, J. (eds.): *Handbook of the History of Logic* (to appear)

Rahman, S. and Roetti, J. (1999): 'Dual Intuitionistic Paraconsistency without Ontological Commitments', *Contribution to the Congress: Analytic Philosophy at the Turn of the Millenium,* p. 120-126

Rahman, S. and Rückert, H. (1998a): 'Dialogische Logik und Relevanz', *FR 5.1 Philosophie, Universität des Saarlandes*, memo No. 27, December 1998 (new version in this volume, p. 79-104)

Rahman, S. and Rückert, H. (1998b): 'Die Logik der zusammenhängenden Aussagen: ein dialogischer Ansatz zur konnexen Logik', *FR 5.1 Philosophie, Universität des Saarlandes*, memo No. 28, December 1998

Rahman, S. and Rückert, H. (1998/99):'Die pragmatischen Sinn- und Geltungskriterien der Dialogischen Logik beim Beweis des Adjunktionssatzes', *Philosophia Scientiæ* (3) 3, p. 145-170

Rahman, S. and Rückert, H. (1999): 'Dialogische Modallogik (für *T*, *B*, *S4* und *S5*)', *Logique et Analyse* 167-168, p. 243-282 (new version in this volume, p. 45-78)

Rahman, S. and Rückert, H. (2000/01): 'Eine neue dialogische Semantik für lineare Logik', previously unpublished manuscript (new version in this volume, p. 141-172)

Bibliography

Rahman, S. and Rückert, H. (2001a): 'Preface', in Rahman, S. and Rückert, H. (eds.): *New Perspectives in Dialogical Logic*, *Synthese* 127 (1/2), p. 1-6

Rahman, S. and Rückert, H. (2001b): 'Dialogical Connexive Logic', in Rahman, S. and Rückert, H. (eds.): *New Perspectives in Dialogical Logic*, *Synthese* 127 (1/2), p. 105-139 (new version in this volume, p. 105-140)

Rahman, S., Rückert, H. and Fischmann, M. (1997): 'On Dialogues and Ontology. The Dialogical Approach to Free Logic', *Logique et Analyse* 167, p. 357-374 (new version in this volume, p. 31-44)

Rahman, S. and Tulenheimo, T. (2007): 'From Games to Dialogues and back: Towards a General Frame for Validity', in: Majer, O., Pietarinen, A. and Tulenheimo, T. (ed.): *Logic, Games and Philosophy: A Foundational Perspective* (to appear)

Rahman, S. and Van Bendegem, J. (2002): 'The Dynamics of Adaptive Paraconsistency', in Carnielli, W., Coniglio, M. and D'Ottaviano, I. (eds.): *Paraconsistency*, New York, p. 295-321

Read, S. (1988): *Relevant Logic. A Philosophical Examination of Inference*, Oxford

Read, S. (1993): 'Formal and Material Consequence, Disjunctive Syllogism and Gamma', in Jacobi, K. (ed.): *Argumentationstheorie. Scholastische Forschungen zu den logischen und semantischen Regeln korrekten Folgerns*, Leiden, New York, Köln, p. 233-259

Read, S. (1995): *Thinking about Logic*, Oxford

Restall, G. (2000): *An Introduction to Substructural Logics*, London, New York

Rosser, J. and Turquette, A. (1952): *Many-Valued Logics*, Amsterdam

Routley, R. and Montgomery, H. (1968): 'On Systems Containing Aristotle's Thesis', *Journal of Symbolic Logic* 3, p. 82-96

Rückert, H.: (1999a) 'Wodurch sich der dialogische Ansatz in der Logik auszeichnet', in Mittelstraß, J. (ed.): *Die Zukunft des Wissens*, Konstanz, p. 644-648

Rückert H. (1999b): 'Dialogue Games and Connexive Logic', in Baltag, A. and Pauly, M. (eds.): *Proceedings of the ILLC Workshop on Logic and Games*, Amsterdam 1999, p. 37-38

Rückert, H. (2001): 'Why Dialogical Logic?', in Wansing, H. (ed.): *Essays on Non-Classical Logic* (Advances in Logic – Vol. 1), New Jersey, London, Singapore, Hong Kong, p. 165-185 (new version in this volume, p. 15-30)

Rückert, H. (2004): 'Logiques Dialogiques 'Multivalentes'', in Rebuschi, M. and Tulenheimo, T. (eds.): *Logique & Théorie des Jeux*, *Philosophia Scientiae* 8 (2), p. 59-87 (new version in this volume, p. 173-198)

Russell, B. (1905): 'On Denoting', *Mind* 14, p. 479-493

Sinowjew, A (1970): *Komplexe Logik*, Berlin

Smullyan, R. (1968): *First-Order Logic*, Heidelberg

Toulmin, S. (1958): *The Uses of Argument*, Cambridge

Bibliography

Van Bendegem, J. (2001): 'Paraconsistency and Dialogue Logic: Critical Examination and further Explorations', in Rahman, S. and Rückert, H. (eds.): *New Perspectives in Dialogical Logic*, *Synthese* 127 (1/2), p. 35-55

Van Benthem, J. (2007): *Logic in Games* (to appear)

Van Fraassen, B. (1966a): 'Singular Terms, Truthvalue Gaps and Free Logic', *Journal of Philosophy* 63, p. 481-494

Van Fraassen, B. (1966b): 'The Completeness of Free Logic', *Zeitschrift für mathematische Logik und Grundlagen der Mathematik* 12, p. 219-324

Venn, J. (1881): *Symbolic Logic*, New York

Walton, D. (1984): *Logical Dialogue-Games and Fallacies*, Washington D.C.

Walton, D. (1985): 'New Directions in the Logic of Dialogue', *Synthese* 63, p. 259-274

Wansing, H. (1994): 'Sequent Calculi for Normal Modal Propositional Logics', *Journal of Logic Computation* 4, p. 125-142

Wansing, H. (1998): *Displaying Modal Logic*, Dordrecht

Weingartner, P. (2000): 'Reasons for Filtering Classical Logic', in Batens, D., Mortenson, C., Priest, G. and Van Bendegem, J. (eds.): *Frontiers of Paraconsistent Logic*, Baldock, p. 315-328

Weingartner, P. and Schurz, G. (1986): 'Paradoxes Solved by Simple Relevance Criteria', *Logique et Analyse* 113, p. 3-40

Wittgenstein, L. (1953): *Philosophical Investigations* (edited by Anscombe, G. and Rhees, R.), Oxford

Woods, J. (1988): 'Ideas of Rationality in Dialogic', *Argumentation* 2, p. 395-408

Zucker, J. and Tragesser, R. (1978): 'The Adequacy Problem for Inferential Logic', *Journal of Philosophical Logic* 7, p. 501-516